Essential Articles 10

Editors: Christine Shepherd & Chas White

The copiable resource for issues and controversies

www.carelpress.com

CAREL PRESS

Introduction

Welcome to Essential Articles 10, the latest volume of this highly praised series.

The major difference from previous editions is that Essential Articles has now become an annual publication, in a bound format. This change allows us to respond quickly to customer demand for background information on the most current issues and reflects the rapid pace at which we all expect to access information. It is also a response to requests from our customers, who prefer a slimmer, conventional volume which can be placed on a library shelf.

Publishing annually also means a stronger connection between Essential Articles and its sister publication, Fact File. On publication of Fact File 2008, a guide will be available on the web to link statistics in Fact File to relevant articles in Essential Articles.

This means you will find Essential Articles indispensable for browsing and researching. Students researching with Essential Articles can quickly find relevant and appropriate material, rather than wasting hours on fruitless internet searches. Because it can be copied, it's also invaluable in the library and the classroom for exploring today's issues and controversies; considering opposing views; looking at models of the best writing and gaining an insight into the press.

We have selected pieces of writing that offer opinions on current affairs rather than news stories. Even where the details have changed, the opinions contained in the articles remain both valid and valuable. For example, the recent spate of shootings of young people is reflected in features which analyse the factors which have contributed to the events. We have also included a section called Modern Britain which includes topics as varied as integration, swearing and the dominance of football.

Some issues which recur constantly in the Essential Articles series are presented with a different emphasis. In Environment, for example, the phrase 'carbon footprint' has become current, one article in this edition analyses Liz Hurley's extravagant marriage in these terms.

Many articles are wide-ranging and, as previously, we have provided an index to make researching easier.

While each volume in the series can be considered as a separate item, all ten volumes taken together make up a unique resource on important issues and controversies, offering balanced argument, personal accounts, strong viewpoints and humour. A free digital, searchable guide to the whole series is available on our website.

Published by Carel Press Ltd
4 Hewson St, Carlisle CA2 5AU
Tel 01228 538928, Fax 591816
info@carelpress.com
www.carelpress.com (for a free digital guide to the series)
This collection © 2008 Christine A Shepherd & Chas White

Acknowledgements

Additional illustrations: Adrian Burrows
Designers: Adrian Burrows, Anne Louise Kershaw, Debbie Maxwell, Dean Ryan
Editorial team: Anne Louise Kershaw, Debbie Maxwell, Christine A Shepherd, Chas White
Subscriptions: Ann Batey (Manager), Brenda Hughes, Anne Maclagan

We wish to thank all those writers, editors, photographers, cartoonists, artists, press agencies and wire services who have given permission to reproduce copyright material. Every effort has been made to trace copyright holders of material but in a few cases this has not been possible. The publishers would be glad to hear from anyone who has not been consulted.

Once again, we are particularly grateful to Dan Hedley of The Independent and Laura Hitchcock of PA for their helpfulness and efficiency. We'd also like to thank Jack Croal of the Apple Centre, Manchester, for his invaluable help.

Cover design: Anne Louise Kershaw

Front cover photos (clockwise from top left)
Natallie Evans, PA Wire/PA Photos, pg 159
African elephant, Shutterstock, pg 20
Lifeguard in burkini, Surf Life Saving Australia, pg 35
Power station, Shutterstock, pg 177
Head illustration, Shutterstock, pg 127
Oscar Pistorius, AP/PA Photos, pg 44
Joanna Dyer, PA Wire/PA Photos, pg 191

Back cover photos
Ashley Cole and Cheryl Tweedy, PA Archive/PA Photos, pg 142
Rescued child labourer, AP/PA Photos, pg 184
Nicola McKeown and Connor McCreadie, AP/PA Photos, pg 75
Muslim women, PA wire/PA Photos, pg 132
Amillia Sonja Taylor, AP/PA Photos, pg 167

**British Library
Cataloguing in Publication Data**
Essential Articles 10: the resource for issues
   1. Social problems 2. Social sciences – Study and teaching
   I. Shepherd, Christine A   II. White, C
082
   ISBN   978-1-905600-11-3

Printed by Finemark, Poland

Jenny (who has autism) suffered extreme mental bullying and she lashed out. The school just excluded her
page 31

Contents

CLOTHES

DISABILITY

> She can command a wage of £17 per month, but to earn this amount she must work between 60 and 90 hours each week
> page 34

DRUGS

EATING DISORDERS

EDUCATION

ENVIRONMENT

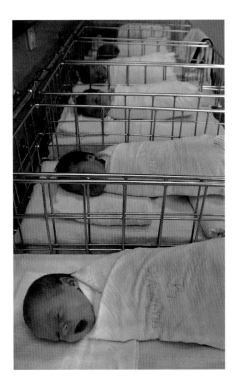

I became so ill that my body began cannibalising its own organs ... and I could barely get up the stairs
page 53

FAMILY

FUTURE

Contents

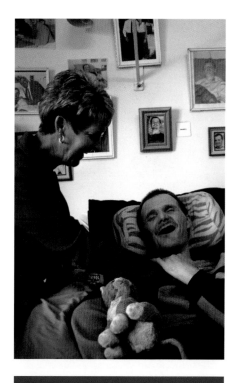

I'm definitely never going to have children... If we're serious about cutting levels of consumption... then we've simply got to stop making new consumers
page 69

Contents

Connor now weighs 14 stone... a miserable little boy entombed in a block of blubber
page 74

Contents

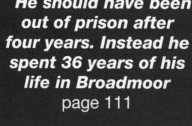

He should have been out of prison after four years. Instead he spent 36 years of his life in Broadmoor
page 111

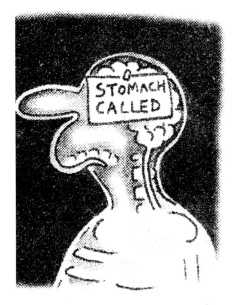

Some women actually prefer abortion to contraception as a means of controlling their fertility
page 161

Contents

WORK

I found him in a terrible state, struggling to breathe and with little blue bruises all over his body. His blanket, nappy and a bag of clothes we'd brought were missing
page 188

YOUNG PEOPLE

What is so thrilling about killing a deer?

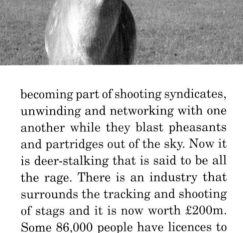

Terence Blacker

An exciting new sport is becoming popular in America. Enterprising safari owners have realised that there is good money to be made from the internet and are bringing the joys of hunting animals into the home. A variety of mammals – antelope, wild pig, deer and others – roam in an enclosed safari park where there are a number of rigs with webcams and remote-control .22 rifles. Online hunters can, at a click of the mouse, shoot an animal and, for a fee, be sent its mounted head. It is now possible to be a successful sportsman, with a wall covered in trophies, without actually leaving the house.

There are social benefits to the new sport, according to its supporters. By keeping a distance from his prey, man is becoming more evolved and civilised as a hunter, moving from bare hands, to a blade, to a gun and to a computer. It is a marvellous opportunity for the disabled. Shots deemed to be unethical or likely to wound can be over-ruled by an online assistant.

Although there seems little likelihood that computerised hunting will reach these islands, it does point up why the new popularity of shooting here is cause for niggling concern. Last month we heard that ambitious, fun-loving business folk were increasingly becoming part of shooting syndicates, unwinding and networking with one another while they blast pheasants and partridges out of the sky. Now it is deer-stalking that is said to be all the rage. There is an industry that surrounds the tracking and shooting of stags and it is now worth £200m. Some 86,000 people have licences to shoot deer.

It is all about the countryside, apparently. Those who shoot stags are essentially enjoying life in the wild. "The reasons people do it," a recent convert has explained, "is to see nature and understand it".

Does anyone seriously believe that? Was David Cameron, recently revealed to have been a deer-stalker in his time, doing no more than adding a bit of fun to a walk in the countryside? Common sense suggests that, when it comes to the hunting of a large mammal, the killing of it – a socially accepted form of extreme violence – is an essential part of the thrill.

There are the online hunters in America who experience not so much as a sniff of the outside air as they enjoy their sport. A man who runs a big-game hunting agency in Africa once told me that he was startled by the type of people who wanted to shoot game. Many of them were not remotely interested in wildlife but were middle-aged men, showing off to younger girlfriends.

It is not so far from the kind of inadequates who yearn for trophies from the "big five" species in Africa to David Cameron and his other stalking enthusiasts in this country. The sport is all about the joy of killing a large, magnificent animal.

Clearly, in the case of deer, there is a practical problem of landscape management to be addressed – their numbers are increasing at an unhealthy rate, causing damage to trees and the rest of the environment. But the culling of them should not be an excuse for encouraging rifle-toting stalkers to "see nature and understand it".

I should confess a personal bias – I have shot a stag and disliked the experience. At a time when we fret about violence and animal welfare, it seems perverse to accept the shooting of deer as an acceptable even desirable recreation. It is a blood-drenched sport which brings out the worst in its participants.

The Independent 14 March 2007

Should we give in to our children's pleas for pets?

Rachel Carlyle

There's nothing like children nagging for a pet to make you feel like Cruella De Vil. After all, there are only so many times you can extol the benefits of a goldfish when what they really want is something furry. An Andrex puppy would be top of the list, closely followed by a mewing kitten with big eyes and an oversized head (a bit like Barbie, really, but more needy). After completely failing to convert my daughter to the joys of goldfish ownership, we are at a stalemate: I've said no pets, she sulks. Nowhere are my deficiencies paraded more than on the way to school, where every cat en route is lovingly stroked and petted, no matter how mangy and unappealing.

As it turns out, my approach may well be wrong. There's a whole raft of studies that have proved that having a pet actually benefits children. One showed that kids aged between five and 11 who kept pets were healthier and more emotionally balanced than those who didn't. They were also more kind and patient. "If you are kind to animals, you tend to be kind to humans too," said Dr Deborah Wells, a psychologist who specialises in animals. She believes a pet can help children's self-esteem because it loves you unconditionally – even when you're convinced that your parents hate you and you're definitely adopted. It's also

a cheerful companion to them: one survey discovered that a third of children with pets went to them when they felt unwell, 85 per cent used them as a playmate and 37 per cent had their pet beside them when they were doing their homework. In adults, pets have been shown to lower their owners' blood pressure and stress levels, so there's no reason to think they won't do the same for children. In one rather bizarre bit of research, children with pets were even shown to have more stable immune systems and be less prone to minor illness, hence they had almost two weeks more schooling each year that non-pet owners.

But just as I am feeling like relenting, friends have warned me off. They say a child's interest in the pet wanes incredibly quickly once they have got their way – and it will always be the parent who is left to clean out the rabbit hutch, feed the cat and take the dog for walks. One said: "The kids had badgered me for at least a year to get a dog, and when I finally caved in, their interest was incredibly short-lived. Tara, the oldest, had been reading dog-rearing manuals at bedtime for several months, but even she had lost interest after the first few weeks and complained about going out on long walks."

Animal experts say a parent should never assume that the child will look after the pet, and should never get one unless they are happy to do the work themselves. It's also unrealistic to give a child under five or six a pet thinking that they will understand the responsibility involved: they won't. And, strangely, they warn that even if a child has constantly nagged for a pet, once they have an animal it can take up to a year for them to accept it, especially if it's a boisterous puppy.

If you do say yes, consider carefully which might be the best animal for your situation. It's now regarded as a myth that pets cause allergies in children (in fact, all the evidence shows that children who are exposed to a pet in their first year of life will end up being healthier and stronger). But if your child is asthmatic or already prone to allergies, you might be better off with our rodent friends. "Cats, dogs, and horses – in that order – appear to be the worst offenders for allergies," says GP Dr Rob Hicks, author of Beat Your Allergies: 52 Brilliant Ideas to Find Relief and Feel Free (Infinite Ideas) "Small furry animals, for example hamsters and rabbits, are less likely to cause problems."

The RSPCA points out that dogs are probably the most expensive (at nearly £10,000 over their lifetime) and time-consuming and are also completely unsuitable if you're out of the house all day. A cat is clean and can be a good companion, but will probably damage furniture and carpets. Of the assorted small, furry creatures, they advise steering clear of rabbits because they can be lonely on their own but aggressive with other rabbits; hamsters are nocturnal, which isn't such a good bet for those under 10; rats and guinea pigs are good but get lonely on their own; and mice can smell.

Which, I'm afraid to say, leads us right back to the goldfish.

Sunday Express 19 November 2006

Rescue me
Britain sees sharp rise in unwanted pets

Trapped between walls, stranded in a river, stuck in a hole or simply unwanted, the RSPCA rescued nearly 150,000 domestic, wild and farm animals from dangerous and distressing situations in 2006.

The number of animals rescued by the RSPCA just because their owners did not want them any more increased by 44%.

Top of the league for the second year, cats were the most unwanted pets. Despite their apparent popularity – more households in Britain own one than any other domestic animal – the RSPCA rescued nearly 3,000 unwanted cats last year, more than double the number of unwanted dogs.

RSPCA annual rescue figures in 2006 also showed:

- overall the most animals were rescued because of sickness and injury
- the Society rescued more wild birds than any other type of animal
- animals in road traffic accidents increased by more than 2,000 – from 7,711 to 9,885
- more cats were rescued from road traffic accidents and being stuck up trees than any other domestic or wild animal
- the RSPCA responded to more than one million calls from members of the public

Andy Foxcroft, chief officer of RSPCA inspectorate, said: "We rescue a staggering number of animals from a wide range of difficult, distressing and often surprising situations each year. But what strikes me particularly about our latest figures is the huge number of animals we rescue simply because their owners no longer want them.

"With the new Animal Welfare Act now in force – which means owners are legally obliged to find out about their pet's particular needs and care for it properly – we really hope more people will consider the full responsibility they are taking on before getting an animal. Hopefully this will mean the RSPCA rescuing fewer unwanted animals."

Typical RSPCA rescues in 2006 include:

- a cat rescued from the bumper compartment of a van, after being driven around Birmingham all day
- a fox cub entangled in a football net
- a terrier rescued after being trapped all day between a cavity wall
- a kitten rescued from a two-inch gap between his house and another building
- a sheep stranded in stormy weather on the banks of a river
- four puppies dumped in a cardboard box in woods

Source: RSPCA

Caring and cruel:

our attitude to animals just does not make sense

W F Deedes

Oh dear, the cat's in trouble again. It has discovered that the peanuts my daughter puts out in canisters for small birds are an excellent stalking ground. Three times in the past week it has ambushed blue tits and laid them on the mat at the back door. There is something a little Dr Jekyll and Mr Hyde about cats. When snoozing after a night's hunting or at the foot of the bed, they are a picture of innocence and tranquillity.

Winston Churchill loved to see the cat at the foot of his bed – though how the animal survived the cigar smoke that clouded Winston's bedroom as he worked off the pillows most mornings, we will never know. Why, I asked a member of my household after the blue tit episodes, do we blame the cat when it kills a small bird but applaud it when it catches a mouse? "Mice are dirty little animals and can contaminate our food," she replied. "They are vermin. Little birds are not."

I have been meditating on this observation. It does not wholly explain our contradictory attitude towards animals.

When I see a squirrel gathering acorns for winter storage, I see it as an endearing animal. When it raids the aforementioned bird table, I see it as a rat with a bushy tail. Hunting foxes, indulged by a minority, is treated as reprehensible. So increasingly is shooting pheasants or partridges, indulged by another minority. Fishing, which means hauling in a fish by means of a hook in its mouth, is popular and is seen as perfectly respectable The decline in religion has raised the status of animals. As long as the human tribe was separated from the animal tribe by its spirituality, they stood apart. Without the spiritual element, humans are different, but not all that superior. Some animals are at least as intelligent as some human beings and, come to think of it, a faithful pair of swans seem more moral than certain human beings.

Being cruel or neglecting animals is abhorrent and debases those who are guilty of it. I have particular sympathy for the donkeys of this world. I have seen so many of them over-worked and ill-treated. But we do not think twice about swatting hard-working bees, though many are superstitious about killing spiders. Badgers, which are friendly-looking beasts, have countless friends and defenders, though they are suspected of contributing to tuberculosis in cattle.

The great dividing line will always be between those who think experimenting on live animals in the interests of human beings is justified and those who regard it as vile, and will go to criminal lengths to harm those whom they hold directly or remotely connected with establishments engaged in such research.

Many years ago, as a junior minister in the Home Office, I had tenuous responsibility for this activity. My office was troubled by the correspondence we received about it. Well, I said, we have an inspectorate for these establishments and the public is entitled to know that, where experiments on live animals are carried out, the rules are strict and the inspectors are watchful. We must make sure they are.

I still believe that is the right answer. It will not satisfy the extremists who make experiments on animals an excuse for war against human beings, but if we want these experiments to continue in our interests, then there must be – as I hope there are today – strict regulations and a strong system for enforcing them.

Daily Telegraph 9 December 2006
© Telegraph Group Limited 2006

The essence of dogness

Crufts celebrates only a small, shallow section of the canine race. Real dog lovers prefer mongrels

Roy Hattersley

Dogs are for life, not just for exhibition. I became convinced of that when I visited Crufts four years ago. My conviction is reinforced every time the annual show comes around and is publicised by pictures of potential winners from exotic breeds. Being one myself, I am instinctively on the side of mongrels. But it is not my highly developed egalitarian instinct which has turned me against the canine perfection that comes from pedigree. I just find the idea of loving a dog because of its appearance inherently repulsive. Dogs should be loved because they are dogs. Nothing less. Nothing more.

My dog Buster happens to be extremely handsome – he has the shape of a small alsatian and the coat of a Staffordshire bull terrier. But we no more chose him for his good looks than for his other qualities – extraordinary intelligence, phenomenal loyalty and remarkable affection. He needed a good home and we wanted a dog. We paid to have him, but the money went to providing a refuge for other canine waifs and strays. Buying and selling dogs, as a commercial enterprise, seems to me an unattractive way of earning a living.

Crufts is a highly commercial enterprise. The casual visitor could be forgiven for believing that it exists solely to promote the sale of dog food. And half of the owners with dogs on show hope that, by winning a cup or a rosette, the puppies they breed will sell at a premium. Breeding dogs is, in itself, a morally dubious activity. So many unwanted strays and outcasts need good homes that we ought to look after them before we actively engage in production of the pedigree alternative.

Believe me, I have nothing against pure-bred dogs themselves – despite the unhappy experience we had when we bought a Yorkshire terrier for my mother. We were assured that Magnus – just the last of the nine names on his pedigree – would live to be 12. Since my mother was 83 at the time, we assumed that he would remain her companion for the rest of her life. He died of a heart attack at eight and she lived to be 97. He was lovely, though unreliable. I brought him home inside my coat because he was cold as well as tiny, and I almost kept him for myself. But I would have been just as reluctant to part with him if, instead of having a fringe dangling engagingly over his eyes, he had been (in Crufts' exacting terms) as ugly as sin.

My mother's last dog was – though, to be fair, we chose her for her looks. Distress at the loss of Magnus resulted in a refusal "ever to go through that again". So we went to the local RSPCA refuge and found a dog that could be represented as too pathetic to be decently rejected. Sally – smooth-haired at the front and long-haired at the back – had such a clear dividing line running round her middle that she looked as though Dr Frankenstein had sewn two half dogs together. After six years of happy companionship, she survived my mother and now lives out her retirement on a friend's farm. What, I wonder, do the luminaries of Crufts think should have happened to her?

I know what I would do if I was offered a lost borzoi or a homeless shih-tzu. Assuming that Buster agreed, I would welcome them with open arms. But when I see the "Best of Breed" listed on the Crufts website, I wonder how its enthusiasts would react to the worst of breeds. In my experience, the most unprepossessing mongrel still exhibits all the qualities that makes dogs irresistible. The tail may be too long, the ears unpricked and curve of the spine less than classical. But they are all dogs. And it is the universal dog – the essence of dogness – that makes, or ought to make, us want them.

All civilised people – whether they are dog lovers or not – deplore the employment of a poodle or a dalmatian as a fashion accessory. The exhibition of a flawless labrador or an impeccable corgi is only one step away from treating dogs as "positional goods" – something which is not of value in itself but is acquired to illustrate the owner's special status. There are some beautiful dogs at Crufts – as well as stall after stall of canine trash, which no dog owner needs. But do not think that the show is a celebration of the whole canine race. The real dog lovers are people who go to dog rescues and ask if they have a potential friend in need of care and protection.

© The Guardian 12 March 2007

The Observer 11 March 2007

The tale of the tail continues

Even after the docking ban comes into force controversy persists

Possibly originating with the Romans – who believed that tails were the source of rabies – the practice of removing dogs' tails was boosted in the 1790s. Amongst the inventive methods used to finance the wars against the French, there was a tax on dogs (alongside the better known taxes on windows and wig powder). Working dogs were exempt, and thrifty citizens had their dogs' tails docked to establish their working credentials. Later, when the Kennel Club (established 1873) began to set standards for the various breeds, docking became enshrined as the normal practice for certain dogs. All this, however, was before the concept of animal welfare had entered the national consciousness.

Docking is done at a few days old. The base of the puppy's tail is encircled by a rubber ring, causing the blood supply to be cut off, or the tail is removed with surgical scissors or a knife. From the 1990s this procedure could only be carried out by a vet and now, with the passing of the Animal Welfare Act, only on working dogs from specified breeds.

The reasons for tail docking, and the extent to which it is painful, are hotly disputed. To those who oppose it, docking is an unnecessary, painful mutilation which deprives a dog of an essential body part and a means of communication. Supporters of the practice see it as a harmless and virtually pain free procedure which prevents later injury to dogs working in the undergrowth. Amongst those who opposed the ban, and whose dogs are exempt, are the police and armed forces.

By the end of April 2007 tail docking for cosmetic reasons was illegal in most of the UK (the legislation for Northern Ireland was delayed) – but controversy and confusion remain. In Scotland there are no exemptions for working dogs while in England and Wales some breeds – spaniels and terriers, for example – may still be docked.

The dog world remains divided. While the Anti-docking Alliance is angry that any exemptions still exist, the Council for Docked Breeds argues that dogs will suffer when they inevitably injure their tails. They argue that breeders will go out of business rather than comply with the law, leading to the extinction of some breeds. Both these groups might regard the partial exemption as a victory for the Countryside Alliance and the British Shooting and Conservation Society whose gundogs will still be docked.

The RSPCA has, naturally, been an opponent of tail docking and the Royal College of Veterinary Surgeons has a policy of opposing docking except for medical reasons or for working dogs. While in the past the Council for Docked Breeds could discreetly connect members with sympathetic vets, the Animal Welfare Act now requires documentary proof that the dog will be working.

The effect of the ban on show dogs will take time to work through. There are different regulations for shows where the public pay and where they do not, different rules for dogs docked before and after the ban and it is still possible to enter a docked dog in a show of working dogs.

What is certain is that the Act will result in changes to the appearance of some breeds and, in time, Crufts, the world's most famous dog show will only be able to welcome canines who can show very clearly how happy they are to be there.

Sources: various

The eagle that came to visit

Hamilton Wende

Photo: John Dale

The crash was terrifyingly loud

I was sitting upright naked in bed in my hotel room when a spray of glass shards shot across the room covering the bed and floor. It left me utterly disorientated.

My mind raced back to the war zones I had covered. Explosions or gunfire that I had experienced in Baghdad, Congo, or the townships in South Africa all came flooding back to me.

But this was a quiet Sunday morning in downtown Lusaka, the capital of Zambia, a country that has never known war, and it just did not make any kind of sense.

My hands were shaking slightly and my head spinning as I threw back the covers and scrambled out of bed.

Lying on the carpet below the shattered window was an eagle. It was, well, spread-eagled on its back amid the shards of broken glass.

Hauntingly beautiful

For a moment I stood there, transfixed, staring at this bizarre phenomenon.

The great sandy-coloured bird looked almost human in its semi-conscious distress. Its large wings were fully extended to the length of my own arms, its feet opening and shutting uncontrollably, its eyes fluttering half-open.

There was something hauntingly beautiful in the deep brown colour of its eyes, in the curve of its sharp talons and in its long scythe-like beak that would tear the flesh of my face and arms to shreds in panicked incomprehension if I picked it up.

I did not know what to do next. I knew I had to act before it regained full consciousness.

First I ran into the bathroom and wrapped a towel around my waist, partly to protect my dignity and partly to protect everything else.

Panicky moments

I then tried to open the door, which led onto a balcony so the bird would have an escape route. But the door kept slamming shut, on an automatic spring, so somehow I managed to wedge it open with a plastic waste paper basket.

All the while the eagle was beginning to wake up and stare at me with increasingly bright and it seemed to me, angry eyes, as if it blamed me for its predicament.

A lonely life for Golden Boy

Finally, I slipped on a pair of sandals and grabbed another towel. In a sliding, and certainly indecorous, series of panicky movements, I rushed across the sea of broken glass and wrapped a towel around the eagle.

I held it in my hands for a few moments, aware of the strange paradox of vulnerability and power contained in its warm, surprisingly light body. Its head was held straight on its shoulders. It was clearly coming to. I threw it gently out through the remains of the window. It stretched its wings and flew unharmed into a nearby tree.

As I got dressed I found myself wondering what extraordinary circumstance had brought an eagle to crash through my window. There seemed something both wonderful and vaguely disturbing about it.

Bad omen

My Zambian colleague was visibly distressed when I told him. "It is a bad omen," he said. "Most people here believe that something terrible will happen to you now."

I did not want to believe him, but secretly I was uncomfortable. Eagles and omens have been part of both African and Western mythology since earliest times and we cannot shake off our primal psychological feelings that easily.

The front manager was both fascinated and appalled. "I must make an immediate physical inspection," he said, and soon my room was filled with hotel staff staring open-mouthed at the litter of broken glass and feathers.

The story spread quickly through the hotel, becoming a kind of Aesop's Fable for the age of air-conditioning.

"We have found the bird," the security manager told me at breakfast. I was escorted to a room beneath the kitchen where, with a dramatic flourish, he pulled a dead pigeon out of a drawer.

"No," I told him. "It was an eagle. A big eagle". I spread my arms out to make my point.

"I told you so," a young security guard said triumphantly to his boss. "It was chasing that little bird. The pigeon hit the window first and then the eagle crashed through the glass."

The case had been solved.

Seeking protection

But there was still the lingering omen to be cleared up. They gave me a new room, and all the next day, the staff looked at me curiously. "No birds this morning?" one of the elevator technicians asked.

Finally, the young security guard came to me in the lobby. "You must not be worried," he said, "about the meaning of what happened. It is a good sign. That pigeon was seeking your protection. It means you are man who has kindness."

Of course, I had not the heart to point out the irony that it was the pigeon which died, and the eagle which was saved.

BBC Radio 4, From Our Own Correspondent
24 March, 2007

Over a remote corner of the Lake District a magnificent bird with a six foot wingspan soars and glides in an impressive mating display. But the spectacular swooping and turning is in vain: his mate died three years ago and there is no female eagle within hundreds of miles – ten year old Golden Boy is the last golden eagle in England.

The golden eagle was exterminated in England and Wales by 1850, but a hundred years later Scottish eagles found their way to the Lake District. Hopes were high for their reintroduction when they first bred in 1969. But the population declined; since 1996 no young have fledged. Golden Boy and his mate were the last breeding pair and recently their egg laying had stopped.

Eagles pair for life, but if one of the pair dies the survivor will accept a new mate. However the obvious idea of introducing a new female from Scotland's more robust population is probably not practical. Golden eagles are very territorial and in the unlikely event of a female being captured for release in the Lakes, she would probably try to return to her home range, possibly at the cost of her life. The only hope for Golden Boy is if an eligible female arrives of her own accord.

While Scotland is home to 430 breeding pairs of golden eagles, even here they are not secure. The encroachment of humans threatens their ranges, with increased tree planting and inappropriately sited windfarms being particular problems.

These impressive birds of prey hunt by flying low and striking swiftly Their live prey is mainly rabbits, hares and grouse – anything larger could only be taken when it is already dead. Scare stories of eagles carrying off dogs and children are unlikely to be true since the maximum that they can lift is 4-5kg. Nevertheless, not everyone welcomes them – birds have been poisoned, (though two anonymous donors expressed their disgust by pledging £10.000 as a reward for information). Since they lay only one clutch of eggs each year, the eagles are also very vulnerable to egg collectors.

While Golden Boy continues his undulating flights above the Haweswater estate all his admirers and protectors can do is to hope that history repeats itself and, as in the 1950s, a bird finds its way to his remote, beautiful but solitary home.

Sources: RSPB and others
http://www.rspb.org.uk/

A sad tail with an artificial ending

Fuji the bottlenose dolphin showcases the world's first artificial fin

Photo: PANA JIJI/PA Photos

The star attraction of the Okinawa Churaumi Aquarium in southern Japan had delighted visitors for decades. Fuji the bottlenose dolphin, who has been a resident at the aquarium since 1976, is one of the main reasons why the aquarium gets so many visitors each year. Then an unknown disease destroyed her tailfin and it was feared she might never swim or leap through the water again.

Fuji had suffered from the mystery disease since 2002. What started as a loss of appetite and discolouration of her tail quickly developed into something much worse. Following intense treatment with antibiotics and transfusions for 60 days, Fuji thoroughly recovered from the disease although she lost 75% of her tail flukes.

Unable to swim, Fuji became quickly depressed and staff feared she might soon die if nothing was done. Although doctors at the aquarium had cured the disease, they could do nothing about the fin. But, thanks to three years of constant work by an acrylic sculptor, Fuji now has the world's first artificial tailfin, and a total new lease of life.

Veterinarians from the aquarium first turned to Bridgestone, the company which makes tyres for Formula One cars to see if they could come up with a rubber replacement for the lost fin. In 2003 they developed the first fluke cast out of silicon, but when tested on Fuji it did not work well because of attachment problems and because Fuji did not like wearing it.

The aquarium then turned to Kazuhiko Yakushiji, a famous acrylic sculptor, to see if he could help. He experimented and found a better way of attaching the fin using carbon fibre reinforced plastic. Following a lot of hard work, his efforts finally paid off as he developed a tail which would comfortably attach to Fuji's to enable her to swim again.

> **Unable to swim, Fuji became quickly depressed and staff feared she might soon die if nothing was done**

As with most wild animals, dolphins do not like foreign objects attached to their bodies, but because this attachment would again allow Fuji to swim, the mother of three had to go through a programme of rehabilitation training which included training her to become accustomed to the regular medical check-ups she'd now be needing.

First the dolphin was trained to show her fin to staff for inspection, then gradually things were attached to her fin to prepare her for her artificial fin until she was comfortable and staff could attach it without any distress to Fuji.

Once the artificial fin was attached, Fuji had to go through her second stage of rehabilitation. Although the fin was on, Fuji didn't swim straight away. She had been used to just floating in the pool and being hand fed by the trainers and so had to be re-trained to swim with her new tail. Trainers took time to train her patiently and her sessions are now open to the public to watch.

Fuji can now swim, jump and will happily allow keepers to giver her regular health checks. Although she cannot say how the artificial tail feels, keepers at the aquarium say her playful noises show she is happy again. According to their latest blood

> **Her playful noises show she is happy again**

test results, Fuji is now healthier than ever. Despite this, they continue to look into further developing and improving the artificial tail and hope that research done will give further insight into the function and mechanism of a dolphin's natural tail flukes.

Sources: Various

DNA detectives

Has new scientific research come in time to hunt out the ivory trade and save the African elephant from extinction?

A scientific breakthrough may have the potential to save the tens of thousands of African elephants who are hunted for their ivory. By analysing DNA taken from a seizure of illegal ivory, researchers at the University of Washington's Centre for Conservation Biology have created a genetic map of the African elephant. By tracing the geographical origin of the elephant they are able to work out the areas targeted by poachers.

The African elephant population decreased from 1.3 million to 500,000 individuals in the eight years between 1979 and 1987. This prompted a global ban, in 1989, on the sale of ivory, brought in by the Convention on International Trade in Endangered Species (Cites), and the African elephant was listed as an endangered species. Eighteen years on, however, the illegal trade in ivory has reached the highest levels ever reported.

Some crime syndicates are finding that ivory has become not only more lucrative, but easier to move than illegal drugs.

When the ban was introduced, a kilogram of ivory could sell for $100. Prices dropped to around $10 dollars, but then continued to increase, rocketing to $850 (£440) this year, meaning the largest tusks can sell for thousands of dollars. With such a financial incentive, poachers are more attracted than ever.

More than 23 tonnes of illegal ivory were seized between August 2005 and August 2006, most of it from recently killed elephants. Researchers say the actual weight of smuggled tusks will be ten times this amount. This would mean that about 234 tonnes of ivory were exported from Africa that year and, despite the global ban, at least 23,000 elephants were hunted for their tusks last year alone.

Samuel Wasser who led the study at the University of Washington in Seattle, said the seizures suggested that poaching is taking place on a scale unseen since the ban was first introduced. As well as elephants living in the savannah habitat, forest elephants add another challenge. Logging, road building and the bushmeat trade have recently made forest elephants more vulnerable to poaching. Poaching at this rate will clearly drive the species rapidly into extinction.

The work of the researchers in developing a genetic map will allow wildlife authorities to pinpoint poaching hotspots and potential trade routes.

In order to get suitable DNA the ivory first has to be reduced to powder. Previous attempts to do this through heat had destroyed the DNA but researchers borrowed a technique used by dentists to grind teeth to dust. By using a machine that freezes the ivory at -240°C, they would be able to make it brittle enough to be turned into powder, and the DNA was preserved.

Dr Wasser and his team put the theory to the test to trace the source of one of the largest shipments of ivory intercepted in recent years. The consignment contained about 6.5 tonnes and was seized in Singapore in 2002. It contained 532 tusks, with an average weight of 11kg. The shipment also included 42,120 ivory cylinders, known as hankos. These are used to make stamps bearing personal seals and carry great prestige in South Asia. The hankos alone were worth about $8.4 million.

Researchers had collected elephant dung from across Africa to extract the DNA enabling then to produce a map detailing the genetic make-up of the continent's elephants. Once the DNA of the ivory was known, Dr Wasser compared it to the map. The samples tested matched the genetics of elephants from Zambia and its surrounding savannah. Zambia's director of wildlife has now been replaced, and significantly harsher sentences introduced for those convicted of ivory trafficking.

Although the discovery has influenced policy in Zambia, further international action is urgently needed. The information gathered from genetic tracking, should allow conservationists to protect elephants better where they are most at risk from poaching. Telling authorities where greater enforcement efforts are needed will help to identify trade routes used to move ivory inside and outside Africa. Such results will force nations to be more responsive to the poaching in their country.

Sources: Various

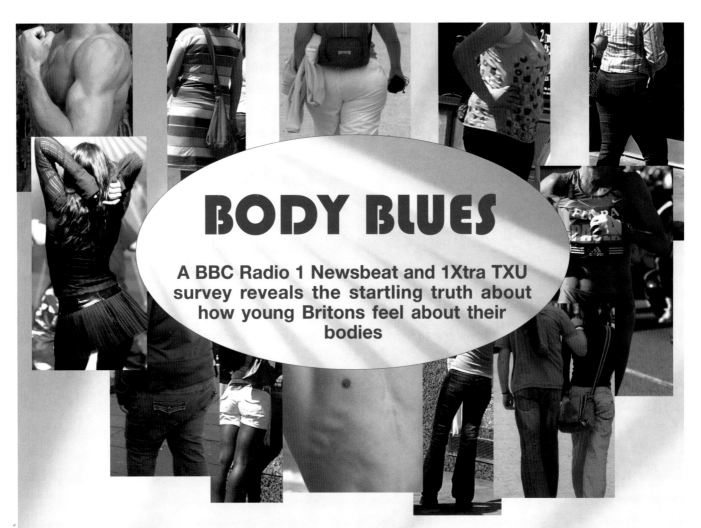

BODY BLUES

A BBC Radio 1 Newsbeat and 1Xtra TXU survey reveals the startling truth about how young Britons feel about their bodies

Almost 25,000 people completed a 16-question survey via the Radio 1 Newsbeat and 1Xtra TXU websites, between 26 January and 9 February 2007.

The vast majority, 85%, of respondents, were aged 17 to 35.

Body Image

Almost a third (31%) of size 12 women describe their body as either overweight or fat, rising to two-thirds (66%) amongst size 14 women.

Half of the women surveyed (50%) said that there are "lots they would change" about their body, while more than one in ten said that they "hate" their body.

In comparison half of the men (49%) said that they are "ok" with how they look, and one in ten are "very happy" with their appearance.

More than half (53%) of the girls, aged 12 to 16, feel that their body image either stops them from getting a boyfriend or means that they cannot relax in a relationship.

Given the choice of three different female body types, both men and women rated a curvy body as the best.

Plastic Surgery

More than 50% of female respondents said they would consider having plastic surgery, compared with less than a quarter of men. Of those women, 36% would opt for breast enhancement, and 32% would go for liposuction.

Size Zero

Despite heated debate, less than 1% of respondents said that they were size zero (UK size 4). The survey suggests they are more likely to hate their body than size 12 women.

Diets

Forty-three per cent of the women say that they have skipped a meal to try and lose weight, whilst 8% have made themselves sick.

More than one in five female respondents said that they were on a diet, compared to fewer than one in ten men.

Weight Watchers was by far the most popular diet (with almost 20% of the dieters following it), but Atkins has plummeted in popularity with only 1% opting for the low carbohydrate eating plan.

Boys Bulking Up

On protein supplements, 20% of young men in their early 20s say that they have taken them, compared to 11% of over 35s.

When asked to rate photos of differently shaped male bodies, almost 80% of men favoured a very muscular physique.

In response to the survey the Radio 1 website has been bombarded with comments. These clearly mirror the survey results as the girls talk of wanting to be thinner and the boys more muscular. There are hundreds of comments such as "I'm a size 8 but my friends say I'm fat' and "in my teens I was skinny and lanky and couldn't wait to put weight on'. These show the obsession we have with our body image is clearly not going to go away.

This is the world's most beautiful couple...

Perfect woman: Naomi Campbell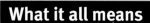

The vital statistics

Body mass index
20.85

Bust girth to height
49.3%

Waist-chest ratio
1.4

Leg-to-body ratio
1.4

Calf girth to height
19.5%

Height
175cm

Thigh girth to height
29.7

What it all means

"Super beautiful" women have waists a third smaller than their hips and three-quarters their bust measurement. They have longer legs, and slimmer thighs and calves than the average woman.

Perfect man: Christian Bale

The vital statistics

Body mass index
26.5

Waist-chest ratio
0.6

Leg-to-body ratio
1

Height
188cm

What it all means

The physically ideal man is more than 6ft tall, with legs the same length as his upper body. The leg-to-body ratio of 1 makes him appear more muscular, which is why the ideal BMI for men is higher than for women.

Photo: Michael Germana Starmax/EMPICS Entertainment/PA Photos

Photo: Paul Smith EMPICS Entertainment/PA Photos

...and we have the figures to prove it

Roger Dobson

It is the holy grail of the fashion and beauty industries: a scientific blueprint for the most beautiful women, and men, in the world.

Researchers have thrown away the old vital statistics and, instead, focused on how the dimensions of different parts of the body relate to height and body mass index (BMI) to give the perfect physique. Perhaps surprisingly, two of the most important measurements are the girth of the thigh and the slimness of the calf.

The researchers, from the University of Gdansk in Poland, studied the vital

statistics of 24 finalists in a national beauty competition, together with those of 115 other women. They said that while weight, height and hip ratio were normally used to assess female attractiveness, these might not throw up crucial differences between the super-attractive and others.

For men, scientists said height, BMI, waist-to-hip and waist-to-chest ratios were key measures.

Super-attractive women had a thigh-to-height ratio some 12 per cent lower than other women, giving them a more slender look. Skin-fold tests on the calf showed 15mm of

fat compared with 18mm in other women. The study also showed that the average super-attractive height was 5ft 9in, with the waist 76 per cent of the size of the chest, and 70 per cent of the size of the hips. Models built like Naomi Campbell came closest to the ideal.

"Attractiveness of a woman's body is one of the most important factors in mate selection, and the question what are the physical cues for the assessment of attractiveness is fundamental to evolutionary psychology," said Leszek Pokrywka, who led the study.

The Independent on Sunday 11 March 2007

The BMI myth

It's long been accepted as the most accurate indication of good health, but now the efficiency of the body mass index is being questioned

by Peta Bee

What do Brad Pitt and Russell Crowe have in common with most members of the England rugby and football teams? Those perfectly honed, toned bodies, of course. Except if you rely on the most widely used measurement of fatness, the body mass index (BMI) – which classifies this collection of supremely fit-looking individuals as either overweight or obese. So concerned have some researchers become with such inaccuracies, that they are calling for the BMI to be replaced with more accurate measures of health status.

Devised by the Belgian statistician Adolphe Quetelet, the BMI has been used to define weight for more than 100 years. It is used by hospitals and doctors' surgeries, insurance companies, university researchers, drugs companies and slimming clubs; and professions such as the fire and police services

require prospective employees to have a BMI that does not exceed healthy recommendations.

Part of its appeal is its simplicity of calculation: weight in kilograms is divided by height in metres squared – someone with a BMI of less than 18.5 is considered underweight, between 18.5 and 24.9 is "normal", 25 to 29.9 is "overweight" and 30 or greater is clinically obese.

But the measurement's downfall is that it does not take into account body composition – whether or not excess weight is fat or muscle – which is why fit people often find themselves in the fat category of the BMI rating system. Among those leading the call for the BMI to be replaced is Dr Margaret Ashwell, a visiting research fellow in nutrition at Oxford Brookes University and a former member of the government's Food Advisory Committee. "The important thing to consider is how body fat is distributed around the body, as the real problems occur when fat accumulates in the central abdominal region," Ashwell says.

Now scientists from the renowned Mayo Clinic in Rochester are questioning the accuracy and usefulness of the BMI. Reviewing data from 40 studies involving 250,000 people with heart disease, they found that while severely obese patients had a higher risk of death, overweight people had fewer heart problems than those with a normal BMI.

Because muscle is denser than fat, many physically fit people are mistakenly classified as "overweight", while they are actually less likely to die young than a "normal" weight individual whose excess weight is mostly fat.

Dr David McCarthy, a senior lecturer in human nutrition at London Metropolitan University, looked at waist circumference as a predictor of obesity in a study of children published last year in the International Journal of Obesity. It was found that the average waistband of two-year-old girls has increased by more than 5% in a decade, while that of boys has grown by 4%. The measurements represented a far greater increase in fat than had been suggested by studies using the BMI.

We want people to understand that a fat middle is bad news

But if BMI is outdated and inaccurate, what else might be used in its place? Tim Cole, a professor of medical statistics at the Institute of Child Health at Great Ormond Street Hospital, says that "body mass index is a cheap and cheerful way of measuring fatness but is not terribly good in detail". Cole suggests that a waist circumference measurement "is more informative, in that it is a direct measure of the part of the body that tends to accumulate fat". Having a waistband of more than 88cm (35in) in women and 102cm (40in) in men indicates the highest risk of cardiovascular and metabolic disease. There is an increased risk of the diseases for women with measurements of more than 80cm (32in) and men whose measurement is over 94cm (37in).

"Measuring waist circumference can help identify patients at higher risk of these problems," says Dr David Haslam, a GP and chair of the National Obesity Forum. "Yet surveys we have carried out show that many people, including some doctors, are unaware that this measurement is a good health predictor."

Ashwell recommends a waist:height ratio "that is applicable to everyone, even children". She has developed her own chart that is already being used by some practice nurses, heart charities and private medical companies such as BUPA.

"Interestingly, when you work out the number of people who are obese using the waist circumference or waist:height ratio, there are more UK men at risk than women. This underlines the problems with the BMI, which suggests the opposite to be true."

Getting out a tape measure is a simple way to keep tabs on your fatness at home, but what else is available? Dr Beckie Lang, spokesperson for the Obesity Resource and Information Centre (ORIC), says that skin caliper tests, such as those performed at gyms, can give an accurate measurement of body fat "provided the test is done by someone experienced as it is prone to error". Otherwise, body-fat scales, such as Tanita, are "fairly accurate", she says. "They work by sending a very small current through the body when you stand on the scales," Lang explains. "Muscles conduct the current, fat resists it and a computer inside the scales converts these figures to arrive at your body fat percentage."

Ashwell argues that GPs, insurance companies and the general public need to become used to a different way of thinking. "What we want is for people to understand that a fat middle is bad news," she says. "It is not how much you weigh, but where the excess fat gathers that causes problems."

© *The Guardian 28 November 2007*

Fatmen Slim (with liposuction's help)

Three-fold rise in surgery as men follow women's lead and fork out £3,000 a time to stave off mid-life crises

Jonathan Thompson

Middle-class men desperate to be slim are fuelling a near three-fold increase in liposuction operations, new figures show.

Weary of dieting or shuttling to the gym, men are following the example of thousands of female counterparts and having their excess fat vacuumed away.

Statistics compiled by the British Association of Aesthetic Plastic Surgeons, show a 280 per cent rise in male liposuction in the UK over the past two years, to 494 procedures last year.

Experts believe that the trend has been driven by an increasing obsession with body image combined with greater awareness, acceptance and availability of cosmetic surgery.

"Men are catching up with women in everything, from the way they dress and smell, to a willingness to have procedures like this done," said Adrian Richards, a consultant plastic surgeon at AR & Associates on Harley Street.

"Everyone has a bit of their body they would change in an ideal world – and now more men are realising they have the power to do exactly that."

Mr Richards said he has seen male liposuction patient numbers double at his own clinic over the past 12 months, with the neck, chin, flanks, abdomen and chest – the dreaded man boobs, or "moobs" – the most common areas for treatment. In its simplest form, liposuction involves the diluting or breaking up of fatty deposits in these parts of the body, before vacuuming them away. A typical procedure will cost upwards of £3,000.

Another leading Harley Street cosmetic surgeon, Dalia Nield of the London Clinic, said she too had noted a dramatic rise in the numbers of men demanding liposuction.

"These men have been living with unwanted fat for years and years," said Ms Nield. "If you feel like you have the hips of a hippopotamus, this can make a big difference to your life. Liposuction is a liberation for these people: they're able to wear T-shirts and take them off at the beach without being self-conscious."

James Spencer, a 45-year-old financial director, paid £6,000 for liposuction last year and describes it as "one of the best decisions I've ever made."

"It wasn't a case of wanting to lose weight – it was a case of trying to shift fat in an area I just couldn't lose it from at the gym," said Mr Spencer, from south London. "The result has been fantastic – a totally flat tummy. It makes you look better, feel healthier, and keeps you feeling at the top of your game professionally, particularly when you have ambitious younger people coming up beneath you. There is an element of me that says I have cheated a bit, but I have an entirely new wardrobe – and absolutely no regrets."

The Independent 18 March 2007

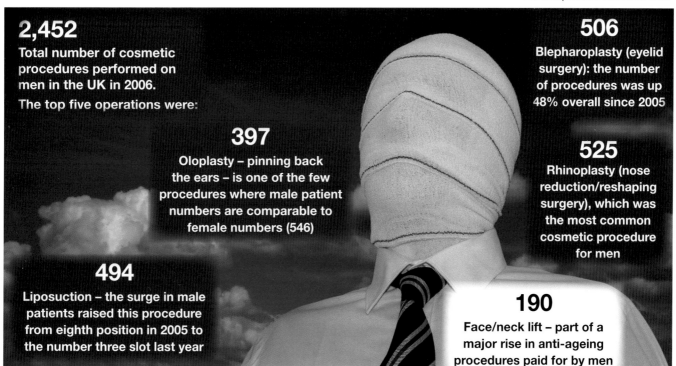

2,452
Total number of cosmetic procedures performed on men in the UK in 2006.
The top five operations were:

397
Oloplasty – pinning back the ears – is one of the few procedures where male patient numbers are comparable to female numbers (546)

494
Liposuction – the surge in male patients raised this procedure from eighth position in 2005 to the number three slot last year

506
Blepharoplasty (eyelid surgery): the number of procedures was up 48% overall since 2005

525
Rhinoplasty (nose reduction/reshaping surgery), which was the most common cosmetic procedure for men

190
Face/neck lift – part of a major rise in anti-ageing procedures paid for by men

Zero appeal: why thin doesn't sell

Advertisers love skinny models, but women see real body shapes as healthier, more credible and smarter, say researchers

by Amelia Hill,
Culture and Society correspondent

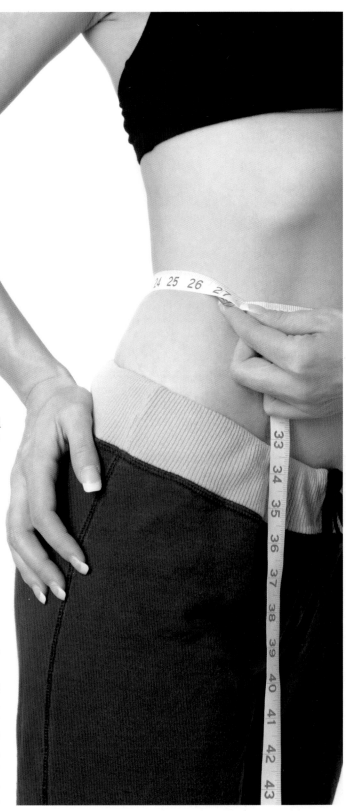

They have been banned from the catwalk, blamed for devastating women's self-esteem and suspected of suffering eating disorders. Now ultra-thin models face another accusation: that they're no good at their job.

New research has found that instead of being admired by women, excessively slender models are regarded as less ethical, knowledgeable and truthful than their larger peers, such as the ones in the widely praised Dove adverts. 'The advertising and fashion industries are reluctant to use larger models because they say that thinness sells,' said Dr Helga Dittmar, of the Social Health Psychology Research Group at the University of Sussex. 'But our research has shown that thin models are less effective in selling products than average-size models.'

Dittmar asked 800 women aged from 18 to 30 to rank the effectiveness of adverts featuring slim models with a UK size eight dress compared with those using size 14 models. She said she expected women to find thin models more convincing and persuasive. 'Instead there was a strong message that models were evaluated more positively when they were average-sized,' she said.

The findings come after London mayor Ken Livingstone said the city's Fashion Week will not receive £620,000 in crucial funding from the London Development Agency unless it bans all models below a certain body mass from the catwalks. The row erupted after Madrid said models at its fashion shows must have a BMI – a ratio of height to weight – in line with United Nations health guidelines. Livingstone's announcement was backed

good for your skin. great for your look.

new

Dove Dove

Body Lotion with
Self-Tanning Agents

Photo: LexisPR / PA

'The only item that ultra-skinny models were better at selling was diet aids'

by the Culture Secretary Tessa Jowell, who said that the use of ultra-thin models pressured girls to starve themselves.

A BMI of 18.5 or below is currently classed as underweight by the World Health Organisation. The average catwalk model is 5ft 9in tall but weighs just 7st 12lb, giving a BMI of only 16. Size-zero women (a US measurement equal to UK size four) weigh not much more than 7st 2lb. Hyper-thin Hollywood celebrities such as Nicole Richie, daughter of singer Lionel Richie, and actress Lindsay Lohan are examples of the trend.

If the ban were implemented in London, top models such as Lily Cole, Erin O'Connor and Irina Lazareanu would probably be barred. Also falling foul would be some of the world's most famous models: Giselle Bundchen is reported to have a BMI of 16 and Kate Moss apparently has a BMI of about 15.

Dittmar, who co-authored the Economic and Social Research Council study with Dr Emma Halliwell, head of the Centre for Appearance Research at the University of West London, said: 'Only the tiniest percentage of women can ever hope to achieve the bodies shown in most advertising. There are well-grounded fears that images of size-zero models spark a body dissatisfaction in women which can have a number of significant consequences, including negative self-perception, depressed mood and disordered eating. The message we received very strongly was that thin models have a negative effect on the self-esteem of women, which affects the effectiveness of the advertising message overall.

'Compared with ultra-thin models, those with an average, healthy body size were viewed as more credible, more trustworthy, and more knowledgeable than their skinnier peers by all women, whatever their profession, age or personal weight issues,' she said.

The reaction to the adverts held true for a range of different products, including bodycare items, make-up and food. The only item that the ultra-skinny models were better at selling was diet aids. However, a spokeswoman for the Premier Modelling Agency said: 'Statistics have repeatedly shown that if you stick a beautiful skinny girl on the cover of a magazine you sell more copies. We supply the women the advertisers, our clients, want. The clients would say that they are selling a product and responding to consumer demand.

'At the end of the day, it is a business, and the fact is that these models sell the products.'

© The Observer 15 October 2006

The lies that led to death and devastation

When Lucy Cochrane was accused of bullying, her school was obliged to investigate. But the allegations were false – and now Lucy's parents are dead. What went wrong?

Sarah Ebner reports on a tragic case

The Children's Commissioner, Sir Albert Aynsley-Green, has warned that relentless bullying is driving some children to the brink of suicide, while the number of children counselled by ChildLine about bullying rose by 12 per cent last year.

But what of those children who are accused of bullying, but aren't guilty? Just as it took years to recognise that charges of assault against teachers can be false, so people are starting to realise that accusing another child of bullying may simply be a way of getting them into trouble. And that trouble can have devastating results.

At the end of last year, Michael and Jane Connor were convicted of the murder of another set of parents, Maureen and Alex Cochrane. Their daughters, Natalie Connor and

Lucy Cochrane, had been at the same schools and at some stage had fallen out.

Lucy, who has learning difficulties, was regarded by school staff as a pleasant but vulnerable girl who was bullied by Natalie. However, it was Natalie who claimed to her parents that Lucy was the bully, accusing Lucy of assaulting her at a dance class at school. A subsequent police investigation found the contentions to be entirely baseless, but they still had to be investigated.

Natalie's allegations, which were described during the Connors' murder trial at Manchester Crown Court as "groundless and an invention", goaded her parents and contributed to the ill-feeling between the families. The Connors plotted to set fire to the Cochranes' house

Jane, Michael and Natalie Connor (top row, Left to right); Maureen, Alex and Lucy Cochrane

and Michael Connor subsequently poured petrol through the letter box, killing both parents and seriously injuring Lucy.

Michael and Jane Connor were convicted of double murder, and Natalie Connor was convicted of manslaughter and causing grievous bodily harm with intent and arson.

Clearly this was an extreme case, but the prosecution lawyers agree that the false bullying allegations exacerbated the situation. Such claims are not entirely unusual.

"Contrary perspectives and malicious reports will always be part of bullying disputes," says Sir Albert, while John Stead, education adviser for the NSPCC and a former head teacher, agrees that false accusations are "certainly something that you come across".

However, he adds, when a child makes a false accusation, it is often a cry for help.

"It's never straightforward," says Stead, who is also the Anti-Bullying Alliance co-ordinator for Yorkshire and Humberside. "Sometimes it's quite deliberate because a child wants to get someone else into trouble, but sometimes it may be that the child is unhappy because of something else, such as other children not playing with them. Occasionally there's almost a sense of delusion – the child actually believes they are being bullied."

Still, Stead is keen to emphasise that he believes most bullying accusations are true. "The danger is that children who are being bullied are ignored," he adds.

Joanna Ross (not her real name) accepts that it's important not to

dismiss children who accuse others of bullying. However, she is also concerned that increased openness about the subject of bullying may be leading to false accusations. She's convinced that more care is needed with young children.

Ross's son Leo, 10, was accused of seriously bullying a younger boy towards the end of last year. The trouble began in the summer term when class teachers discussed bullying and then asked the children to fill in forms saying whether they had been bullied. One child – who was friendly with, and in the same class as, Ross's younger son, Callum – said that he had been bullied, by Leo and two of his friends. This boy, David, said that the older boys had told him to go away and said they didn't want to play with him.

Callum Ross says their teacher told David, then seven, that

such behaviour was not bullying. However, the forms were filled in, and Leo and the two other boys were accused.

"Everyone thought it was minor," says Ross. "I spoke to David's father and he said that his son simply wanted to join in with the older boys and then when they didn't want him to, he would poke, prod and kick them. They would respond by cuffing him and telling him to go away. Neither of us was really concerned."

After the summer holidays, there were new, more serious allegations. David accused the boys of punching him, kicking him and kneeing him in the groin. He also said that they had "threatened to bully him more than he'd ever been bullied before".

"It was quite ironic, because one of the boys he had accused had been off sick on the days he specifically said some of these things had happened, so I really thought they couldn't be true," says Ross. "Still, it was awful. The previous term I had told Leo to keep away from David, and he assured me that he had, but as one of the oldest boys in the school, the younger ones want to play with him and his friends. David's father then came to speak to me and said he hadn't been concerned before because it was rough and tumble, but that now he felt it was getting serious. He thought there was no smoke without fire.

"He also said that the bullying had gone on for two years, even though for a lot of that time, David had been coming to my house to play with my younger son. He alleged that three times a week Leo and his friends had been kicking him, punching him and threatening him. He also said that they had been bullying his sister, Ruby, and held her upside down, threatening to drop her on her head.

"I was really worried about the whole thing, but most of it just didn't ring true. It's not simply that

"The danger is that children who are being bullied are ignored"

I would defend my own son, but the fact that when I started asking around, no one had seen any of this so-called bullying. The children attend a very small school, but none of David's friends knew anything about it, none of the teachers said that David had seemed unhappy or hurt and, despite him accusing Leo of forcing his head into the toilet on more than one occasion, no one had seen him with his hair wet or in tears."

John Stead says that falsely accusing another child of bullying is one way to seek attention.

"There aren't any easy answers when you've been falsely accused," he adds. "The biggest way we protect against false allegations is to look into it as soon as possible."

Ross agrees that, once the allegations had been made, the school had to look into them, and that they did so fairly. At this point Ruby admitted that she had made her story up, but David stuck to his.

"I think he was in a bit of a trap," says Ross. "His father had asked him many times if the accusations were true and he could have got into more trouble if he'd backed down."

However, Ross has a problem with the way the school initially went about encouraging the reports of bullying.

"The school gave out these forms and a lot of children felt they needed to fill them in," she says. "I think the

school handled that badly, and I also felt the onus was on me to disprove everything. I thought they should have given my son some defence mechanism."

"Schools need to talk about what is and what isn't bullying and encourage children to talk about it," says Stead. "And I do believe we should be asking children every year how safe the school is. But I'm not sure we should be asking them to specifically name people."

Joanna Ross has some sympathy towards her son's accuser because of his age, and also because she thinks he might well have been unhappy.

"The family had moved a lot and were actually about to leave again to live abroad," she says. "It probably was disconcerting for David. His mother sent me an e-mail saying that they weren't going to pursue the accusations, that she didn't want any bother and that they would leave school a few weeks early. She also said that only the boys would 'know the truth' of what had happened.

"But that view has left my son and his friends under a cloud. If the school had actually believed David, my son would have been expelled. It's left him vulnerable and having learnt a funny lesson, that you can say bad things and get away with it.

"You have to take bullying seriously, but you also have to analyse it. Parents have to accept that children can be mean, but that's not necessarily bullying. There are noticeable symptoms when it comes to a child being bullied, but David wasn't unhappy, crying on the way to school or upset during the school day.

"If a small child picks on a big child they are in a win-win situation. If a big child lashes out, then he'll be accused of bullying. I've told Leo that he must now always walk away."

The Independent 8 February 2007

B is for bullied

Autism, including Asperger syndrome, is a lifelong developmental disability that affects the way a person communicates and relates to people around them. People with autism experience difficulties with social interaction, social communication and imagination – known as the 'triad of impairments'.

In 2006 The National Autistic Society (NAS) carried out the largest ever survey on autism and education.

My son was bullied to the point of wanting to end his life and has self-harmed. He attends therapy to help him deal with this. We feel he will never recover from these feelings.

Who gets bullied?

Bullying can take on many forms, including name-calling, physical violence or social isolation. According to the survey, two in five children with autism have been bullied.

It's the same group of people just annoy me all the time. They do a range of different stuff – chucking stuff at me, paper and stuff in class... not usually in break time... Happy slapping me once, that got seriously dealt with... They got detention and badly shouted at.

Why children with autism can be vulnerable

Some children with autism can appear to be locked in their own world, while others may be eager to make friends but lack the social skills to fit in with their peer group. Children with autism have difficulties with non-verbal behaviour, such as making eye contact, using and interpreting facial expressions and body language. They may act in ways which seem unconventional or strange, as a result of not understanding social rules and norms. Some children with autism also have difficulties with physical co-ordination, or have sensory difficulties, such as an under- or over-sensitivity to certain smells or noises. Others have special or very narrow interests in certain topics.

A lot of teasing and children copying the way she walks, etc. She is aware of it and confidence is affected. She would self mutilate, scratching herself etc.

Children with autism may not fit in easily with their peers and can be more susceptible to bullying than others. Because of the nature of their disability, children with autism may not always be able to identify when they have been bullied, particularly with more subtle forms of bullying. If another child appears to be friendly, then a child with autism may trust them even when that child later acts in malicious ways.

Carl doesn't tell when he is being bullied. I have to figure it out, sometimes from bruises. His teachers don't seem to notice – perhaps because of inadequate playtime supervision.

"I've seen for myself the devastating impact that bullying has on children with autism. Every child with autism has the right to feel safe and secure at school. We need to act now to make this a reality."

**Professor Sir Al Aynsley-Green,
Children's Commissioner for England**

Because children with autism often find it difficult to understand social rules, when other pupils take advantage of this, it can make it even more difficult for children with autism to develop their social understanding.

How bullied children can face exclusion

A child with autism may lack the social skills to handle difficult situations, and can be easily led or provoked by bullies. A classic pattern for children with autism who exhibit challenging behaviour is that prolonged, low-level bullying and teasing from other children triggers a sudden and seemingly disproportionate response.

Jenny (who has autism) suffered extreme mental bullying about her severely autistic sister, and because of her poor social and language skills she lashed out. The school refused to address the issue and just excluded her for her retaliation.

Children with autism can sometimes be the perpetrators of bullying too. There may be a wide range of reasons for this, including reasons related to their disability, such as not being able to understand other people's point of view.

Effects on the family

Bullying does not just impact on children with autism. Their brothers and sisters may also experience bullying about their sibling's disability.

His younger brother (at the same school) is bullied because of his older brother and therefore he even joins in and he bullies his younger brother at home.

Bullying policies

In the Department for Education and Skills (DfES) guidance for schools, *Bullying: don't suffer in silence: an anti-bullying pack for schools*, different types of strategies are suggested for different forms of bullying.

This includes putting in place effective recording systems; multi-agency working with police, youth services and others.

Strategies for bullying on the grounds of disability focus more on helping the bullied pupil to deal with the bullying. Strategies include teaching assertiveness and other social skills; role-playing in dealing with taunts; and providing special resource rooms at playtimes and lunchtime.

There is a danger that the contradiction in the advice on tackling bullying sends out the message that bullying on the basis of race, gender and sexual orientation is unacceptable, but that bullying on the basis of disability is a problem that needs to be dealt with by the bullied child.

No allowances are made (by the school) for a different style, her need to withdraw, her terror from bullying peers. They said she was a natural 'victim' and brought it all on herself. The bullying was simply 'the rough and tumble of everyday life in school'.

*© The National Autistic Society 2006
http://www.autism.org.uk*

What can you buy for 5p in Bangladesh?

Aida Edemariam

There is a certain inevitability to the news that workers in six Bangladeshi factories that supply Primark, Tesco, and Asda are under-remunerated. The deals at these shops have been so good, the clothes so on-trend, the scope for instant gratification so high that we have on the whole refused to believe that perhaps £8 cocktail dresses do not leave much of a margin for four weeks' holiday, health insurance and a 40-hour working week for those who make them, even when the exchange rate is as obliging as it tends to be in the developing countries where these workers live.

According to the Primark supplier code of conduct, "wages and benefits paid for a standard working week meet, at a minimum, national legal standards or industry benchmark standards, whichever is higher. In any event wages should always be enough to meet basic needs and to provide some discretionary income."

A minimum wage in Bangladesh is officially £12 a month, though the living wage is calculated by economists there at £22 a month. The least skilled garment workers can make only £7 or £8 a month; the most skilled can hope to earn only 2,400 taka (£16), or an average of 7 taka (5p) an hour for an 80-hour week.

Skilled garment workers in Bangladesh can earn as little as 5p an hour

The following is a list of what 7 taka can buy:

1. A roadside haircut
2. One and a half a Benson & Hedges cigarettes
3. Sixty cigarettes handrolled locally (beedi)
4. One very small bar of soap or a miniature sachet of shampoo
5. Three rotis and a bhaji
6. A hairband
7. A three-minute local phone call
8. Three candles – for use in the power cuts that have been so frequent that in September people took to the streets in protest; 200 were injured when police responded with rubber bullets, batons, and tear gas.
9. Three return crossings of the Buringanga river, which hugs the capital, Dhaka. It is dangerously polluted with factory effluent and sewage, 80% of which is untreated.
10. A bus trip halfway across the city.

So – not a lot, really.

The TRUE cost of cheap clothes

War on Want's report *'Fashion Victims: The true cost of cheap clothes at Primark, Asda and Tesco* forms part of an ongoing campaign for corporate accountability. It looked specifically at workers in Bangladesh who make the clothes sold by bargain retailers and it concludes that the demand for low cost goods is the driving force behind appalling pay and working conditions.

The report deals with workers such as Lina who began working in a garment factory at the age of 13. She moved from her village to Dhaka to get a job and help her parents make ends meet. Now 22, she works in a factory that supplies Primark (www.primark.co.uk), Asda (www.asda.co.uk) and Tesco (www.tesco.com). As she can operate a sewing machine she can command a wage of £17 per month, but to earn this amount she must work between 60 and 90 hours each week.

Primark, Asda and Tesco each buy tens of millions of pounds worth of clothing from Bangladesh each year, an unsurprising fact since the Bangladeshi workforce is the cheapest in the world. All three retailers signed up to a code of conduct which states that:

Workers shall not on a regular basis be required to work in excess of 48 hours per week and shall be provided with at least one day off for every 7 day period on average.

Overtime shall be voluntary, shall not exceed 12 hours per week, shall not be demanded on a regular basis and shall always be compensated at a premium rate.

War on Want, however, found workers regularly employed for 12 to 16 hours per day and for 80 hours a week. The minimum they found was 10 hours per day, six days per week. One worker, Ifat, whose factory supplies all three brands, had worked an incredible 140 hours of overtime during August 2006. When interviewed, workers said that continuing until 11pm was common. Overtime is compulsory, a refusal to work long hours would result in the sack, and workers feel they are often cheated of their extra pay

The majority of garment workers are women – especially young women – the most vulnerable and the easiest to exploit. Uneducated and looked down on, they are afraid to speak out about the difficulties they face. They are systematically paid less for the same work than their male colleagues. Long hours mean they finish work late at night, perhaps facing a dangerous walk home. Most workers, male and female, are not aware of their rights and a climate of fear means that no one in these factories dares form a trade union. Wal-Mart, Asda's owner, has a reputation for 'union-busting' in the United States and Tesco has also been overt about its desire to avoid unionisation.

The audits which the retailers use to establish their credentials as responsible retailers are superficial. Generally done in a few hours, the factories have ample time to prepare for the audit visit and workers have been coached and intimidated by their managers to ensure they said the right things.

Audits also usually miss working conditions for home workers and in subcontracted workplaces – used by factories when they have too many orders to fill at once.

War on Want is asking people to apply pressure on both retailers and government to ensure that companies are held accountable for their actions.

*Source: Fashion Victims:
The true cost of cheap clothes at Primark,
Asda and Tesco, War on Want*

Shop smart:
Next time you go shopping, remember the true cost of clothes sold by Primark, Asda and Tesco. Instead of filling your wardrobe with clothes that need replacing each year, shop for ethical alternatives that will stand the test of time.

Contact the companies:
Members of the public can contact Asda, Primark and Tesco directly and voice their concern about their impacts on local communities and workers

Contact the UK government:
A binding framework of regulation could be used to stop UK companies and their suppliers continuing the abuse of workers overseas.

Join War on Want:
Follow their work at www.waronwant.org

Also:
Clean Up Fashion
www.cleanupfashion.co.uk

Clean Clothes Campaign:
www.cleanclothes.org

Burkinis on Bondi Beach

This is the **burkini**, a swimming costume designed specifically for Muslim women and it's already being worn by Muslim Australian lifesavers.

Photo: Courtesy of Surf Life Saving Australia

Costing £65, it's a semi-fitting two-piece swimsuit consisting of straight legged trousers and a top that connects to a head cover. All burkinis are 100% polyester, UV protected, chlorine resistant and water repellent and available in two fits. Slim fit combines the trousers with a thigh length top whilst the modest fit top goes down to the knee.

The swimsuit, along with a wider range of sportswear for Muslim women, was the brainchild of Aheda Zanetti, the woman behind the Ahiida sports label. Migrating to Australia from Lebanon with her family at just 2 years old, she faced a lot of challenges, "as an active person who liked to participate in community activities and sport, I found myself restricted due to cultural and religious beliefs. As years went by, I noticed there are younger girls and women that are embracing Islam and obeying their Islamic belief in dressing modestly, in turn, having to miss out on opportunities, and taking part in any sporting activities that Australia has to offer." And so the Ahiida label was born.

The company states that it bases all its designs on four main principles: Freedom, Comfort, Confidence and that all garments are Easy to get on and off without the need for pins or ties. The freedom is for Muslim women to chose to participate in sporting events whilst maintaining their beliefs. Garments are also light in weight, don't restrict movement and so offer ultimate comfort. Finally, by providing appropriate clothing, the company believe they can give Muslim women the confidence that will bring out the best in them, so that their performance is the focus and not their clothing.

> **"Freedom, for Muslim women to participate in sport, whilst maintaining their beliefs"**

Aheda came up with the design, as an extension to their sportswear range, after Surf Life Saving Australia began a recruitment drive to attract more Islamic lifeguards, particularly women, to their team. This was a response to the riots in the previous year between Lebanese Muslim teenagers and white Australians on Sydney's Cronulla beach. Many Islamic women responded and became lifeguards and they can now be seen sporting their red and yellow burkinis on Bondi Beach daily.

However, the burkini isn't the first Muslim swimming costume, though it does seem to be the most forward thinking and effective. In 2000, the "sharia swimsuit" was being sold all over Cairo, with Egyptian women flocking to buy the high-necked costume with sleeves and a small skirt, which was worn over long trousers. Then Egypt revealed the "swimming hijab" and only last year there was the launch of a Turkish swimwear collection called Hasema, consisting of a neck-to-ankle body-suit with hood. This appeared to be based on a tracksuit in design, whilst the burkini seems based more on a wetsuit, and fits in with the general style of other swimwear.

So will the success of the burkini extend beyond Bondi Beach? Well Ahiida sportswear has received plenty of positive feedback which has been posted on their website. Heba, from the USA, said "I was finally able to go to my aqua aerobics class, and I love the swim suit! I came home so happy and excited after my class. I've been telling everyone about it. It's so lightweight; dries so quickly and it looks great. I received compliments by non-Muslims. I even had someone ask where I got it from! I don't look like a fool in the water anymore, and I'm not weighed down by all the heavy wet clothes I used to wear." Similarly Helen, UK, said "It far exceeded my expectations as light and comfortable to wear, with no retention of water. I have worn it on the beach during our July heat wave, and have really enjoyed swimming in the sea for the first time since my conversion to Islam."

Source: Various

Bloody fashion victims

Fur is officially out. **Jenny Rhodes** reports on the companies who have, and have not, signed to a new retailer commitment against fur.

Each year the worldwide fur industry kills more than 40 million animals in the name of fashion. Farmed fur contributes to more than 85% of the total world trade in fur, with most fur farming taking place in Northern Europe and North America. Opinion polls carried out in the last 10 years in the UK have consistently shown that 75-76 per cent of the population is opposed to fur farming, with MORI polls showing that 76 per cent supported an outright ban.

Fur farming was banned in England and Wales on the grounds of "public morality" by the Fur Farming (Prohibition) Act 2000 which came into force on 1 January 2003. Scotland and Northern Ireland followed suit with similar legislation. Italy, Austria, Sweden and the Netherlands have all introduced measures to curtail or ban fur farming. The UK, along with 88 other countries, has also banned the use of the steel-jawed leg-hold traps, the main method used to trap wild animals for their fur.

Dressed to kill

Campaigners against the fur trade believe that it is morally wrong to kill an animal for fashion whether it is trapped or farmed. Fur clothing, they believe, is a trivial and non-essential luxury item obtained through the infliction of prolonged suffering on wild animals. Some consumers assume that fur farming is the same as any other type of intensive farming. This isn't the case. Mink and fox (the main species farmed for fur) are wild animals and have substantially different welfare requirements to domesticated farm animals. It is impossible to keep wild animals in barren captive environments without imposing suffering.

Prior to the banning of fur farming in the UK, the Farm Animal Welfare Council (the UK government's independent advisory group on farm welfare issues) declined to issue a welfare code for mink and fox farming as fur farming was not considered acceptable as practised. It was felt that, had a government-approved welfare code been issued, this would have implicitly condoned the industry.

SHE NEEDS HER FUR MORE THAN YOU DO

THE HUMANE SOCIETY OF THE UNITED STATES.

Occasionally religious groups have argued that animals are put on the planet for human benefit therefore wearing fur is acceptable. However Judaism, Christianity and Islam do not condone the use of animals without moral restraint.

Consumer confusion

Shoppers have for years been confused by companies and designers who claim to go fur-free only to renege on the commitment at a later date. Famously, Naomi Campbell represented Peta (People for the Ethical Treatment of Animals) in its 1997 ad campaign proclaiming "I'd rather go naked than wear fur," only to be sacked for subsequently wearing fur on the catwalk. Peta now includes Campbell in its gallery of "fur hags".

A losing battle

According to the British Fur Trade Association the trade is worth £400-£500 million a year to the UK. The International Fur Trade Association (IFTA), which exists to protect fur trade interests and promote a positive image of the industry, states that worldwide fur sales continue to increase. Yet, in August 2006, IFTA resorted to global campaigns in Vogue, Elle and Wallpaper to prop up the industry's reputation. The magazines were selected "as they represent the worldwide voice of fashion and lifestyle, and have a unique and trusted dialogue with the readers."

According to IFTA "Each campaign explores a different aspect of fur. Vogue: High fashion, luxury without measure and the tempestuous beauty of fur. Elle: Striking glamour and the dynamic allure of fur. Wallpaper: The sensuous appeal and hedonistic beauty of fur. The underlying message that unites these beautiful images is fur as the choice of the strong, stylish woman with a sense of individuality". IFTA's campaign may attempt to bolster the opinion of the influential fashionistas, but at high-street level it is having little or no effect.

UK shoppers still remain hostile to buying and wearing fur, with high-street retailers remaining responsive to customers on this issue. Inditex, owners of Zara, adopted a formal policy against the use of fur in its products in all 2,064 of its stores only three days before a planned international day of protest against the company.

Fur Free Retailers

The Fur Free Alliance (a coalition of over 35 animal protection and environmental organisations) have launched the Fur Free Retailers scheme represented by Respect for Animals in the UK. The scheme provides consumers with reliable assurance that anything purchased from a Fur Free Retailer certified store will be fur free.

The scheme involves retailers:
1. Signing the retailer commitment against fur.
2. Developing an internal system to ensure vendors don't supply the company with items that contain real fur, including credible assurances that faux fur (including trims and accessories) are not animal fur.

Three retailers, the Co-operative Group, Marks & Spencer and Topshop all signed up for the launch of the scheme, with invitations going out to other retailers subsequently. Topshop's Buying Director Karen Finn stated that "Topshop is delighted to sign up to the Fur Free Retailers Initiative. We have a long standing anti-fur policy and we feel very strongly about the use of real fur in fashion and believe that the breeding of animals for their skins can not be justified. To create the look we use high quality faux and artificial furs". Katie Stafford, Sustainable Development Manager at Marks & Spencer, also welcomed the initiative "as it will help consumers interested in these issues to choose products from retailers that have made a pledge to only sell fur free products".

The Fur Free Retailers logo will be available for all retailers who sign up to the initiative to display instore and on company websites.

Faux pas

When shopping, watch out for coats, boots, hats, gloves and jumpers with fur trim. Even cheap items can be made from real fur.

A few quick tips for telling real fur from fake fur are:

1. Feel – real fur is soft and smooth, faux is coarse
2. Look – real fur has several layers with thin hairs forming a dense sub-layer and a leather base, faux is simpler with most hairs having the same length and colour
3. Pin test – real fur has a leather base which is hard to push a pin through, with faux a pin easily goes through the base
4. Burn test – carefully pull a few hairs and hold to a flame, real fur singes and smells like human hair, faux melts like plastic and smells like burnt plastic. It also forms small hard plastic balls at the ends.

Ethical Consumer November 2006
www.ethicalconsumer.org
0161 226 2929

Take Action

- Support Co-op Group, Topshop and Marks & Spencer who have signed up to the Fur Free Retailers scheme
- Boycott retailers who stock fur: Dune, Harrods, Joseph, Nine West
- Ask retailers not signed up to Fur Free Retailers scheme but who claim not to stock fur to sign up
- If you own real fur and don't know how to dispose of it, Respect for Animals will take donated fur items and use them to use to educate consumers about the fur trade.

Each year the worldwide fur industry kills more that 40 million animals in the name of fashion

CRUELTY JUST ISN'T MY STYLE...

NASTASSJA KINSKI MOUSSA

BELLERIVE FOUNDATION
P.O. BOX 6 · 1211 GENEVA 3
SWITZERLAND
TELEPHONE: (022) 46 88 66
TELEX: 429835 MURO CH

Links

Respect for Animals – www.respectforanimals.org 0115 952 5440

Fur Free Alliance – http://infurmation.com

Coalition to Abolish the Fur Trade – www.caft.org.uk 0845 330 7955

I'm not a coat.

Be Fur-Free in the New Century.

THE HUMANE SOCIETY
OF THE UNITED STATES
2100 L Street NW, Washington, DC 20037
www.hsus.org

'I wouldn't have been able to do it...'

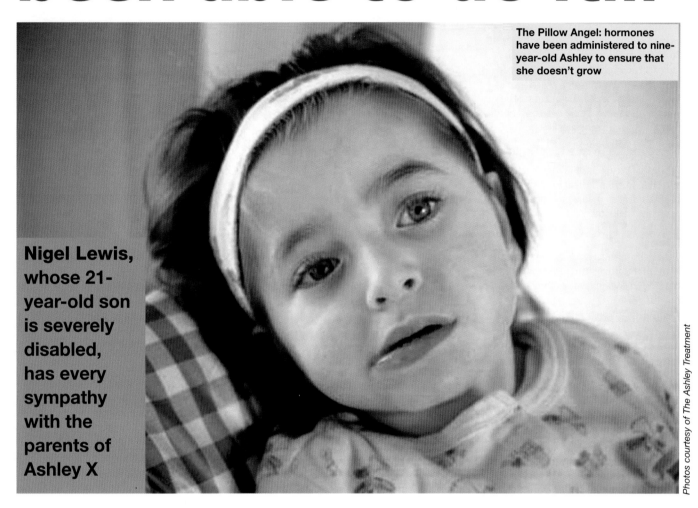

The Pillow Angel: hormones have been administered to nine-year-old Ashley to ensure that she doesn't grow

Nigel Lewis, whose 21-year-old son is severely disabled, has every sympathy with the parents of Ashley X

Photos courtesy of The Ashley Treatment

She is known as the Pillow Angel and her story is one of the most moving and morally perplexing most of us will ever come across: Ashley X, the severely disabled little girl from Seattle who, thanks to modern science, will remain a child for ever.

Her parents' decision to ask doctors to administer hormones to their nine-year-old daughter – who is in a vegetative state because of a rare brain condition and cannot walk, talk, hold her head up or swallow food – to stop her growing, has sparked an intense ethical debate.

One can only imagine what a harrowing week it has been for them since they tried to explain the treatment and their reasons for pursuing it via the internet.

This followed the furore caused by the publication of a paper in a medical journal written by the doctors who treated Ashley X, describing the case (although the family were not named). Ashley's parents feared that if their daughter matured naturally, she would become too big and too heavy for them to lift or move easily.

High doses of oestrogen, which cause bones to fuse, will restrict Ashley's height to 4ft 5in, while her breast buds and womb have been removed surgically. Her parents are adamant they have done the right thing.

While they have had many messages of support, they have also been harshly criticised. I neither support nor condone the specifics of their decision, but I do feel deeply for them. My wife and I know all too well the anxieties they face in trying to do the best for their child.

Our son Andrew was born with severe disabilities. The official term used to describe his condition is spastic quadriplegia with multiple learning difficulties. In Andrew's case, this means he has no voluntary movement.

Initially, my wife and I looked after Andrew at home with the support of carers, visits to a respite centre and a local nursery school for disabled children. Even when he was tiny it was incredibly hard work, especially when our second son Matthew, who was perfectly healthy, was born when Andrew was three and a half.

Caring for Andrew was a 24-hour job that was both emotionally and physically draining. By the time he was five we'd come to the painful realisation that we couldn't cope with him at home. We found a good residential school where he stayed until he was 19, coming home every holiday. Two years ago, he moved home to a full-time residential care home near us.

He is now 21 and his life expectancy is no more than 30. Making him as comfortable as possible is all that matters. As a natural consequence of Andrew's disabilities, he weighs only 33kg and is the size of a 10- or 11-year-old.

The desire of Ashley's parents to keep her small struck a chord with me because there is no doubt in my mind that Andrew's small size makes caring for him easier.

Nevertheless, it's still very tricky to lift him; his body is rigid and he can't help you by clinging on, so he's a dead weight.

An adult weighing 12 or 13 stone would present a far greater problem. However, I don't think I would have been able to do what Ashely's parents have done. Surgery and hormone treatment are significant interventions and I would not have wanted to take such drastic action.

But if Andrew's doctors had told us when he was five or six that they could arrest his growth then, we would at least have thought it through. You naturally want to know about anything that might help your child.

What it is harder to judge though, is whether it would be worse for Andrew himself if he was bigger.

Modern lifting equipment enables adults with severe disabilities to be taken out and about and parents and carers do everything necessary to give them all the experiences they can, even if it is more physically demanding.

The physical impact of keeping severely disabled children small is only one aspect of this debate. There is another factor.

In their blog, Ashley's parents say that they feel it is more dignified for their daughter to have a body that is better suited to her cognitive state, and our own experiences suggest that many people, perhaps subconsciously, share this view.

We make regular trips to the hospital with Andrew where lots of people say things like, "poor little chap". It somehow seems more acceptable to others that Andrew looks like a child. But whatever the driving factors behind Ashley's parents' choice, it is something only they have the right to decide.

Making the right decisions for a child is the most important thing for any parent, but when that child will always depend upon you for everything, it becomes even more significant. In my view, unless you have had a severely disabled child, you cannot possibly begin to imagine the choices you might find yourself making.

I wish Ashley X and her family well.

For information about support for disabled children and their families, www.nch.org.uk

The Daily Telegraph 8 January 2007
© Telegraph Group Ltd

The "Ashley Treatment", Towards a Better Quality of Life for "Pillow Angels" By Ashley's Mom and Dad

Ashley's Story

Our daughter Ashley had a normal birth, but her mental and motor faculties did not develop. Over the years, neurologists, geneticists, and other specialists conducted every known traditional and experimental test, but still could not determine a diagnosis or a cause. Doctor's call her condition "static encephalopathy of unknown etiology", which means an insult to the brain of unknown origin or cause, and one that will not improve.

Now nine years old, Ashley cannot keep her head up, roll or change her sleeping position, hold a toy, or sit up by herself, let alone walk or talk. She is tube fed and depends on her caregivers in every way. We call her our Pillow Angel since she is so sweet and stays right where we place her—usually on a pillow.

Definitions

Pillow Angel:
Affectionate nickname for Ashley X, now generally refers to people with a cognitive and mental developmental level that will never exceed that of a 6–month old child as well as associated extreme physical limitations, so they will never be able to walk or talk or in some cases even hold up their head or change position in bed. Pillow Angels are entirely dependent on their caregivers.

Ashley Treatment:
A collection of medical procedures intended to enhance the quality of life of Pillow Angels. It includes limiting adult height through high–dose estrogen therapy, and for females it includes a hysterectomy and breast bud removal prior to the estrogen therapy in order to prevent discomfort associated with menstrual cramps and developed breasts. It is generally acknowledged that Pillow Angels are most comfortable and attain the highest possible quality of life in the loving care of their own family. The Ashley Treatment improves the quality of life of Pillow Angels, including helping their families continue to care for them at home. The treatment was first applied to a Pillow Angel named Ashley at Seattle Children's Hospital, and was first discussed in a medical article published in October 2006 and in a blog by Ashley's parents published on January 2nd 2007. The treatment was widely publicized by the media worldwide in early January 2007 and was the subject of controversy.

http://ashleytreatment.spaces.live.com/blog

If only right-to-lifers cared as much about the living

The case of little Ashley hides the truth that progressive medical research and treatments are being scandalously denied us

Mary Riddell

Ashley X was never destined for marvels. Her mind is locked in infancy and she cannot walk, talk, eat or raise her head. Undaunted, her parents and her surgeons have made her the heroine of a medical fairy tale in which she will have the body of a child of nine for as long as she lives.

Her womb and breasts have been removed and hormone treatment has halted her growth and limited her weight to 75lbs. The decision by Ashley's father to write an awesomely intimate blog detailing, and commending to others, his daughter's drastic treatment has prompted what the media call worldwide controversy.

That is not strictly true. Disabled groups are broadly against the intervention. Some families facing similar problems are in favour. As one parent of a teenage daughter wrote: 'Please don't judge until you've tried wrestling a 220lb scared child out of the bathtub by yourself.' But the fuss has actually been rather slight by the screechy standards of debates on human engineering.

In America, where Ashley lives, the right to abortion is under constant threat. George W Bush, in the first veto of his presidency, killed a bill to provide federal funds for embryonic stem cell research. In Britain, the government appears to have bowed to pro-life pressure over fusing human DNA with animal eggs. Despite some emollient words from Tony Blair, scientists believe that a ban* will be imposed this week, so depriving people with Alzheimer's and motor neurone disease of the hope of medical breakthrough.

By contrast, the Ashley Treatment, as her parents call it, has been nodded through, untested by other doctors and unmediated by any public debate or court of law. A shockable society is curiously unappalled either by this casual approach or by the shadow of eugenics that hangs over British social improvers of the left. America's sterilisation of 64,000 'imbeciles' carried on long after Nazism, until 1963, and Sweden ran a similar programme for 40 years.

Maybe routine panic about 'designer' humans has been overridden by an equally customary ambivalence about the human calendar. While, for example, the decision by Patricia Rashbrook to have a baby at 62 was greeted as an affront to nature, turning back the clock is an obsession of 21st-century time-surfers. When so many pay to have age scalpelled from their faces, who dares forbid a gravely damaged child the luxury of surgery that, according to her parents, will make her happier?

Besides, the parents claim, a girl's body is 'more appropriate and more dignified' to a child with a vestigial mind. But will that be so when Ashley, who is expected to have a long life, is a pre-pubescent 60-year-old? The public, in general, is prepared to sanction her adulthood being carved away without consent and this is why. Her parents have done what few in their position can. They have dared to dream, for themselves and for their daughter. They have procured a narrative and a future for a 'pillow angel' who, however grey and wrinkled, will never lose her childhood innocence.

Deprived of all other powers, Ashley has the ability to hold back time. Her fate has invited not only compassion, but also a touch of envy, especially from parents of disabled children. Ashley, a living doll, bears little resemblance to the heavy, incontinent, sleepless, hormonal, infantile adolescents for whom their parents care with a desperate and equivocal love.

  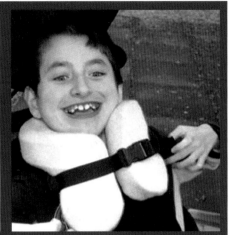

Here she stops: Ashley as a baby through to today, aged nine. She'll get no bigger

The state, in many cases, offers almost nothing. The Children's Commissioner for England correctly calls services for the UK's 770,000 disabled children 'a national scandal' and campaigning groups are demanding that Gordon Brown reverses a shaming neglect. Only one in 13 families gets help from their local social services, 55 per cent are living on or near the poverty line and eight out of 10 parents are at breaking point.

Henrietta Spink understands their struggle. She has fought as far as the House of Lords to get adequate help for her two profoundly disabled sons, now 15 and 18. But local authorities can still decide what assistance to give and she is 'screaming inwardly for freedom'.

Her younger son cannot wipe his bottom, but he can try to make off with the family car. In her darker moments, she wishes that this child, once given a 1 per cent chance of survival, had died at birth.

But that despair, she says, is always overridden by love. Much as she abhors the shabby deal for disabled children and their families, she does not believe Ashley's treatment to be justified. Other parents, though, say they would jump at the chance of similar operations if British law allowed it.

Ashley's surgery, I believe, was permissible, but only just. Modifying human beings without permission is a sinister business, for all the Peter Pan gloss invoked by her parents. There was something unsettling, too, about a medically explicit blog that stripped every last stitch of privacy from a disabled child. But, for me, the clinching argument in the parents' favour is that outsiders are far too prone to foist high-minded edicts on those enduring the unthinkable. Ethics stripped of tolerance and compassion are diktat with a nicer name.

Ashley's fate has invited a touch of envy, especially from parents of disabled children

Or, as Ashley's father puts it: 'The God we know wants Ashley to have a good quality of life. Knowingly allowing avoidable suffering. . . can't be a good thing in the eyes of God.' If only the followers of his deity were always so pragmatic.

Lord Joffe's modest bill on assisted dying was blocked, disgracefully, partly in the name of God, and religious groups were last week cited as prime movers against stem cell work which involves using animal eggs as recipients for human DNA. If society is less worried by the customising of Ashley X than by life-saving research involving scraps of 'Frankenbunny' tissue, then we are truly on the edge of madness.

Human life, it seems, is sacrosanct only at the entry and the exit barriers. What happens in between, by way of surgical intervention and society's neglect, is neither here nor there. Hence the row over recent guidelines by the Nuffield Council on Bioethics, recommending that babies born before 23 weeks should not be resuscitated, given the grave disabilities the few survivors are likely to face. 'Baby butchers,' screamed the outraged. Yet the council talked perfect sense.

The dying are being forced to cling to intolerable existences, long past the stage of mercy and reason, while more and more seriously disabled children are surviving, only to be denied even basic care. Right-to-life campaigners, though scrupulously kind to embryos, pay far too little heed to the rights of human beings to good lives and tolerable deaths. So do not be too shocked by Ashley X. Her rare case may be disturbing, but spurious morality and budget cuts can inflict more damage than a surgeon's knife.

The Observer 7 January 2007

*May 2007 overhaul of the Human Fertilisation and Embryology Act contains a proposal to reverse this ban.

Time to drop the 'disabled' label?

Agnes Fletcher examines how the debate around definitions of disability relates to the modern sense of being disabled

There have been lists of the most powerful women, gay men and lesbians, black and minority ethnic Britons in the media for some time. Yet the concept of disabled influencers, which Disability Now (August issue) established with its Influence List, (*www.disabilitynow. org.uk/people/opinion/opinion_aug_ influence.htm*) raises questions of definition and identity. For those of us on the panel choosing the list, the debate was not just about types and impact of influence, but the very idea of being a disabled Briton.

Panel members differed on how to define "disabled" in this context: all those who meet the current definition of disability under the Disability Discrimination Act; only those with a significant level of impairment; or only people who embraced a "disabled" identity from a rights perspective.

There was heated debate over the possible inclusion of Gordon Brown, who is blind in one eye and requires information in large print. Some wanted to exclude him because he does not identify himself as "disabled", others because they did not believe that he is "disabled enough", others because they believed he had not faced discrimination.

When I first found out about the

'Allies were important but were there to support, not to speak'

disability movement 14 years ago, there was a very clear boundary between who was a "disabled person" and who was not. Activists placed themselves on one side of what seemed like a clear line in the sand. There was an emphasis on differentiating impairment from "being ill." You just could not be "a person with a disability" – unless you were Irish, American or Canadian.

Allies were important – but were there to support, not to speak. Talk of the particulars of impairment was frowned upon. If you had an impairment but did not embrace your "disabled" identity, you were letting others down.

Such unwritten rules shored up an important sense of solidarity, badged "disabled by society," and common purpose – at a time when progress on civil rights was so slow. Undoubtedly, they were part of what created the Disability Discrimination Act and later amendments.

I, like many, found the social model of disability on which they drew, both politically inspiring and personally liberating: you were "in"

after years of being "out". But where is identity politics now, and how can disability organisations ensure that they represent different experiences and accommodate different ways of thinking about disability?

Research from the Department for Work and Pensions shows that around half of those covered by the DDA do not consider themselves to be "disabled people" and Disability Rights Commission research found many people meeting the definition actively rejected the term, especially young people.

We should not drop the idea of disability – but there may be different, less exclusive, ways of ensuring that people know who you are talking to and what about. So, the DRC has explored terms such as "people who are disabled or have long-term health conditions", "people with rights under the DDA" and "people/families affected by disability or long-term health conditions" – the latter reflecting that being the parent, partner or child of a disabled person can also affect your life chances.

Through our emerging Disability Agenda for the Commission for Equality and Human Rights (CEHR), government and others, we have positioned disability equality as a way of tackling some of the major

6th in Disability Now's Influence List:
Tanni Grey-Thompson competes during the
200m during the Visa Paralympic World Cup,
Manchester, May 2007

Photo: Gareth Copley PA Photos

public policy challenges today – of demographic change and the "care crisis", of child poverty and of wasted potential because of an unskilled and underused workforce. We have tried to demonstrate the broader impact of social justice for disabled people.

Part of this approach is demonstrating that change is possible, acknowledging individual achievements and contributions. Not all of us will be a Gordon Brown or David Blunkett – achievement comes in many forms – but we are in a catch-22 if every time we hear about success, we decide the person concerned cannot "really" be disabled, has not sufficiently embraced their "disabled" identity or has not faced sufficient disadvantage to count.

Public life has mostly seen people forced to hide health and disability issues – JFK with his back condition, Churchill's depression, or Tony Blair's "heart scare", which meant double duty at the gym to prove his fitness.

We should encourage people to acknowledge their experience of impairments and health conditions and note their achievements. While people who are disabled or have long-term health conditions must always, directly or through advocacy, have a voice, hearing from parents, partners and children is valid too.

The advent of the CEHR means we need to make links across equality strands and understand that identity in Britain is increasingly multiple and fluid, not singular and fixed for a lifetime.

The experiences of a white family that contains a child with autism will differ from those of an 85-year-old Bangladeshi man with arthritis living in an institution or an HIV-positive parent of African descent. Our respect for them, support for their needs and celebration of their achievements should not depend on the specifics or the severity of impairment – or their embracing of any label. They may be unwilling or unable to unite around a single disability identity.

The time is coming to acknowledge that of those ten million people who meet the definition of disability in the DDA, the variety among them – their gender, age, sexuality, parent or carer status and religious or ethnic background – is greater than their commonality. The prospect of converting them to a 'disabled/not disabled' worldview will be small; and their sense of disadvantage may be based on the perspective that whole families can be affected by the poverty and discrimination associated with disability.

Who knows, perhaps in a few years the most influential British disabled person will be Cameron's young son Ivan, who has cerebral palsy?

Agnes Fletcher is assistant director of communications for the Disability Rights Commission and was a member of the disabled panel that chose Disability Now's list of the UK's most influential disabled people.

Disability Now November 2006
www.disabilitynow.org.uk

Heartwarming tale may NOT have happy ending

James Porteous

"PEOPLE ASK ME ALL THE TIME if I wish I had the rest of my legs," said Oscar Pistorius this week. "No. I guess it's a kind of an inconvenience, having to put on different legs to do different things, but there's nothing that anyone else can do that I can't do."

Quite. In fact there's plenty that Pistorius, thanks to the miracles of modern technology, can do a hell of a lot better than people with normal legs. Such as run the 100m, 200m and 400m.

The double amputee from South Africa holds the Paralympic world records at those distances. Now he wants to take on the "able-bodied", a phrase he finds offensive for obvious reasons.

At the national championships in Durban last week he was second in the 400m competing against able-bodied athletes.

The fastest man on no legs wants to show that a horrible accident or a congenital birth defect need not

The attitude from able-bodied athletes is motivated by a fear of being beaten by a disabled person

Oscar Pistorius, left, races to victory in a time of 11.27 in the final of the 100m at the 2005 Paralympic World Cup in Manchester
Photo: AP /Jon Super

hold people back in any walk of life, a heartwarming tale that already has Hollywood and Tom Hanks interested.

But here come the International Association of Athletics Federations killjoys: The Herald's athletics correspondent, Doug Gillon, reported this week that they are reviewing their rules as a direct consequence of his achievements and that he is not likely to be allowed to run against the able-bodied.

That's right, banning a double amputee from racing "normal" folk because it's not fair – on the normal folk. A novel argument.

On the surface, of course, it seems ridiculous. But look a little closer and you realise that the IAAF have got this one right. The problem is that Pistorius – who had his legs amputated as a one-year-old because he was born without fibulas and his parents wanted him to walk rather than spend life in a wheelchair – has a massive advantage over his rivals. Okay, it still sounds ridiculous.

The springy blades allow Pistorius to stride higher and longer than would be humanly possible without prosthetics

Oscar Pistorius carries his two artificial legs on the way to the start of a race
Photo: AP/Fred Ernst

Pistorius is able to walk, run, drive a car and do anything that anyone else can because he possesses a range of high-tech artificial legs that he can strap on according to his purpose. When running, he whips out his "Cheetahs", carbon fibre prosthetics made by an Icelandic engineering firm called Ossur which have blades rather than feet.

The springy blades allow Pistorius to stride higher and longer than would be humanly possible without prosthetics.

At the 2004 Athens Paralympics, single and double amputee classes were merged. Pistorius won in 21.97, three massive strides ahead of the single amputees. He had fallen in the heats and got up and still qualified.

Understandably, many disabled athletes are upset at the IAAF's stance. They feel the attitude towards Pistorius from able-bodied athletes is motivated by a fear of being beaten by a disabled person. But thanks to his amazing metal legs, Pistorius not only is not disabled on the track, he is super-enabled.

The Herald March 25 2007

STOP PRESS

At the third Visa Paralympic World Cup in Manchester in May 2007, Oscar Pistorius took home two gold medals, winning the 100m and 200m in his class, and breaking the Championship record over 100m in 11.64 seconds.

Becoming blind as an adult forced Chris Parkington to relearn old skills and find new strengths

The Person that's Me

Sometimes I wonder who I really am. I've been Donald and Della's daughter, and Lindy's older sister. I've been Wilf's wife, Daniel's mother and Annette's mother-in-law. I've been Mrs Parkington or "Miss" to countless schoolchildren of all ages. And now? Now I am a statistic. I am not a common statistic, as I am both totally blind and in a wheelchair; but a statistic all the same. And because of this, many professionals believe they know exactly what I need. They haven't asked me. They just know, because that is what the textbooks told them when they were training. In social services reports my disabilities are listed in black and white, for all to see. Not my abilities; just my disabilities. When I attended a social services day centre for a couple of days a week for three years, all possible sources of risk were removed from my life. Woodwork, cookery, sewing – all were reduced to the skill level of a five-year-old. "Don't use those scissors; they are sharp!" – it was as if I had never studied dissection and learned that a blunt instrument is dangerous, not a well-sharpened one. No wonder that most blind clients soon came to believe that almost all household chores were beyond them. So I ask again: who am I? As a person I am an artist, a crafter, a musician, a writer and a scientist. I design and make greetings cards which I sell for a local charity. I am an active volunteer for several local, regional and national organisations, including Stockton Blind People's Voice, the North Tees Primary Care Trust health forum and Skills for Care.

Many things I have been involved in the past have helped me since I lost my sight in 1999. Having taught children to read made it easier to learn to read Braille. Having crafted meant that, once I regained the confidence to use my crafting tools and materials, I found my fingers could feel what my eyes had seen. I learned how to use a computer and screen-reading software to write and read e-mails, and from these made many new friends across the world. They have taught me more about living with sight loss than any professional has. Being blind hasn't made me a better person. However, I have become far more aware of other people and their needs. I have listened to the way in which I have been spoken to, treated or told I should be grateful for what I have when I have tried to improve things for myself or others.

Now I use my experiences to empower myself: to speak for those without a voice and for those too afraid of recriminations to tell the truth. Working through Skills for Care I want to spread the word that everyone deserves a say in what happens to them, and where they wish their place to be in the world, whatever their abilities or disabilities. Who am I? I am me!

Chris Parkington uses a wheelchair and is blind

Community Care 30 November-6 December 2006
www.communitycare.co.uk

Surge in solvent abuse

Thousands of school children are risking their lives sniffing glue and aerosols

While public attention has focused on drug use, solvent abuse has dramatically increased, new research from the institute for Public Policy research (ippr) has revealed.

The report shows that cannabis remains by far the most common drug amongst young people, with 12% of 11 to 15 year olds having taken it in the last year. However, while the use of cannabis and class A drugs has risen slightly over the past seven years, the use of other stimulants has risen considerably. The number of children using poppers has almost doubled from 84,000 young people to 144,000 while, astonishingly, the number abusing glue and solvents has increased sevenfold from 28,000 to 168,000.

Solve It, the only national charity dedicated solely to tackling solvent abuse, says that the average home contains about 50 products that could be abused. So while parents may think they know what to look for when it comes to drug abuse – such as cigarette papers and needles – the bathroom cabinet or cleaning cupboard has plenty to offer for solvent abusers.

According to the Solve It website, VSA (volatile solvent abuse) kills at least one young person a week in the UK, yet in 23% of deaths users showed no evidence of previous abuse. Shockingly, solvent abuse kills more 10-16 year olds than all illegal drugs put together, with butane lighter refills linked to over half of all VSA deaths.

Despite this, recent anti-drug campaigns have focused on the dangers of ecstasy and other drugs without even touching on solvent abuse. Glue sniffing was the plague of the 1980s yet the number of abusers dropped considerably following various campaigns to deal with the epidemic. Now, after the issue has been overlooked for too long, figures have risen again.

VSA can lead to powerful hallucinations and, even though it can lead to damage to the lungs, liver, kidneys, brain, heart and central nervous system, young people are risking their lives just for the buzz it provides. A single occasion of solvent abuse can kill, but because VSA can get a young person high in 15-30 seconds, they may put themselves in a potentially tragic situation very quickly. With more and more products becoming available for the home that can potentially be abused, parents and guardians need to be aware of the situation.

According to the ippr report, developing social skills and strong adult role models are crucial in keeping kids off drugs, drink and cigarettes. Figures on the Solve It website show that 2,000 people have died as a direct result of VSA and most of them were under 18. With all media attention being paid to drug abuse, how are parents to know about this threat? Julia Margo, a senior research fellow at ippr said, "This is a real hidden tragedy. All the focus has been on cannabis and cocaine and trying to turn children away from hard drugs. But children will use whatever they can get their hands on."

Solvent abuse can happen anywhere at any time: if a parent or teacher were to search through a young person's things, marker pens and other abusable items wouldn't raise alarm. Glues and solvents such as deodorant and hairspray are not illegal and no parent would surely want to stop their children from using such products.

Barbara Skinner lost her son Darren in 1988 because of VSA and in 1989 set up Solve It to help prevent other people from suffering the same fate as her son. She says on the website "As a responsible parent, (and qualified nurse) I had informed my children about the dangers of smoking, alcohol, and illegal drugs, yet before my son's death my knowledge of VSA was non-existent, this type of substance abuse was not discussed."

The shock of her son's death made her realise that education was the way forward and she began to "learn and then inform children, young people, parents and professionals of the consequences of VSA. Solve It was born and prevention through education was its main objective." Campaigners believe that because solvent abuse no longer dominates news headlines that police, teachers and parents may not be aware of its dangers.

"Those involved in, or at risk of becoming involved in, VSA are also vulnerable to becoming victims of crimes ranging from theft to physical and sexual abuse," says Barbara Skinner. "When people see evidence of other drug taking they tell someone. But we have forgotten about volatile substance abuse, so no one thinks to look closely at aerosols to see if there are teeth marks or nozzles missing. We have to become more vigilant. More than 2,000 young people have died in the past 30 years due to VSA. If any other drug taking had caused so many deaths we'd be beating down the door of government."

Source: various

The Facts

- The number of young people given Anti-Social Behaviour Orders due to their VSA is increasing.

- Crimes committed by young people whilst high on these substances include murders, rapes, assaults, thefts and vandalism.

- The vast majority of drug users have admitted that VSA was their "Stepping Stone" to illegal drugs.

- The youngest person to die from VSA was a 7 year old – the oldest 80 years old. Volatile Substances are easier for young people to access than illegal drugs.

- There is no such thing as a typical sniffer. Those who abuse these substances can come from any social, cultural and ethnic background.

Britain 'needs a more realistic approach to heroin addicts'

Heroin should be prescribed to long-term addicts to prevent them from committing crimes to feed their habits, the head of Britain's police chiefs has suggested.

Ken Jones, the president of the Association of Chief Police Officers, also admitted that current policing tactics are failing to combat a "hardcore minority" of heroin addicts.

He called for a political consensus on the issue of heroin prescription on the NHS, and a more "realistic" approach to tackling long-term drug abuse. Mr Jones argued that by prescribing heroin the police would be able to significantly reduce overall crime and prevent deaths from overdoses.

The former chief constable of Sussex is the most senior police officer to give his support to heroin prescription and his controversial view is likely to be criticised by organisations opposed to any form of drug liberalisation.

Mr Jones, who is head of the organisation that represents the most senior ranks of the 43 police forces in England and Wales, said: "You need to understand there is a hard core, a minority, who nevertheless commit masses of crime to feed their addiction. We have got to be realistic – I have looked into the whites of these people's eyes and many have no interest whatsoever in coming off drugs. We have to find a way of dealing with them, and licensed prescription is definitely something we should be thinking about."

The most common treatment for heroin abuse in Britain is methadone, a synthetic drug similar to heroin but less addictive. Heroin prescription is used in Switzerland and the Netherlands, where it has been credited with turning offenders away from crime.

In the UK only a few hundred of the 40,000 registered heroin addicts are currently being prescribed heroin as part of a limited experiment. Heroin addicts commit on average 432 crimes a year, costing a total of £45,000, according to research. Mr Jones's organisation, ACPO, has said officially that it will await the outcome of the current limited trial before making a formal policy statement.

But Mr Jones said: "I was a drugs officer and we have to be realistic. There is a hardcore minority who are not in any way, shape or form anxious to come off drugs. They think 'I am going to go out there and steal, rob, burgle and get the money to buy it'. What are we going to do – say 'OK we are going to try and contain this by normal criminal justice methods' and fail, or are we going to look at doing something different? Start being a bit more innovative. It is about looking at things in a different way without turning away completely from the current position."

He added that drug prices in some areas of the UK had reached a historic low, which he conceded was a good indicator that drugs were readily available.

He said: "I am not in any shape or form a legaliser, but what I am concerned with is that we have to shape up to some tough realities. We don't have enough treatment places for those who want to go on them. What we need is a cross-party consensus which considers the overwhelming public view to be tough on the roots of drugs, as well as treating its victims."

UK drug facts

40,000
addicts registered in the UK

200,000
addicts estimated to be living in the UK

£30–£100
price per gram of heroin on the streets of the UK

2,200kg
of heroin was seized and taken out of the supply chain in Britain in 2005–06

90%
of heroin in the UK comes from Afghanistan

12,687
deaths were related to drug misuse by males from 1993 to 2004

3,401
deaths in 1993–2004 among females, with heroin/ morphine most commonly mentioned substances

744
people died of heroin-related causes in 2003–04

200
deaths related to methadone, the heroin substitute, in 2003–04

Studies on heroin prescription in the Netherlands and Switzerland found significant reductions in illicit drug use among those receiving the treatment. Both the Swiss and Dutch reported a drop in the crimes committed by their addicts.

The widespread prescription of heroin in Britain was phased out in the 1960s. GPs in England and Wales have the legal power to prescribe heroin, but do so extremely rarely.

The UK has 327,466 hardcore "problem drug users" who are regularly using either heroin, crack or cocaine. A report by Glasgow University last year found that fewer than 4 per cent of heroin addicts beat their habit with methadone. There are an estimated 40,000 problem heroin users using methadone.

Mr Jones said that he knew of one region where many years ago doctors had prescribed heroin to try to deal with problem addicts. "There are junkies who are alive today who would have been dead now," he said. "Their lives are stable, yes, their addiction is being maintained, but far better they are being maintained than them trying to get their fix off the street from crime. Heroin is an incredible stimulator of crime and I think we are foolish if we don't acknowledge that."

On a separate issue, Mr Jones also called for the introduction of a written constitution to remove any suggestion that the Government is using the police for political purposes. He argued that without written rules the police service will always be vulnerable to the suggestion that it is being manipulated by ministers at the Home Office.

He argued: "There used to be much more clear water between us and the Government, there has to be for public confidence to remain. The minute that the public perception is that we are now being politically directed by the government of the day, then some of that confidence will leak away.

"There is the unease sometimes that we are being misused, but I don't see any evidence of that. If there was a much clearer demarcation in terms of a constitution then I think we would be less vulnerable to those suggestions.

"But people have nothing to refer to, if someone from a particularly political persuasion says why are we doing this, or that, then I would like to be able to refer to a written constitution."

A liberal experiment that is sweeping the world

In the shadows of Frankfurt's gleaming glass towers an undistinguished six-storey building serves as a safe injection area for heroin addicts.

Along with the heroin room, there is a medical station, a counselling centre, a crack-smoking room and on the top two floors, a 24-hour shelter, complete with a cafe run by the addicts.

By the late 1980s Frankfurt's police had lost the battle to control drug use. When Deutsche Bank AG decided to build its new headquarters near the red light district, city officials decided that the last thing they wanted was bankers rubbing shoulders with addicts.

Frankfurt is one of about 40 cities in Europe and Australia where safe injection sites have been embraced by police and health officials as an essential tool of urban drug policy.

Berlin has set up mobile safe injection sites in vans that travel to areas where addicts congregate. Sometimes they are accompanied by a second van with medical and dental facilities. Only America demands a fundamentalist line in the so-called "war on drugs" and balks at prescribing heroin to addicts.

The introduction of heroin-injecting centres in Switzerland has reportedly led to an 82 percent decrease in its use since 1990.

According to a study published in the medical journal *The Lancet* it has "changed the image of heroin use as a rebellious act to an illness that needs therapy... Heroin seems to have become a 'loser drug,' with its attractiveness fading for young people".

"It is time for England to catch up with Holland, Germany and Switzerland, and provide a small amount of this high-cost treatment as part of the mainstream service," said Michael Farrell, consultant psychiatrist at the National Addiction Centre in London.

In North America, Vancouver has a major heroin problem. Emaciated prostitutes can be seen shooting up outside soup kitchens.

Now with preparations for the 2010 Winter Olympics in full swing, the Canadian city, routinely voted the world's most attractive to live in, has a potential public relations disaster on its hands.

Despite the US muttering dark threats, the city has opened a heroin administration clinic and is watching nervously to see whether the area attracts even more drug use and lawlessness or helps mitigate the uglier side of heroin addiction.

Supporters say that injection centres reduce drug use in parks and that there are fewer discarded syringes on the streets. A review by the EU's Monitoring Centre for Drugs and Drug Addiction concludes: "[The] longer the exposure to consumption rooms, the greater the reduction in high-risk behaviour."

The United Nations' narcotics control, which adheres to Washington's hard line on drugs, flatly opposes injection facilities.

Leonard Doyle

The Independent 19 February 2007

The magic ingredient:

Hash brownies, dope stir fry... Cooking with the cannabis granny

She's just been busted for the second time, but Patricia Tabram's unusual (and illegal) cottage industry goes on.
Ian Herbert joins her in the kitchen for a masterclass in class C culinary delights.

Patricia Tabram at Carlisle Crown Court

Photo: Owen Humphreys PA Wire/PA Photos

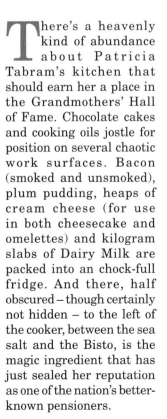

There's a heavenly kind of abundance about Patricia Tabram's kitchen that should earn her a place in the Grandmothers' Hall of Fame. Chocolate cakes and cooking oils jostle for position on several chaotic work surfaces. Bacon (smoked and unsmoked), plum pudding, heaps of cream cheese (for use in both cheesecake and omelettes) and kilogram slabs of Dairy Milk are packed into an chock-full fridge. And there, half obscured – though certainly not hidden – to the left of the cooker, between the sea salt and the Bisto, is the magic ingredient that has just sealed her reputation as one of the nation's better-known pensioners.

The finely ground marijuana is kept in an old Bramwells pickle jar by the sink, and it looks almost interchangeable with the nearby jars of mixed herbs when Mrs Tabram reaches for it during a morning's initiation in the art of cooking with cannabis. But Mrs Tabram's miserliness with the teaspoonful which she eventually scoops out from the jar suggests that her belief in the liberal use of cannabis does have its limits. A quarter of the spoonful makes it to the mixing bowl from which she will assemble the ingredients for her unique "claggy" – a Northumbrian form of fudge brownie. "I've special scales to measure it," she says. "One small dose like this will give me five hours free of pain."

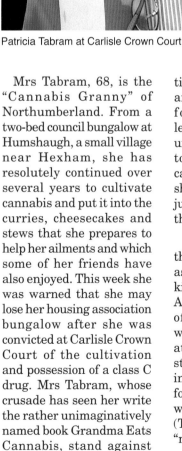

Mrs Tabram, 68, is the "Cannabis Granny" of Northumberland. From a two-bed council bungalow at Humshaugh, a small village near Hexham, she has resolutely continued over several years to cultivate cannabis and put it into the curries, cheesecakes and stews that she prepares to help her ailments and which some of her friends have also enjoyed. This week she was warned that she may lose her housing association bungalow after she was convicted at Carlisle Crown Court of the cultivation and possession of a class C drug. Mrs Tabram, whose crusade has seen her write the rather unimaginatively named book Grandma Eats Cannabis, stand against the cabinet minister Peter Hain on a pro-cannabis

ticket at the last election, and become a figurehead for the campaign to legalise cannabis, remains undaunted. "It's not going to stop me cooking with cannabis for one minute," she says. "The law and good justice just do not exist in this country any more."

Granny she might be, but this former chef is evidently as uncompromising in the kitchen as in the courtroom. After she throws a pinch of cannabis into a bowl with a quantity of butter at the kitchen table, her student is ready to throw in a few sweet ingredients for the cannabis "claggy" we are making together. (The word is Geordie for "messy", which may well prove appropriate here.) But Mrs Tabram removes

"One small dose like this will give me five hours free of pain"

the cannabis mix. The weed, it transpires, is best cooked after 24 hours sitting in butter or fat, so this one is for another day. Instead, there is some she prepared earlier. It is sitting among five ready-made cannabis mixes placed into flowery teacups back in the fridge. A few whirls of flour and a little mixture-beating later, and the cake is placed in the oven.

"The police have always known where to look," Mrs Tabram says, amid all the industry. "They'll ask me 'Is it in the hot chocolate Pat?' And of course, there it is every time." She opens the lid on a Cadbury's hot chocolate jar in which the green specks are also unmissable. (Eight heaped teaspoonfuls of chocolate to a level one of cannabis is apparently the ideal ratio for a satisfying beverage.) When Northumbria Police raided her home in October 2005, they also found four cannabis plants in a store cupboard. Mrs Tabram showed them a further 20 tubs of pre-frozen cannabis stews and soups in the freezer, though she says they declined to take them because they did not want to deprive her of food. She was charged only six months after receiving another six-month jail sentence – suspended for two years – when convicted of possessing 31 plants and blocks of cannabis worth £850.

Despite the second conviction, Mrs Tabram's determination is becomingly an increasingly awkward problem for Northumbria Police. Her beliefs about the medicinal value of cannabis and its superiority to prescription drugs (which she says make many of the elderly ill), mean that only jail will stop her from her cultivations. Her first trial judge observed that this would only make her a martyr, an opportunity she is all too ready for. "Emmeline Pankhurst had to go to prison three times before women got the vote", she says, whisk in hand, "so I am not going to be worried about it."

Her actions have contributed to a strong pro – cannabis campaign here, where she is supported by Mark and Lezley Gibson, campaigners from neighbouring Cumbria, who were convicted last year of making and distributing cannabis-laced chocolate bars to multiple sclerosis sufferers. Mrs Tabram's own experience with cannabis began amid what she describes as a near-suicidal depression five years ago, a result of the death of her husband, David, from cancer, and pain suffered following two car crashes. She had not appeared from her bungalow for days when two friends brought her out of her despair when she least expected, she says, by offering a cannabis spliff without telling her what she was smoking. Mrs Tabram was astonished by the effect. A chef and former restaurant proprietor, she was soon seeking out cannabis recipes from a shop in Newcastle.

Her first effort, cannabis scrambled egg, left her violently sick after she applied a whole teaspoonful to the plate and suffered what users know as a "whitey" or blackout. But soon she began cooking up cannabis chicken and leek pie and cannabis chocolate cheesecake. "I was in so much pain and the cannabis brought me back to life," says Mrs Tabram. Opponents of her point to the profound psychological effects cannabis can have. But Mrs Tabram also speaks of the contradictions in drug sentencing, in which the wealthy enjoy rehab while "the working classes" are seeking something that works, a life free from pain.

"To offer someone a slice of cake means they can charge me with supply"

She wants to talk some more but the rich array of vegetables arranged near the cannabis pot are suddenly a distraction. Can carrots, cauliflower and cannabis really mix? Suddenly Mrs Tabram is offering a teaspoon over and I am ladling another small quantity of cannabis/cooking oil mix into a pan, for conversion into what can only be described as dope stir fry. The sequence is all-important for this one, it transpires. Fry the soya beans, sprouts and cabbage with our special green ingredient, then throw in the celery, mushroom and

spring onions as well as chicken squares. A touch of chilli oil at the end will make all the difference too, Mrs Tabram predicts. But that will have to wait because the cake – literally a "claggy", messy, soggy and flecked with green spots – is ready.

Mrs Tabram also now offers some unwelcome news, which quashes a cherished hope that I would soon be eating some of "claggy". "To offer someone a slice of the cake means they can charge me with supply," she says. "I couldn't possibly do that." She then leaves the room for an unspecified reason – and it seems that the risk of her catching me in flagrante eating a slice which contains a whole 0.1g of cannabis, is probably worth taking. I take a piece. With one obvious difference, it is like any other self-respecting grandmother's fudge brownie.

"It will take two slices to alleviate back pain for you," warns Mrs Tabram, back in the room and evidently tolerating my imposition. "A tall bloke like you would need a whole 0.2g for five hours' pain relief."

It seems likely that she will also be tucking in for some time yet. Though the local Milecastle Housing Association will hold a meeting to decide whether to evict Mrs Tabram, she is quite prepared to turn such a decision into plenty more public embarrassment for the authorities.

"I've got a tent and a little camp cooker and I can sleep on the piece of grass outside," she says. "Let them see what it looks like to throw an overweight old granny like me out of their council bungalow. "

The Independent 10 March, 2007

'I was entirely alone'

Tom Dodds, 19, tells how his quest for a 'manly' body became an obsession that almost killed him

Anorexia is seen as a 'women's problem'. But eating disorders in men are widespread and on the increase

Photo posed by model

The summer of 2005 was baking hot. Wimbledon was over, and Bob Geldof was telling the world how to make poverty history. Somewhere among all this, I was wrapped within my own little world. I knew these things were happening, but like the AS levels I was about to take and my part-time job stacking shelves in Waitrose, they were on the edge of my vision, almost a different place in another world. While most of the boys in my class were going out drinking and having fun, I was fixed rigidly in a solitary regime of weight loss.

Every morning I would wake before anyone else in the house, swing myself out of bed, drop to the floor and perform 60 press-ups. I focused my eyes on the dull blue carpet, getting nearer then further, nearer then further, trying to ignore the pain. Next came 100 sit-ups. By the time I had finished, my back would bleed but I didn't care. Breakfast was one Weetabix with skimmed milk, eaten on my own in the front room before another 60 press-ups while the rest of the house began their day around me. At school I couldn't concentrate and I spent my time between lessons walking around the town, trying to keep moving in order to burn more calories. Lunch was an apple; the sandwiches my parents made me take with me in the hope that I might eat them went to the pigeons in the square. In the evening I would eat only vegetables before more press-ups, sit-ups, and exercises with the dumbbells I had liberated from my elder brother's room. I followed this ritual every day, religiously, relentlessly, alone and scared. I think I knew what was happening, but didn't know what to do about it.

The common perception of anorexia is that it is a "women's problem", largely the preserve of teenage girls. Newspapers have been full of stories about the dangerous effects of stick-thin models and skeletal celebrities on young women. However, eating disorders in men are widespread and on the increase. Many cases go undiagnosed because no one realises that it is even a problem. All the literature and self-help guides on the subject, their weight tables and lists of symptoms, are written for women. At the time when I was looking for help, this only enhanced my feelings of isolation and shame: I was motivated by a desire to appear manlier, but society seemed to view my illness as inherently feminine.

I didn't want to be thin. I wanted to be lean and muscular. Specifically, I wanted to look like Christian Bale in American Psycho, which I had seen earlier that year at a friend's house. I think we all admired his muscularity, but only I really *wanted* it. I lusted after a six-pack and massive arms. It wasn't about wanting to emulate skinny models in magazines but about trying to be more self-assured. I associated all those gleaming, chiselled torsos with masculinity and confidence as well as discipline and focus. I had been overweight when I was younger, which had made me an easy target for bullies at my all boys' school where athleticism and machismo were highly prized and being in the rugby team seemed the greatest service to the school. I always felt unattractive and worthless; even after I dieted and lost weight the label of being "the fat one" never really went away.

When I arrived in the sixth form the stresses multiplied. I wanted to be an actor, and to show everyone that I was worth something. Like the rest of my peers, I started taking some of my lessons at the local girls' school but this only made me feel worse. Girls never seemed to talk to me, something I had not yet worked out was connected to the fact that I never talked to them, being too shy. I still saw myself as physically undesirable. At 17, the pain of this was exquisite, like a fine needle threading through the heart. Achieving the perfect body would stop all these problems, would somehow transform me.

That was when I began cutting back on what I ate, slowly swearing off more and more food. I also started to exercise more. I saw myself as a model of healthy living – superior to all my lazy friends. I stopped going out at night and didn't see anyone outside school. I wanted to concentrate only on pushing myself to the limit, to find out where the limit was. I was entirely alone and I never revealed my problem (by now, at over a stone underweight I had recognised it as such) to any of my friends or colleagues. It was my mother who first realised I had anorexia. I just wanted to ignore it and pretend there was nothing wrong. Inside I was terrified and so, so alone, but I refused to show it: it seemed like another sign of my weakness.

When people at school mentioned that I had lost weight I merely told them I was wearing a belt, or just denied it. Most of my classmates and teachers didn't notice and I was just

I was at death's door, and so close that I could look through his letterbox

living in my own little bubble. All my problems seemed to disappear, so intently was I focusing on weight loss, and in a way life became much simpler – but at a price. I became so ill that my body began cannibalising its own organs for protein and I could barely get up the stairs. I looked like someone from a POW camp; every bone stuck out and I had no muscle left. I couldn't see a way out and could think only about the terrible hunger; it was what drove me on, relentlessly, towards catastrophe. It felt as though time had stopped for me but the world was still going, as though my life was standing still, stretching out on every side. It is still all a bit of a haze but I can remember thinking that I was going to die, and hoping that I would collapse and be taken to hospital before I did. I was at death's door, and so close that I could look through his letterbox.

I still don't know exactly why I made the decision to change. It was a warm and sunny day, and there was no one about to see my moment of awakening. I was walking down the street, making my way to music class at school. But I never did get there. I suddenly realised that all I needed to do was eat, so I did. I rushed home and ate everything I could lay my hands on – cheese, bread, cereal, jam. The feeling was exhilarating, like tasting food for the first time.

I was soon put on a re-feeding programme but I hated being told what to eat so I ignored it. Instead I was determined to recover my own way and although this made things difficult, I am glad I did. With the help of my doctor and family, I slowly put on weight, which was physically very painful at first as my body adapted, but I persevered. I

was very lucky – had I carried on as I was, I would almost certainly have collapsed as a result of the massive strain my organs were under.

Nearly two years on, I still haven't told most of my friends what happened and I rarely mention it to those who do know. Most people are still oblivious to there ever having been a problem. This is not because I am embarrassed or ashamed but more because I feel that it is something people would view as "weird". Most think that, because of the close association of anorexia with women, any men who have it are some sort of freakish anomaly. I hope that in sharing my experiences I have opened some people's eyes.

I am 19 now and taking a diploma to become a personal trainer. Obviously, exercise and healthy eating are still a big part of my life and anorexia never goes away. You don't recover from it, you merely learn to live with and control it. I still exercise a huge amount, working out with weights four to five times a week to help me bulk up, and I have trouble sitting still for a long period of time even now. I have to be constantly vigilant for any sign that my old ways are returning.

I suppose I am still unhappy with my body – I now think it is too skinny so I guess I just can't win. In the past couple of months, though, I have put on about half a stone of muscle and I am getting a bit bigger every day. I don't want to look like Christian Bale any more, though. I know I have my own unique body with its own strengths. Unfortunately, I am still pretty rubbish with women, but am not quite as self-conscious as I was. I have also not given up on acting entirely but it is such a hard industry to succeed in that I am not sure I can make it. I will just have to wait and see. I feel that I have learned a lot about myself and what I am capable of – and to have survived is an accomplishment in itself .

© The Guardian 26 February 2007

The thin gene

Breakthrough links bulimia to testosterone

Scientists have established that the eating disorder that plagues young women could be genetic, and treated by the contraceptive pill.

Thin celebrities such as Victoria Beckham are 'very negative role models', says the mother of a girl who died of anorexia

Louisa Felton and **Paul Bignell**

Bulimia may be caused by hormones, according to new research, which suggests that up to a third of women suffering from the condition could be treated with the contraceptive pill.

Scientists investigating the causes of food disorders have discovered that one in three patients who had bulimia also suffered from hormonal disorders which gave them unusually high levels of testosterone, the male hormone.

Bulimia, which causes sufferers to eat excessive amounts of food and then regurgitate or purge it out of their systems by throwing up or use of laxatives, was widely accepted to be caused by depression, stress or self-esteem issues.

However, because testosterone hormone levels are directly linked with the regulation of appetite, scientists believe that higher levels of the hormone are directly linked to increased levels of hunger.

The researchers tried reducing testosterone levels by giving sufferers the Pill, which boosted their levels of oestrogen, the female hormone. Half of the women who were given the Pill saw decreased levels of sugar and fat cravings and their feelings of hunger lessened. By the end of the trial three of the subjects were free of bulimia.

Dr Sabine Naessen, who led the research at the Karolinska Institute in Sweden, the world's largest medical research school, said yesterday: "We have shown that one third of female bulimics have metabolic disorders that may explain the occurrence of the eating

Photo: Mark J. Terrill/AP/PA Photos

disorder. These disorders may in certain cases express the hormonal constitution of a patient, rather than any mental illness."

British experts gave a cautious welcome to the research yesterday. Steve Bloomfield, a spokesperson for the Eating Disorders Association (EDA), said: "The danger I would foresee is lots of people thinking that this will cure bulimia in the way an aspirin may cure a headache."

Claire Evans, clinical director at the Riverdale Grange Hospital, Sheffield, a specialist centre in the treatment of eating disorders and alcohol, also welcomed the research. She called for more work to be done before the Pill is accepted as a treatment for bulimia, saying "in many cases the psychological aspect would still be there" even if hormonal imbalances were corrected.

Most bulimics are treated with antidepressants and cognitive behavioural therapy (CBT) – a treatment that tries to change the behavioural patterns associated with over-eating.

According to Dr Joan Brunt from the Eating Disorder Service, St George's Hospital, London, around 2 per cent of the population in the UK suffers from the condition. Some 85 per cent of these will be girls in their late teens.

High-profile figures such as Diana, Princess of Wales, Oprah Winfrey and Sharon Osbourne, have spoken of their battles with bulimia. Like the majority of sufferers, they attribute their illness to emotional trauma.

Former bulimic Liselle Terret, a 37-year-old lecturer, yesterday said the cause of her illness went back to her family life and her mother, who was a "secret eater": "I was bullied by my brother and was a tag-along at school. Family life was not easy either," she said.

At the lowest point, Ms Terret, who began forcing herself to throw up at the age of 14, found she could

THE FACTS

Bulimia is an eating disorder that leads to a cycle of binge eating and purging – usually by vomiting.

RECOGNISED BY Professor Gerald Russell in 1977, the condition is often less about food and more to do with psychological issues and feelings of a lack of control.

RATES OF bulimia are highest in Western countries. The disorder, almost nonexistent in Eastern cultures, is seeping into other cultures through Western movies and television.

WOMEN ACCOUNT for 90 per cent of bulimia patients, with gymnasts, dancers and cheerleaders most at risk because their roles make it imperative that they be extremely thin.

make herself vomit on cue, up to five times a day. With no one to talk to, she felt alone: "Every time a medical magazine would come through the post I would search to see if I could find answers to what was wrong with me."

Ms Terret's bulimia continued through university. She saw many psychotherapists who helped her cut back on vomiting, but the core psychological issues were still tightly locked away: "I took safety from everything in the toilet and I managed to hide it for a long time."

Today, she is a lecturer in applied theatre at Goldsmiths College in London, and learned how to overcome bulimia through performing arts.

Ms Terret can relate her own experiences to Dr Naessen's research: "They may have a point about the hormone imbalance – during my periods, when I was emotional, happy or sad, I would vomit. It became my life ... it didn't matter what the emotion was; I would be sick."

Mother of teenage girl who died of anorexia, weighing just four stone, blames Victoria Beckham

The mother of a teenage girl who died from anorexia has singled out Victoria Beckham as setting a bad example to young, impressionable girls by leading them to believe thin is glamorous.

Rosalind Ponomarenko-Jones, whose 19-year-old daughter, Sophie Mazurek, weighed just four stone when she died, condemned skinny models and thin celebrities such as Mrs Beckham for promoting an unhealthy image.

Ms Ponomarenko-Jones, 46, said: "These girls and celebrities such as Victoria Beckham are very negative role models. Sophie knew that but she wanted to be like them."

Originally 8½ stone, Sophie developed anorexia at 17. She died last month from heart failure caused by malnutrition.

"Sophie spent a fortune on celebrity magazines showing who was looking thin or fat," said Ms Ponomarenko-Jones, a housing support officer from Snead, Powys. "She was just a normal girl but the anorexia got out of her control."

A spokesperson for Mrs Beckham said it would be "inappropriate to comment on somebody's loss".

The Independent on Sunday 7 January 2007

Give Us Our Voice in Class

Hannah Couchman

(West Midlands deputy representative on the English Secondary Students Association executive)

Despite the cliché that it is the students that make a school, many students feel they have little or no "student voice". Student voice is about students having a genuine influence on decision-making through being properly represented in their schools.

It can involve anything from students participating in staff appointments to their choosing their own timetables – and it's something that can certainly be found if students feel they are being ignored.

Last April, 120 students at Flegg High School in Norfolk went on a walkout protest, claiming that the decision to shorten their lunch break to half an hour was made without consulting them. Their walkout resulted in the police being called. It is unacceptable that students have to resort to such measures to assert student voice – and that 10 pupils were suspended after the protest.

Ironically, many of the protesting students should have been receiving citizenship education, which requires pupils to study democratic processes. By avoiding consultation with their pupils, schools are failing in their duty to ensure young people understand the importance of their own views. Encouraging involvement in school decisions is

Encouraging involvement in school decisions is one step towards reducing political apathy among young people

one step towards reducing political apathy among young people.

Some argue that the level of student voice is already adequate, with the introduction of school councils and similar consultation groups. However, in a National Federation for Educational Research survey, 98% of secondary school headteachers claimed to have a school council, yet only 45% of pupils said they had been involved in electing school councillors – a significant difference.

Encouraging student participation is as beneficial to staff as it is to students. Students may not always describe school as their favourite place, but the more student voice we have in school, the more enjoyable it becomes. Often, classroom behaviour is dependent on the degree of respect held for the teacher.

Teachers who encourage mutual respect in the classroom experience less bad behaviour from students.

Unfortunately, there is an underlying problem that prevents effective student voice – the belief that adults know what is best for young people. Although schools require pupils to show respect to members of staff, little is often shown in return.

The recent education bill should have included a requirement for meaningful consultation with students – the same right that children and young people in Scotland have had since 2000 and young people in care have had for more than 30 years. In its absence, there are various methods that could be employed to ensure that student voice is heard, one being compulsory school councils, as in Wales. However, unless school councils are effective they can tend to be tokenistic and even a barrier to democratic participation. To make sure that schools do not introduce token councils simply to tick a box, there needs to be clear guidelines and it needs to be included in school evaluation and inspections.

Why not let schools lead the way in showing respect to the next generation?

www.studentvoice.co.uk

'We've all seen horror. But our school goes on'

In a city where pupils step over bodies to get to their classes, the teachers face unique challenges. On a trip to Britain, they tell their remarkable story.

By Anushka Asthana
Education Correspondent

AN ASTONISHING picture of life inside Baghdad's schools has been revealed by a group of Iraqi teachers who have travelled to the UK to gain respite from the daily bloodshed they witness. One, Suad Saleem Abdulla, described how she pulled her own children close every morning and said goodbye as if it was the last time she would ever see them. It was a daily ritual shared by parents throughout Iraq, she said. Only then did she start her treacherous 20-minute walk to school.

Suad, who told her story for the first time this weekend, has seen corpses and even 'flying body parts' on her journey to the school where she is head teacher, but carried on walking because she was determined to keep it open.

The 43-year-old is one of 10 teachers, heads and school inspectors who have come to the UK from Iraq's capital after being invited by the NASUWT teaching union. They spoke of teachers assassinated as they walked to work, or kidnapped in front of pupils, and a daily battle to keep the terror outside the school gates. Their stories give a remarkable insight into the lives of Iraqi children who turn up for lessons day after day despite the bloodshed and violence.

Last month, a photographer captured an image of a girl in uniform on a blood-stained step after insurgents launched a mortar attack on her school. To Suad and her colleagues, the image was disturbingly familiar.

A similar attack has been launched four times on Nasser Kdhim Nasser's school in the al-Husseini area of Baghdad, leaving one student dead. 'The atrocities impacted so badly on one boy that he did not come back in, but for most, even though they have seen horror, school life continues as normal. We teach children to paint, draw and sing. Every morning they stand up, raise the flag and sing the national anthem.'

Suad is similarly determined: 'We have no choice. We have to carry on living, we have to go out. These extremists want to stop life and the best thing to them is to stop us going to school and teaching the children. But if they stop that then everything will collapse.'

Each day she has just four hours to teach the 400 pupils before another school takes over the building for the afternoon session. She presides over Arabic, English, maths, art, sport and much more. Two weeks ago, she saw insurgents set up a phony road block near the building so she locked the doors and carried on inside.

To get textbooks and stationery, Suad has to walk to a nearby Unicef building. It is a job none of her staff is prepared to do because those who go there are often targeted by snipers.

Teachers, according to the group, are at particular risk because insurgents want to disrupt education. Mahdi Ali Lefta, the head of the delegation, is from al-Mahmodia, where five teachers were executed in front of children. In Nasser's area, three head teachers were killed.

The issues facing these teachers in Baghdad are barely imaginable to colleagues in the UK. 'The challenges they have got - are workplaces open, can they get members to work? - puts into perspective all the furore over closures because of snow,' said Chris Keates, general secretary of the Nasuwt, which is playing host to the group in Birmingham. 'In Iraq, it's about getting schools open for basic education.'

Yet when Keates talked to the teachers on Friday, their questions were not about security in the face of terror but wage negotiations and pensions. They clapped when they were told they were going to Stratford to see Richard III in Arabic. Back home, few of them venture out beyond 5pm.

'In the evening the roads are deserted as if there is a curfew,' said Bushra Bashar Taleea, a teaching adviser. 'Where I live, the warehouse we use to store basic food for children has been blown up three times. We are afraid but we are conditioned to it because we see it every day. Life is better now because we have got rid of the dictatorship, but we need time.'

Bushra 'jumps' when she hears a bang and constantly calls her family to reassure them that she is alive.

Ali Ahmed Sindal, aged 63, a school inspector, checks on his three sons and daughter every day after work. But Ahmed, who spent four years on death row under Saddam Hussein, was hopeful: 'We are optimistic that all these things will be ended within one year, two years, three years. Then we are expecting a new life, a better life.'

In the meantime, the teachers want to keep improving the country's education system. Mahdi, who has brought the teachers to Britain with the support of the Iraqi Federation of Workers, said he was still planning strategies for teaching a year in advance despite the trouble.

'These people who attack education, attack schools and teachers have nothing in their heart but hate and violence and they want the destruction of Iraq. They have no sense of humanity.'

Teacher Mohamed Seed Hatem said the situation today 'was still better than it was. A bloody dictatorship has gone.'

'The picture represents what has become of Iraqi childhood'

Wisam Sami, 32, a photographer with news agency AFP, took this remarkable picture of a girl leaving her school in western Baghdad after a horrendous mortar attack on 28 January. Reproduced around the world, it is an image that sums up the everyday struggle for normality in Iraq.

'When I arrived at al-Khulud secondary school, there was blood all over the playground. I found out that mortars had fallen as the girls were playing and they had been hit. Some were wounded and one girl had been killed. The girl in the picture witnessed everything and told me what had happened. She was terrified and she was crying. She had to go into the school to get her things because her parents were waiting.

'I saw her coming out and I took the picture. I took it because it represents what has become of Iraqi childhood - wherever children go they see blood. This image shows the contrast between childhood and violence.

'Before the war I used to take portrait pictures [Now] my life has been turned upside down. I went from taking happy portraits to being a war photo-journalist.

'The role of photographers here is to get a message to the world and let it know the truth. The pictures we take cannot lie.'

The Observer 18 February 2007

Students at a number of Scottish schools, including Craigroyston High School, Edinburgh, have rather surprisingly voted to have a school uniform. Those in favour suggest that by disguising inequalities, improving discipline and increasing a sense of community within the school, a uniform enhances academic performance. Opponents suggest that a uniform curbs freedom of expression and point out that the highest performing pupils in Europe, the Finns, do not wear them. Dr Sheila Riddell of Edinburgh University went further, suggesting that uniforms are unpopular in Europe because they have sinister associations – with Nazi youth.

ABSURD SCHOOL UNIFORM CLAIM LEAVES A NAZI TASTE

Brian Hennigan

'You'll grow into it", must be one of the things most children hate to hear. It's one of the things mothers say when foisting a school uniform on them which – for sadly non-fashion reasons – has been bought several sizes too big, affording the child an opportunity to feel both impoverished and a laughing stock. The good news is that you are often surrounded by similar figures who are in danger of being drowned alive in their blazers. On the bright side it is always possible to go camping with the simple addition of a pole.

Incidentally, you'll have to forgive me if halfway through this article I feel the urge to stop and annex Austria. The problem is that I went to a couple of schools where I was required to wear a school uniform. As you may be aware, when Craigroyston High School brought back their uniforms, an educational expert from Moray House noted that: "Whilst we want to have discipline in schools, we certainly don't

want to be bringing up a generation of Nazi Youth".

The fact that I and many others spent our entire school lives in uniform without ever being tempted to create a master race must surely be put down as a lucky escape. We couldn't even get in the local newsagents more than two at time let alone invade Poland. Nevertheless, one shudders to think of the horrors that the St Thomas Aquinas Black Shirts might have visited upon Tollcross.

In journalist William Shirer's magnificent account of the Second World War, The Rise and Fall of the Third Reich, there is no mention of the possibility that if only the Allies had pressed Germany for a casual dress policy in their educational establishments as part of the settlement

reached after the First World War then the 1940s might have been a more joyful decade.

The claim that there is a link between school uniforms and extreme right-wing politics is as nonsensical as a claim that wearing hoodies causes social exclusion and crime. It doesn't, anymore than sticking on a Burberry baseball cap makes you suddenly want to hang around shopping centres trying to look moody.

While the powers of a decent uniform might stretch to making people sit up a bit more, or perhaps want to issue parking tickets in an over-diligent manner, it is ludicrous to suggest that school uniforms could be in any way responsible for an outbreak of fascism.

School uniforms make school children accountable. Making children accountable has been an unpopular idea ever since the notion was first hatched that children are never responsible for anything and should be treated as victims, even when they are sitting at the back of a bus swearing like storm-troopers and making other passengers' lives a misery.

Uniforms are becoming more and not less relevant. Contemporary society is under a process of fragmentation that means more and more of us can do exactly what we want, where we want, when we want, especially in Upper Polmont. The invisible ties that create a society – the fact that everyone used to watch the same programmes at the same time, that everyone worked the same hours – are being loosened. From an early age, children are encouraged to discover their individuality using technologies that can enhance their isolation. Schools must find ways to emphasise that being part of society means conforming to certain rules.

Uniforms are a simple way of exploring the whole concept of membership, both of society and of the smaller units within society of which they are a member. School uniforms can be an important element in teaching responsibility.

Obviously some educational experts might find this concept difficult to swallow. But don't worry – as your intelligence matures you'll grow into it.

The Scotsman 16 January 2007

Ok, you win, I'll wear the uniform but I'm warning you now, it's like completely your fault if I turn out to be a fascist, home-wrecking ball breaker.

The big switch-off

Kate Thomas

We know energy-saving lightbulbs are better for the planet. The trouble is, they're also glaring, ugly and awkward. Or are they?

In the Nineties, when light bulb jokes were still funny, Australians used to tell one about the English. "How many Englishmen does it take to change a light bulb?" Answer: "What do you mean change it? It's a perfectly good bloody bulb! We have had it for a thousand years and it has worked just fine."

Edison's original incandescent light bulb design – patented in 1880 – has been used for 127 years in Britain. It releases up to 95 per cent of its energy in the form of heat, and despite the fact that only the remaining 5 per cent is put to good use, it's still the most popular way of lighting our homes. Energy-saving bulbs use up to four times less electricity to generate the same amount of heat, saving energy, money and the environment.

Eco-conscious Australia has already seen the light, recently unveiling its plans to become the first country in the world to ban yellow incandescent bulbs by 2012 – they will be gradually phased out and replaced by compact fluorescent bulbs (CFLs). Here in Britain, we've been a little slower to get off the mark. But earlier this week, the high street electrical store Currys announced plans to cease selling traditional bulbs. And Chancellor Gordon Brown has taken on the Conservatives for the green vote, with a move to phase out the use of all old-fashioned bulbs by 2011.

So why is Britain so reluctant to make the switch? Well, the energy-saving alternatives don't always seem to be quite bright enough, we say.

They flicker. They hum. Don't they emit more toxic gases than the incandescent type? And it's all very well championing eco-friendly bulbs if you're living in sunny Australia. But here in grey Britain, we say, let there be light!

All Australian households will run on more fuel-efficient CFL bulbs by 2010, using around 20 per cent of the electricity to produce the same amount of light. But we want to know more than simple statistics. What we need are viable alternatives to old favourites.

Lucy Mantovani, a nutritionist, bought her first home last year, a period property in north London. "While my workplace has switched to energy-saving bulbs, I still use yellow incandescent lighting at home," Lucy admits.

"I find I need quite a bright bulb in the kitchen for cooking. But my guilty pleasure is halogen. I've fitted bright spotlights in the ceiling in the hallway, and upstairs in my bedroom I have a gorgeous mother and baby lamp that only takes halogen bulbs.

"Last weekend my boyfriend and I were in B&Q, and as I slung a box of 50-watt halogens into the trolley, I found myself throwing a quick glance over my shoulder, almost as if to check nobody was watching me. I count myself as an environmentally aware person. I recycle and I carbon offset whenever I fly. But I can't find a decent alternative to halogen, even though I get cross with myself for buying the bulbs. They have their wattage splashed across the front of the box, almost like warnings on a cigarette packet."

Lucy should look again. The range of energy saving bulbs available in the UK has greatly improved since the first designs came on the market. CFLs now warm up much faster than older designs, typically reaching 95 per cent of their full light output in under a minute. They still flicker slightly, but new technology has reduced the humming. And instead of those halogens? Once confined to the school physics lab, LEDs (light-emitting diodes) are now available as a sound alternative to halogen lighting. Not only do they produce more light per watt than incandescent bulbs, but LED bulbs have no filament so they don't burn out.

For those worried there may be significant amounts of CO2 and mercury released in the production of CFL bulbs – research is still under way, but speculation abounds – LEDs are a greener bet. Each bulb will light up your life for more than 50,000 hours (incandescent light bulbs typically run for 1,000-2,000 hours). Nigel's Eco Store (www.nigelsecostore.com) sells packs of two LED bulbs – suitable for ceiling spotlights – at £18.99 a pop. Expensive, yes, but on a pay-per-use basis, that's 0.04 pence an hour. Or there's the Osram dot, a bright, handheld, sticky LED that can be attached to any surface and gives 100 hours of light with three AAA batteries (from £5.22).

A number of UK companies are vying to become "the Englishman who changed the light bulb". Mega-man (www.megamanuk.com) offers 14 different types of bulb, including coloured globes, outdoor designs and the Cat's Eye – a bulb that lulls kids to sleep by emitting a soft, sleep-inducing afterglow long after being switched off. Or try eco-designers Luminair. Their range includes attractive – yes, really – coloured CFL globes, with edgy recycled lamps to fit, and they also sell a range of ultra-modern light fittings specially designed for LED bulbs. Proof that, really, Britain is more switched on than we once thought.

The Independent 15 March 2006

My guilty pleasure is halogen. In B&Q I slung a box of halogens in the trolley and found myself checking that no one was watching me

How they work

Traditional bulbs waste a lot of their energy by turning it into heat rather than light. Energy saving bulbs work like fluorescent lights, passing the electric current through gas in a tube, making the tube's coating glow brightly. This means that they use less energy and are cool to the touch.

These use a quarter of the electricity of ordinary bulbs to generate the same amount of light. So where you'd normally use a 60W bulb, you'll only need a 13-18W energy saving recommended equivalent.

How the savings add up

If everyone installed just one energy saving light bulb the CO2 emissions saved would fill 2 million double decker buses. And if each house installed three energy saving bulbs, it would save enough energy to run the country's street lights for a year.

Source: Energy Saving Trust
www.energysavingtrust.org.uk

IT IS A WONDERFUL WORLD: RICHER, HEALTHIER, AND CLEANER THAN EVER

Gloom and doom are in fashion, but, writes Allister Heath, a remarkable collection of economic statistics shows that the reality is much, much cheerier. For all our laments to the contrary, the human race has never had it so good

For billions of people around the world, these are the best of times to be alive. From Beijing to Bratislava, more of us are living longer, healthier and more comfortable lives than at any time in history; fewer of us are suffering from poverty, hunger or illiteracy. Pestilence, famine, death and even war, the Four Horsemen of the Apocalypse, are in retreat, thanks to the liberating forces of capitalism and technology.

If you believe that such apparently outlandish claims cannot possibly be true, think again. In a book which will trigger intense controversy when it is published later this month, the acclaimed American economist Indur Goklany, former US delegate to the United Nations' intergovernmental panel on climate change, demonstrates that on every objective measure of the human condition — be it life expectancy, food availability, access to clean water, infant mortality, literacy rates or child labour — well-being and quality of life are improving around the world.

A remarkable compendium of information at odds with the present fashionable pessimism, Goklany's *The Improving State of the World*, published by the Cato Institute, reveals that, contrary to popular belief, it is the poorest who are enjoying the most dramatic rise in living standards. Refuting a central premise of the modern green movement, it also demonstrates that as countries become richer, they also become cleaner, healthier and more environmentally conscious.

Needless to say, Goklany has already been accused of naive Panglossianism by the doom and gloom merchants, to whom all must always be for the worst in the worst of all possible worlds. This is deeply unfair to Goklany: like the rest of us, he is concerned at the shameful deprivation, disease and misery that continue to affect hundreds of millions of people in sub-Saharan Africa, North Korea and all the rest of the world's horror spots. But he argues convincingly that to recognise their horrific plight should not prevent us from also acknowledging our progress in liberating even larger numbers of people from extreme poverty.

We should be especially proud of the fact that humanity has never been better fed: the daily food intake in poor countries has increased by 38 per cent since the 1960s to 2,666 calories per person per day on average. The population of those countries has soared by 83 per cent during that time, so this is a stupendous achievement which puts the final nail in the coffin of Malthusianism.

Together with a 75 per cent decline in global food prices in real terms in the second half of the 20th century, caused by improved agricultural productivity and freer trade, fewer people than ever before are going hungry. The rate of chronic undernourishment in poor countries has halved to 17 per cent, compared with a little over a third 45 years ago. In wealthy countries, the cost of essential foods has collapsed, with the price of flour, bacon and potatoes relative to incomes dropping by between 82 and 92 per cent over the past century; similar trends are now visible in developing countries too.

There is still a long way to go; but never before in human history have so many people been liberated from extreme poverty so quickly. The number of people subsisting on $1 a day has declined from 16 per cent of the world population in the late 1970s to 6 per cent today, while those living on $2 a day dropped from 39 per cent to 18 per cent. In 1820, 84 per cent of the world's population lived in absolute poverty; today this is down to about a fifth.

Famine and declining life expectancy are problems now limited to the small number of countries unfortunate enough to continue to suffer from horrendous misgovernment by kleptocratic elites or which persist in rejecting capitalism and globalisation. There is only one way to ensure that the most deprived in the poorest countries are fed and clothed: their governments must embrace the market economy, strong property rights, sound money, free trade and technological progress. That is the only road to higher economic growth; and increased wealth is the prerequisite to better living standards.

To see how far we have come, consider that anyone born in Britain during the Middle Ages would have been exceptionally lucky to live to see their 30th birthday. The average person could expect to live only to the age of 22, before succumbing to disease, injury or famine. By 1800, thanks to the Industrial Revolution, life expectancy in Britain had climbed to 36 years, then the highest ever seen but less than the life expectancy enjoyed today in even the most war-torn and deprived countries. By the 1950s the average Briton could expect to live to the age of 69; today this has increased to almost 78 years.

Life expectancy in poorer countries has improved even faster. In China it has surged from 41 years in the 1950s to 71 years today; in India it is up from 39 years to 63 years, almost doubling the average lifespan of 2 billion people. In 1900 average life expectancy around the world was a mere 31 years; today it is 67 years and rising.

Just as remarkably, the gap between poor and rich countries has been shrinking fast. By the early 1950s a child born in a wealthy country such as Britain could expect to live 25 years longer than a child born in a poor country such as Algeria; today accidents of birth matter far less. The gap has closed to 12.2 years, thanks

Fewer people are toiling 18 hours a day in mines; more are working in offices and able to afford holidays

to diffusion and transfer of public health practices and medical advances pioneered in the West.

We are not only living longer; we are also living healthier lives, in poor as well as in rich countries. Disability rates in the leading developed countries have declined strikingly and the onset of chronic diseases has been significantly delayed during the course of the past century — by nine years for heart disease (despite increased obesity), by 11 years for respiratory disease (despite smoking) and by nearly eight years for cancer.

All of these and other improvements to well-being have come despite a hundredfold increase in the use of man-made chemicals, demolishing the oft-repeated but obstinately incorrect claim that pollution, urbanisation and modernity have made life more dangerous. In truth, before industrialisation, at least 200 out of every 1,000 children died before reaching their first birthday. Infant mortality globally is now down to 57 per 1,000, thanks to huge strides made in nutrition, hygiene and medical care in the developing world.

Children are not only much more likely to survive infancy; they are also far more likely to spend their childhood in school. Child labour, while still all too prevalent, has been in steady decline for years. In 1960 a quarter of all children aged ten to 14 were in work, a share which has fallen to a tenth today. Partly as a result, the global illiteracy rate has declined from 46 per cent in 1970 to about 18 per cent today.

There are many other ways in which life has improved across the developing world. Compared with 20 years ago, people are generally more free to choose their rulers and express their views; more likely to live under the rule of law and less likely to be deprived of their life, liberty or property through the whim of a ruler. Social and professional mobility is less circumscribed by accidents of birth and location. Fewer people are toiling 18 hours a day in mines; more are working in offices and able to afford holidays.

When Charles Dickens depicted the industrial town as hell on earth, he was chronicling the dark phase of economic development which some parts of China and India are undergoing today. But the forces that eventually lifted Britain from that Stygian gloom had already been set in motion, as they have in emerging economies today. Remarkably, there is mounting evidence that as countries become richer, they eventually also become greener, cleaner and healthier.

Increased productivity and better technology have allowed us to conserve energy resources, cut emissions of noxious substances such as lead and sulphur dioxide, provide cleaner drinking water and ensure better quality air. London's great smog of December 1952, which killed 4,000 people, is now a mere historical footnote, as is the

Great Stink of 1858, when the Thames was so filthy and polluted that Parliament had to be evacuated.

The widespread view that Western societies are squandering natural resources on an unprecedented scale doesn't stand up to scrutiny. A ton of coal produces 12 times more electricity in modern power stations than a century ago. Energy intensity in the rich countries has been falling by 1.3 per cent a year for the past century and a half. This year the demand for oil from rich countries will actually fall, despite buoyant economic growth. Because one acre of agricultural land produces so much more food today than it did even a decade ago, Western countries have been able to cut back on the amount of space devoted to agriculture. Forests are growing again, replacing fields.

To the doom merchants, however, none of this really matters. Emissions of carbon dioxide and other greenhouse gases are on the rise globally which, they claim, will trigger devastating global warming and a catastrophic relapse in living standards. But Goklany begs to differ. Climate change might exacerbate existing problems, such as malaria, coastal flooding and habitat loss, he acknowledges, but this doesn't justify the heavy-handed interventionism called for in Sir Nicholas Stern's recent report.

In fact, equally rigorous modelling using different assumptions suggests that, for the next 80 years at least, the benefits of faster economic growth in further improving quality of life across the developing world will outweigh any cost of global warming. Some reductions in carbon emissions may eventually be needed, Goklany says, but in most cases it would be cheaper to adapt to higher temperatures than to try to stop them.

Our best bet, therefore, is to allow technology, trade and the global economy to continue growing unimpeded. Such is Goklany's plea: if the present rate of improvement continues, he argues, we could soon be living in a world where 'hunger and malnutrition have been virtually banished; where malaria, TB, Aids and other infectious and parasitic diseases are distant memories; and where humanity meets its needs while ceding land and water back to the rest of nature … even in sub-Saharan Africa infant mortality could be as low as it is today in the United States, and life expectancies as high'.

Hope has become a commodity in short supply in the West. Even though more progress will always be required, our victories over famine and extreme poverty during the past two centuries are civilisation's greatest achievement. It is time we took a well-deserved break from worrying about terrorism, rising crime, social dislocation and all our other problems to celebrate what we have actually got right.

Allister Heath is associate editor of The Spectator and deputy editor of The Business

The Spectator 2 December 2006

Prospect Magazine January 2007

"I'm taking these bottles to recycling, we must all do our bit for the planet."

Nuclear energy

greener than you think?

Twenty years on, wildlife is thriving around the destroyed Chernobyl reactor. Perhaps it's time to reassess our attitudes towards nuclear energy, write **Jim Smith** and **Dave Timms**

Nuclear power stations, and their effects on the environment, remain top of the list of environmental enemies for many people. Discharges from Sellafield into the Irish Sea; 'hot' particles on beaches at Dounreay; and the Chernobyl accident have all contributed to the nuclear industry's unenviable environmental reputation. But recent studies suggest that it's time to re-evaluate nuclear's environmental impacts. If radiation is so damaging to the environment, why are many scientists now describing the radioactive zone around Chernobyl as a rich wildlife reserve? The answer seems to be that radiation isn't the kind of environmental threat we thought it was.

We tend to take an anthropocentric view of environmental risks. Our fear of radiation, heightened by associations with nuclear bombs, is a legitimate fear not for the environment, but for our own welfare. It is well known that people exposed to radiation from the Hiroshima and Nagasaki atomic bombs suffered higher rates of cancer than the average for unexposed populations. The current scientific consensus is that even low-level radiation from environmental pollution could result in an (extremely small) cancer risk to people. Surprisingly though, as far as we can tell, radioactive pollution appears to have little long-term effect on animals and plants in the natural environment.

After the horrific accident at the Chernobyl nuclear power plant in Ukraine on 26 April 1986, a 30km exclusion zone was set up around the destroyed reactor. More than 100,000 people were evacuated from the area to protect them from the radioactive contamination. Twenty years later, the area remains largely uninhabited. Just after the accident, extremely high radiation levels damaged, and in some areas killed, pine trees and other wildlife close to the reactor. But in subsequent years, despite the tragic consequences for the human population, scientists in Ukraine and Belarus have observed a dramatic recovery in wildlife populations.

'Stories of mutant animals roaming the exclusion zone are myths.'

'If radiation is so damaging to the environment, why are many scientists now describing the radioactive zone around Chernobyl as a rich wildlife reserve?'

Wildlife in the Chernobyl zone is now more abundant and diverse than before the accident. The area is now home to large populations of wild boar, wolves and many bird species. Some people are even talking seriously of ecotourism in the area. Though scientists are still researching the subtle genetic and developmental effects of radiation on animals and plants, stories of mutant animals roaming the exclusion zone are myths. We, along with our Belarussian, Russian and Ukrainian colleagues, have spent more than ten years studying fish in Chernobyl's contaminated lakes, but have observed no mutants. Blinky, the famous three-eyed fish from the cooling pond of the nuclear power plant in *The Simpsons*, has no cousins at Chernobyl.

As far as we can tell so far, fish are in fact thriving in the cooling pond of the Chernobyl reactors. One of us, Dave Timms, isn't just a radiation physicist but is also a keen angler. On our last trip to Chernobyl (part of an international project on remediation of the cooling pond), Dave took his fishing rod and caught one of the huge catfish living there. Local Ukrainian scientist and cooling pond expert Oleg Nasvit estimated the fish at 30kg and said it was a small one. The diversity of fish in the cooling pond is amazing: there are 38 fish species, two of which are in the Red Data Book of rare species. However, what is truly amazing is the size of some of the fish. The largest catfish is estimated at over 4m and there are believed to be carp over 50 pounds.

The reason for the wildlife's dramatic recovery is that, except at extremely high levels, radiation does little direct damage to animals and plants. We know that current levels of radioactivity in the Chernobyl zone could lead to a small cancer risk in humans. In most of the zone, this risk is much lower than that from smoking ten cigarettes a day, but is nevertheless high enough for the area to be considered unfit for human habitation. Wild animals, though, rarely die of diseases of old age, such as cancer. They are killed by hunger, predation or human activities. At present, the radiation appears to be having no observable influence on wildlife numbers—it is the land-use changes in the evacuated area that are having the real influence. Hunters, fishermen and forestry workers are a much greater threat to wildlife than gamma rays from radioactive caesium. Catfish grow so big in the cooling pond because food is abundant and, apart from a few scientists, nobody is fishing there.

The tragedy at Chernobyl demonstrated an important environmental lesson: human occupancy and land-use do the real damage to ecosystems. The human population, with its road-building, forestry and farming, did far more damage to Chernobyl's ecosystem than the radioactive pollution does. When people were evacuated from the Chernobyl zone, wildlife moved back into the urban and agricultural environments despite the (to us) high radiation levels.

If the environmental impact of energy generation systems is judged primarily on the area and importance of wildlife habitat affected per unit of energy generated and on climate-changing greenhouse gas emissions, nuclear power compares favourably with other forms of energy generation— even many renewables. Protests calling for a moratorium on wind-farm developments in Scotland have highlighted the lack of environmentally cost-free energy options. Green energy sources such as hydropower and bio-fuels usually take up much more land than nuclear power stations and so might have a greater impact on wildlife habitats. Like many renewables, nuclear power plants emit no important amounts of greenhouse gases. Some studies suggest that, even accounting for the energy used in their construction and decommissioning, nuclear power plants cause no more carbon dioxide emissions than wind farms.

Describing radioactive pollution from nuclear energy as a serious environmental threat therefore gives the wrong impression. If we are really serious about protecting the natural environment, we need to re-evaluate nuclear power's environmental impacts. Debates about the risks of terrorism and of terrible accidents like Chernobyl will rightly continue, and our first priority must be energy saving and increasing exploitation of renewable sources where possible. But, when considering Britain's future energy supplies, we may have to continue to put up with a small (some say insignificant) risk to our health for the overall environmental benefit nuclear power brings.

Chernobyl's effects on people

So far, about 50 human deaths are directly attributable to radiation from Chernobyl. After the accident there were 134 confirmed cases of acute radiation sickness: 28 of those affected died within a few months. By 2002, there had been 4000 cases of radiation-induced thyroid cancer in children and young adults. Though very serious, thyroid cancer is treatable with a 99 per cent success rate. Other cancers will probably increase in future, but these may not be detectable against the background fatal cancer rate of about 20-25 per cent in unexposed populations. A recent report by a group of experts assembled by the United Nations concluded that the best estimate of the final death toll is approximately 4000.

Because of the potential radiation risk, over 300,000 people were evacuated from their homes with huge economic and social consequences. A very large number of people are still affected by the accident, and many people naturally worry about their health. This 'radiation stress' has had a serious psychological impact on the affected populations. But, in fact, radiation risks to the vast majority of people in Ukraine, Belarus and Russia are relatively low. For example, the average radiation dose to people who worked in the Chernobyl exclusion zone in 1986-87 gave them about a 0.5–1 per cent (between 1 in 100 and 1 in 200) higher risk of fatal cancer in later life. A lifetime of smoking gives you a 50 per cent (1 in 2) risk of early death from a smoking-related illness.

■ *Jim Smith is an environmental physicist at the Centre for Ecology & Hydrology, Winfrith Technology Centre, Dorchester, Dorset DT2 8ZD, tel: 01305 213607, email: jts@ceh.ac.uk.*

Dave Timms is a Reader in Radiation Physics at Portsmouth University, Portsmouth PO1 3QL, tel: 023 92 84 22 95, email: dave.timms@port.ac.uk.

The views expressed are those of the authors and not necessarily those of their respective institutes.

Planet Earth, Spring 2006
http://www.nerc.ac.uk

Want to know more?

Chernobyl: Catastrophe and Consequences by Jim Smith and Nick Beresford is available from Springer publishers at: www.springeronline.com or other bookstores.

The Government recently consulted the public about energy policy. You can find out more at http://www.dti.gov.uk/energy/review.

Is it ethical to have children?

What are the environmental implications of having children, asks Simon Birch

How far are you prepared to go to do your bit for the planet? OK, so you buy FairTrade coffee, you've turned the thermostat in the living room down and you've even reluctantly cut the number of flights you take every year. But would you go as far as to make the decision that Katy Craven has taken? "I'm definitely never going to have children," she says. "If we're serious about cutting levels of consumption here in industrialised northern countries then we've simply got to stop making new consumers," explains Katy, 26, who as well as being an environmental activist works as a social worker with young people in care. "No matter how hard you try and live an ethical and low-impact lifestyle, just by having one child you're automatically doubling your environmental impact."

The decision whether or not to have children is clearly one which is very personal, and couples choose not to have children for as many reasons as there are designer buggies down at your local Mothercare. Whether it be religious, health, age or lifestyle reasons, couples have always been deciding not to bring another little person into world. What is more recent, however, is the fact that environmental considerations are now being cited as reasons for people deciding not to have a family. An increasing number of people, albeit a tiny minority made up largely of environmental activists, are taking decisions like Katy's not to have children. They base this on the huge inequality in the use of resources between the industrial north and developing countries in the south. Put simply, a baby born in Bristol is over the period of its lifetime going to use up vastly more resources and have a far greater environmental impact than any baby born in Bangalore. "There are enough resources to feed everyone in the world but not enough to let everyone drive an S.U.V.," says Katy.

The environmental charity WWF has worked out that if everyone in the world were to consume natural resources and generate carbon dioxide at the rate we do in the UK, then we'd need three planets to support us. Mark Fisher not only agrees with Katy, but has gone one step further. "I had a vasectomy 18 months ago because I didn't want to add to the deteriorating environmental situation by bringing another person into the world," says Mark, 35, a health worker and environmental and political activist. "Plus the world's overpopulated anyway with the current population of six billion set to hit nine billion by 2045."

Despite vowing that she'll never have children of her own, Katy is keen to point out that she's not anti-children. "Personally I love children and if I do get the need to have a child then I'll try and adopt one as there are so many children in care desperate for a family," she says.

Katy and Mark's decisions not to have children for environmental and ethical reasons have been praised by Catherine Budgett-Meakin from the Population & Sustainability Network. "I think that their decision is very admirable," says Catherine. "The environmental impact and resource use in countries like the UK is so great that the fewer of us there are the better."

Of course not everyone who's genuinely aghast at the scale of the global environmental crisis would be prepared to follow Katy and Mark in their decision never to have children. Having just one child was what American environmentalist and author Bill McKibben called for in the late '90s in his groundbreaking book Maybe One. According to McKibben the planet won't be able to sustain its ever-increasing population. With the US gobbling up a huge slice of the earth's resources as its population grows, to avoid global catastrophe McKibben called for one parent families as a way to reduce America's birth-rate.

So what do UK environmental and development groups have to say on the subject? Well as it happens, not a lot. In the course of the research of this eco-worry it was virtually impossible to gain any comment from an environmental or development group on the issue of population, largely because nobody was willing to talk about the subject. "Since the term 'population' became increasingly tarnished by the brush of 'coercion' and 'control' during the 1980s it has remained politically sensitive," says Catherine Budgett-Meakin. In the absence of any debate on the issue from the mainstream environmental movement, the last word goes to Mark Fisher: "People need to think seriously about whether they need to bring more kids into a world full of children and one that faces an extremely perilous future."

Ethical Consumer September 2006
www.ethicalconsumer.org

Oddie guide
to saving
the planet

Hedgehogs need their sleep. But warm weather wakes up hibernating hogs and puts them at risk of starvation

ACT NOW WARNS WILDLIFE EXPERT BILL

TURN that thermostat down – or the Scottish crossbill gets it!

If every country emitted as much carbon as the UK we would need three planets just to support our own lifestyles.

But what about everything else – the birds, the mammals, the fish, the flora and fauna – that call this planet home?

The frozen arctic is turning to mud, and baked Alaska is no place for polar bears or snowy owls. Their plight is our warning that time is running out to stop climate chaos.

There's no getting away from it. The world is warming up and our actions are causing it.

Either we make it worse by overheating our houses, wasting energy and pumping out too much carbon dioxide. Or we can help by making small differences to the way we live.

Up to one million types of wildlife will be on their way out by 2050 simply because their habitats will no longer exist.

Unlike us, wildlife doesn't have a choice about whether this happens. The only option for affected species is to move further north or uphill to find a home in a similar climate.

But this isn't possible for all creatures. The dormouse, which lives in little pockets of isolated woodland, will find it particularly hard to cope. Warm, damp winters are no good for creatures who hibernate.

In fact, the signs of change are everywhere. This year has every chance of setting another record high temperature.

Our birds are already noticing the change. Chiffchaffs used to be summer migrants, yet more and more are not bothering to leave for the winter.

Hedgehogs need their sleep. But warm weather wakes up hibernating hogs and puts them at risk of starvation.

Each year, spring is starting sooner. Swallows are arriving here a week earlier than in 1970. And our resident birds are feeling it, too. Eggs don't just hatch when they feel like it. Blue and great tits' eggs hatch when there is an abundance of juicy caterpillars for the chicks.

But climate change is breaking this link. Warmer springs mean birds are nesting earlier and their young are born before there are the insects to feed them. If birds miss the feast, it is harder for them to survive. And not just garden birds. Seabirds like puffins are at risk as their food supply – small fish called sandeels – is reduced as the North Sea warms.

Wetlands are good for birds but droughts put them at risk. Dry springs mean birds that depend on splashing about in shallow water are homeless.

Wading birds such as redshanks, lapwings and snipe all depend on water in the landscape. Snipe use their long beak like tweezers to pull food out of the mud. No muddy water's edge, no snipe.

Climate change means we can expect more droughts, particularly in South-East England. Drier summers are also bad news in the hills, where ring ouzels can't find enough worms. And disappearing ponds mean beasties like great-crested newts will be homeless, too. We need to stop the impact of climate change getting worse – but we are already feeling the effects of the last 200 years of messing about with the climate. We've a lot of work to do to make up for the losses.

It's good to know that conservation organisations like the RSPB are getting on with it and putting new wetlands back into the fens in East Anglia.

Photo: Tim Ockenden/EMPICS

The dormouse, which lives in little pockets of isolated woodland, will find it particularly hard to cope

These will be even more important in the future because the east coast is disappearing before our very eyes. Rising sea levels and storms are eating away at the coastline.

The low-lying east coast is dotted with fabulous nature reserves that are home to rare birds such as bitterns.

Without freshwater marshes, bitterns have nowhere to go.

MANY of them are next to the coast already. One big storm might be all it takes to tip them over the edge. So creating new wetlands is an insurance policy against climate chaos.

If your home is on top of a mountain, your ability to move once the climate changes is restricted. On our highest mountains live birds such as ptarmigans, which are so adapted to life on the snowy tops that they turn white in winter. They will be at risk unless climate change is stopped in its tracks.

So is it all bad news? Well, the future is bleak for ptarmigans, snipe and bitterns. But other birds are making the most of milder conditions. Little egrets were once a rarity but now grace many estuaries and lakes.

Other southern birds could make the same jump. We could see more black kites, cattle egrets, great reed warblers or even the zitting cisticola – a tiny warbler that calls "zitt!"

Sounds great, sitting in the sun being serenaded by songbirds. But while there will be some local winners, as we continue to cook the planet we stand to lose so much more.

So join up with people from the RSPB, WI, Surfers Against Sewage and many more to make your voice heard on global climate change.

Remember, if climate chaos continues the Scottish crossbill will be toast.

Unique to Scotland, as the planet warms the crossbill's highland forests just won't feel like home any more.

And how do they get to this spare planet they'll need?

The Daily Mirror 3 November 2006

How Liz put her (carbon) foot in it

Liz Hurley's week-long nuptials were a big, fat, not-so-green wedding, an exclusive survey shows

By **Geoffrey Lean** and **Rachel Beebe**

Liz Hurley's long-haul wedding has produced a carbon footprint so large that it would take the average British couple more than 10 years to contribute as much to heating up the planet as she and Arun Nayar have done in little over a week. It would take a typical Indian couple a massive 123 years.

A special study, by an Oxford-based footprinting consultancy, suggests the celebrations will release around 200,000kg of carbon into the atmosphere.

The consultancy, Best Foot Forward, reckons this is an underestimate. The couple are not giving full details of the festivities because of a contract with Hello! magazine, but last night environmentalists condemned their "conspicuous carbon consumption".

The nuptials ended on a sour note when a fistfight broke out between journalists and security guards as the couple arrived at Meherangarh Fort, Jodhpur, northern India, for their final wedding feast. The couple's two-night stopover in Mumbai earlier in the week hit problems after the authorities tore down part of a venue built to host the wedding party as it impinged on a popular beach.

The marathon marriage began a week before, with a small civil ceremony in the 15th-century Sudeley Castle on Friday 2 March, and the couple repeated their vows in front of 250 guests in a blessing at St Mary's Church in the castle grounds. After two days of "quiet" celebrations in the Cotswolds, the couple flew last Monday, with 24 guests, in a chartered Learjet to Mumbai. After partying there, they and 250 guests flew in seven chartered jets to Jodhpur, northern India. But at the wedding at the Umaid Bhawan Palace hotel, the head priest refused to perform the ceremony because Ms Hurley has a child with the US film producer Steve Bing, while Mr Nayar is divorced. Today, the newlyweds fly to the Maldives for their honeymoon.

Best Foot Forward says the biggest polluter is the Learjet, which will emit more than 70,000kg on its 12,000-mile round-trip. Accommodation in India adds 18,605kg, and food and drink 18,000kg. Flying in flowers produces 28,250kg, and flying three chefs to India adds 2,377kg. Guests and staff travelling to Gloucestershire released 30,000kg. The bride's flight to Milan for a dress fitting added just 215kg.

The total of 207,849kg assumes the couple take the Learjet to the Maldives, while their guests return to Britain by scheduled flights. If the couple just fly first class, the total drops to 173,578kg, as the impact would be shared among more people.

Key

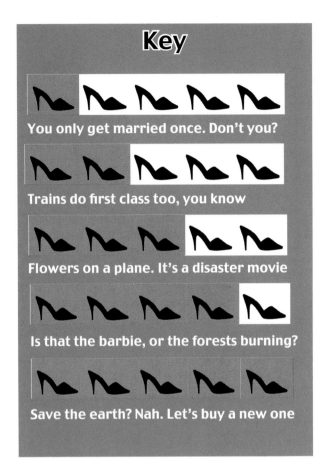

You only get married once. Don't you?

Trains do first class too, you know

Flowers on a plane. It's a disaster movie

Is that the barbie, or the forests burning?

Save the earth? Nah. Let's buy a new one

Photo: UCA BRUNO/AP/PA Photos

Fitting the dress 215kg CO$_2$

Where else does one go but Versace in Milan, darling? At least it was a scheduled flight

The English ceremony 5,196kg

They borrowed a castle. But there was heat, light, food and drink to provide

The Indian festivities 17,143kg

Flowers and chefs were flown in. The press, uninvited, were thrown out

Getting to Gloucestershire 30,038kg

Sir Elton arrived in his personal helicopter. Not many guests came by National Express

Getting to India 66,461kg

The bridal party went by Learjet. The rest went by airline, then boarded hired planes

The honeymoon 70,113kg

Liz and Arun leave Jodhpur and take the Learjet to the Maldives

The Independent 11 March 2007

Time for tough love and a lock on the fridge

Jan Moir

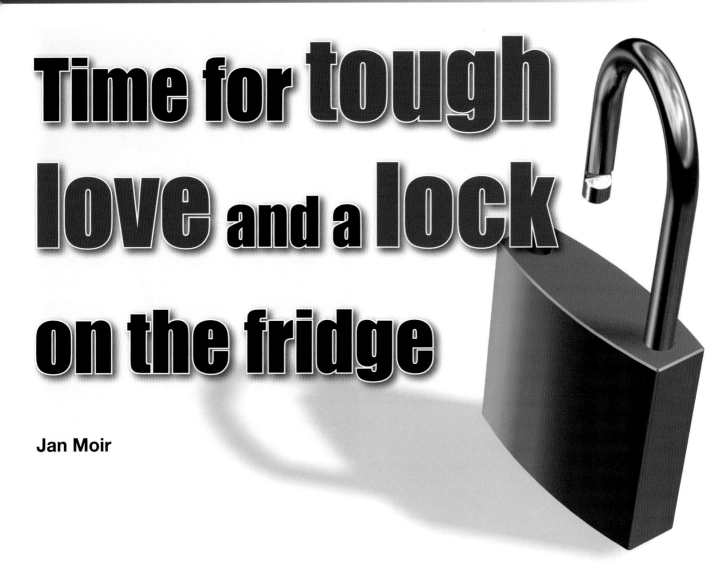

Nicola McKeown is a woman who can't say no. When her son, Connor McCreadie, demands food, she says "yes". She has been saying "yes" since he was born eight years ago, with the result that Connor now weighs 14 stone and might be taken into care because of fears for his health. Despite his mother's claims that Connor has lost weight recently, local health authorities held a conference this week to decide if the boy's future lies with his family or in protective custody.*

Sometimes I wonder about these "authorities", who seem to let malnourished children stippled with cigarette burns and mottled with fresh bruises skip back into the arms of their parental abusers with alarming regularity, while indulging in this modish obsession with obesity instead. Perhaps it is like elephant hunting; the cumbersome and slow-moving target is always much easier to spot? Yet, in Connor McCreadie's case at least, perhaps the North Tyneside health agencies involved are right to be concerned. Connor is not just pudgy; he is nearly four times over the weight he should be. If the reverse were true, and he was four times under the ideal weight, he would be whisked into a hospital quicker than you could say intravenous drip. Yet his health problems could be almost as serious, if allowed to continue.

Connor is a miserable little boy entombed in a block of blubber, bullied at school in the way fatties always are and allowed to cheer himself up with carb-rich snacks every 20 minutes. Why does Nicola allow this? How could she let things slip to the extent that her young son has become so fat that he cannot put on his own socks, or speak without wheezing, or take any meaningful form of exercise? All Connor can do is bellyflop on his garden trampoline, which he does without much joy and with his little flipper hands by his side, like some great, sad sea lion. Then he goes back indoors for another packet of crisps, dutifully provided by mum.

Perhaps, as a single mother struggling with depression and her own weight problems, this situation has become so wretched because there is not much else in life Nicola can give her son except food. So when he demands his favourite chips, biscuits and chocolate, she gives them to him as an act of love and provender. Perhaps, deep down, she even feels good about doing so, somehow validated as a mother, even if her acquiescence in this matter is becoming morbid. For what Nicola is actually doing to her son is killing him softly, and conferring a bleak

He has become so fat that he cannot put on his own socks, or speak without wheezing

Trapped: Connor McCreadie and his mother, Nicola

future on his bloated shoulders. I'm as much against state intervention and nanny interference as the next drippy liberal, but doctors say that if it carries on like this, Connor will be dead by the time he is 30; something drastic has to be done.

In their council house on a cheerless estate in Wallsend, mother and son seem to be locked together in a spiral of mutual despair, unable to help each other out of this pit of bad food and misery – perhaps you won't be surprised to learn that there seemed to be no visible men in the family to offer support. A grandmother does come along in the mornings, to help get Connor and his older sister off to school. She points out that the family have not yet sunk to the level of putting a lock on the fridge, and you think: well, why not? And why not stop filling it with rubbish while they are at it? And if Connor won't eat his vegetables, don't give him anything else to eat until he does, because letting him go hungry won't actually kill him. On the contrary, a little tough love might help save him, and others like him. The latest figures from the Department of Health show that obesity in children under 11 increased from nearly 10 per cent in 1995 to almost 14 per cent in 2003, a national trend that is difficult to digest. A healthier diet, or indeed any kind of diet at all, would help Connor, but this seems beyond the reach of Nicola, who talks vaguely

of buying "exotic fruit", as if it were something you had to order in from another galaxy.

The awful truth is that if Connor were a dog or a horse, he would probably have been taken into care already. Like Rusty the labrador, removed from his owners by the RSPCA last year when his weight ballooned to nearly 12 stone and he could walk only five steps before collapsing. The brothers who owned the dog were given three-year conditional discharges by magistrates, which seems to give credence to the national stereotype that we care more about our dogs than our children.

Meanwhile, out in the margins of society, in unlovely houses with freezers full of oven chips, people such as Nicola McKeown and her family continue to lead lives of quiet chaos and chips with everything.

The Daily Telegraph 28 February 2007
© Telegraph Group Limited 2007

*Connor was allowed to stay with his family and a 'formal agreement to safeguard and protect the child's welfare' was put into place by North Tyneside Council

The grown-ups need to grow up

Tony Sewell

I used to be an inner-city school teacher in the same area where three teenagers were shot recently. I became disillusioned, which can easily happen. Certainly, if the press is to be believed, Britain's streets are breeding the most vicious, disrespectful, morally comatose generation our nation has ever seen.

Yet beneath the hoodies and the Burberry, there is another side to these brazen young individuals who strut the streets drinking, fighting and shooting one another. After a spell in academe, I realised that my real mission in life was to try to create real opportunities for boys who looked like me. I knew that most black boys were extremely intelligent. So two years ago I set up a charity called Generating Genius, which encourages black boys with potential and has them aspire to the scientific professions.

What so many of these boys lacked were high expectations, challenge and a disciplined environment. They are held back by many factors, but what they have in common is that they are all the offspring of adults who do not want to grow up. My generation, born in the early 1960s and later, was the last one to be caned at school and belted at home. Whether it did us good or harm, we swore that when we had children, we would never be so brutal. We wanted our children to be our friends. Instead of giving the little brats a bloody good telling off, we just sat there and listened.

Recently the novelist Tim Lott wrote: "At the heart, our children are as much a riotous, disrespectful, anti-establishment bunch of awkward cusses as the rest of us have always been. And I wouldn't have it any other way."

This is interesting. Here you have a middle-aged man who sees himself in his children. He admires the fact that British children have more attitude than many of their bland Euro-counterparts. In fact, he can see his own childhood replaying itself. But he's forgotten one thing. To rebel against the world, you need some sort of order or establishment to kick against. That was what parents were for. In the daily drama of family life, someone has to play the role of Dad, Mum and rebel child. The trouble is that today we have a whole bunch of adults wanting to play the rebel child. Tim Lott needs to grow up.

It is this liberal misunderstanding of youth rebellion which has led to many children feeling lost and isolated. How can you begin to respect an adult who defines your bad behaviour as "sceptical, knowing, bloody-minded and independent"? Maybe it is just bad behaviour.

Our children want us to be "grumpy old men, who never allow them out after midnight". Now that's how it has always been. We have had too big a diet of middle-class adults trying to "identify" with their children. Anyone laying down the law would be considered a dinosaur. In schools, the teachers that get up my nose are the so called "cool teachers", pathetic specimens trying to be like the children they teach. Although these are the minority, they are still an example of adults abdicating their responsibility.

Last week's report by Unicef, which compared childhoods across 21 OECD countries, found that our children are the most miserable, fat, lonely and frightened, compared with the other developed countries in the study. One of the major problems is a lack of sympathetic adults, whether they are role models or just sounding boards. We need a return of the aunts and uncles we had in the past. These people were not even blood relatives but they were so supportive that we called them Auntie and Uncle. But fear drives everything on this issue. Many potentially significant adults refuse to get involved in their own families. This is because our communities have become fractured; no one can visit without an appointment and everyone claims they are just too busy.

I truly believe that quality "uncle-ing" is a dying art that should be reintroduced to the curriculum of life. The fear of children may be the biggest reason why we see aunts and uncles only when our sons are sweet babies but they disappear when that boy is nearly six foot, his voice has just broken and he has an attitude.

It was MP Diane Abbott in 2002 who caused a row when she said that white women teachers are failing black schoolboys because they are frightened of them. Bad behaviour, she said, goes unchallenged from an early age because staff unfamiliar with black culture are physically intimidated by black children. This, she argues, allows problems to escalate to a stage where the child risks being excluded.

To rebel against the world, you need some sort of order to kick against

What is clear is that in many of our poor-performing comprehensive schools, the teachers are barricaded in the staff room, scared of going out and laying the law down to the children. It is not surprising that in one survey students said their favourite teachers were the ones who had the most discipline. They never really liked these teachers but they felt secure; they knew that they would learn and they knew that these teachers were also secure in behaving like horrible adults.

Generating Genius encourages black boys with potential and has them aspire to the scientific professions

And fear is at the root of the vast alcohol problem, highlighted in today's *Independent on Sunday*. Thousands of children are having to be treated for alcohol poisoning, liver disease or drink-related mental and behavioural disorders. There were more than 8,600 such hospital admissions of under-18s in 2005-06, the highest since records began and a 37 per cent rise on five years ago.

Of course, the aggressive marketing by the drinks industry doesn't help, but our Cool Britannia government is frightened of being accused of spoiling the party. Just as Maggie Thatcher was accused of taking away the milk from our children, New Labour doesn't want to be labelled the government that took away the alcopops from our youth.

It is a strange world we live in, where adults and children dress the same, have the same electronic gadgets and watch the same reality TV. We live in an ever youthful culture where getting old is seen to be sad and undignified. Those of us who are middle-aged are no better than a reformed Eighties band, looking to squeeze one more hit out of our ageing bones.

We need to retire from that infantile stage, unashamedly put on those bed-slippers and show children some leadership.

Tony Sewell is director of the charity Generating Genius
www.generatinggenius.org.uk

The Independent on Sunday 18 February 2007

Best friends? Children need *mothers*

More and more women prefer to be their children's pals, rather than giving them the guidance and discipline they so desperately need – and the results are often disastrous. Why can't they just grow up?

Judith Woods

What makes a good mother? I ask only because it's difficult to tell these days. On the one hand we have Nicola McKeown, tussling with social services over her eight-year-old son, who is so overweight that he may be placed on the child protection register.

On the other end of the social scale, we have the Duchess of York partying poolside with Princesses Beatrice and Eugenie in an excruciating parody of a parent who just can't let go – of her children, or her youth.

Both women love their offspring, of that there is no doubt. But both appear to demonstrate that most modern, most perplexing of family phenomena; the mother so desperate to be her child's best friend that she bunks off her day job and forgets she's supposed to be the grown-up.

McKeown stands accused of overfeeding her 14-stone son, Connor McCreadie, to the point where it constitutes abuse. For her part, McKeown says she tried to make sure he followed a healthy diet but her son "wants chips with everything", loves curry and snacks on junk food all day while sitting at his computer.

A mother – my mother, your mother – wouldn't give houseroom to a sedentary, lardy child who sits at home and crams himself with calories all day. But a best friend would. A best friend would feel his pain at being deprived of that bucket of fried chicken, a best friend would bask in his gratitude at being given another sackful of toffee-drenched popcorn; a best friend finds it impossible to say no.

In his searing cultural evisceration, *Big Babies Or Why Can't We Just Grow Up*, published last year, Michael Bywater wrote about the

Friend or foe? The Duchess of York, above, likes to party with her daughters Beatrice, left and Eugenie

Photo: Ian West/PA Archive/PA

Baby-Boom generation that refuses to take on an adult role and instead readily accepts infantalisation; from politicians, the media, advertising.

I would suggest that even in parenthood huge numbers of thirty and fortysomethings are equally reluctant to take on a role of authority, any sort of authority, and instead take the soft option; the best friend route, where we are the ones cravenly seeking approval from our own children.

No wonder there's an obesity timebomb ticking in a generation of children. We refuse them nothing, whether it's an upgraded iPod, new trainers or gluttonous quantities of food that will eventually kill them.

We can't bear their teenage opprobrium, we bend backwards to please them; listening to their music, desperately (gauchely) seeking to demonstrate that we're every bit as cool as their other best friends. Which we're, like, so not. Which brings me back to the Duchess of York.

Fergie, who for some impenetrable reason was recently named Mother of the Year by the American Cancer Society, was shopped to a tabloid for taking her daughters, then 17 and 15, on a trip to Jamaica where cannabis was apparently consumed (admittedly by other people) in prodigious quantities.

Aside from the fact that Prince Andrew's ex-wife could have dropped by the average north London dinner party and witnessed similar behaviour any night of the week, the hash brownies and magic mushroom tea were the least queasy-making revelations.

Far more disturbing was the claim – by an ex-boyfriend of Bea – that Fergie was wont to telephone friends and summon "the boys" to join her and her daughters as they burnt the midnight oil at some lavish chateau or other in St Tropez.

Being Fergie, it was an international call. Being Fergie's friends, they piled into a car and drove the 400 miles from Zurich without hesitation. After all, a party's a party to weak-chinned wonders the world over. Whether the Duchess of York or her daughters were the main draw is a moot point, but, either way, "the boys" duly pitched up as summoned.

All of which begs the question, what on earth was she thinking? Does she truly believe it's normal for a 47-year-old woman to prance about like a hormonal teenager at a slumber party, coquettishly calling up men to entertain them?

Fergie has been quoted as saying she goes out on the pull with the lovely Bea; a terrifying, Hogarthian image that must surely prompt fathers to lock-up their sons from Schleswig-Holstein to Aruba. Yet Fergie is simply an exaggeration (in this as in many things) of an increasingly common, highly unwelcome trend, particularly among the mothers of daughters. Can there be any more toe-curling phrase in the English language than: "We're not like mother and daughter, we're more like best friends"?

The stock response is clearly meant to be: "Oooh how lovely!" I would venture it ought to be: "Yeuch, how creepy. Stop it. Now."

Mothers aren't supposed to be best friends, they're not supposed to groove away with their teenagers at nightclubs, as if attempting to absorb rejuvenating stem cells by osmosis from their daughters. Nor are they supposed to overindulge their sons by allowing them to eat themselves to death.

The prevailing attitude of Nicola McKeown appears to be: "So what if Connor gets so out of breath that he vomits when he waddles to the bus; he's loved, isn't he? That's the main thing, isn't it?" Well, actually, no, it's not.

Children need more than unconditional love – sometimes, in fact, they even need less. They need boundaries and tough lessons and, occasionally, to feel the chill wind of disapproval, so they can fully appreciate its opposite and strive to earn it. Your kids may rant and sulk and throw the odd tantrum. When thwarted, they may systematically set about destroying any semblance of domestic harmony. But parenthood isn't a popularity contest. It's hard work, grown-up work, that brings with it long-term rewards, very often at the expense of short-term gratification.

That's the thing about best friends, they love you to bits, but they're essentially in it for themselves. They accept you, they embrace you, but they're certainly not responsible for you. That, I'm afraid, is the job of a mother.

Of course the tide will eventually turn, by sheer force of demographics, if nothing else. News that over the past decade the number of women giving birth in Britain over the age of 40 has doubled, from 11,910 to 23,459, can only be a good thing. These mummy-come-latelys will invariably try to join the gang, but surely even the most cosseted daughter would baulk at hitting the tiles with a best friend pushing 60, who runs the risk of breaking a hip on the dancefloor. In the interim, however, a lot of teenagers will continue to endure the indignity of mummy listening to The Killers and borrowing their clothes.

At least when it comes to their wardrobes, Bea and Eugenie are spared. They clearly borrow Fergie's.

The Daily Telegraph 28 February 2007
© *Telegraph Group Ltd*

The Independent 25 February 2007

These touchline tyrants should take their bawl home

By Jim White

In six years coaching my son's football team I have come to the following conclusion: short of excess intake of alcohol, there is nothing that alters the behaviour of adults for the worse as much as youth football.

Every weekend I stand on the touchline and watch allegedly mature adults screaming at their children, abusing match officials, carrying on as if they were eight years old and had just been denied the present of their choice by Santa. And the team coaches are among the principal offenders. In Britain, almost uniquely, youth football works like this: the dad of one of the team players becomes the coach. In the overwhelming majority of cases he does so without any training, experience or scrutiny. Sometimes, the result is little short of child abuse.

Once, in a game my lads were playing, the rather dopey opposition full back gave away a penalty through a somewhat avoidable handball. Instead of explaining what he had done wrong and advising him on how he might avoid such problems in the future, the boy's coach chose instead to bawl profanities in his face. The attack was personal and sustained. The boy was, the coach informed him, useless, fat and stupid. After what seemed like minutes, standing there with his bottom lip quivering and his eyes filling, the boy could take no more. He ran from the pitch in tears and headed into a copse, where he climbed a tree and sat on a branch for the rest of the match. "Good riddance," the coach shouted after him. "We're better off without you, you useless tosser."

It is worth adding that the game did not involve two teams from the grimy inner city. This took place in leafy Oxfordshire. And the lad concerned was seven years old.

Nor was it an isolated example. Such attitudes are everywhere, smothering our national game in an atmosphere than can be as poisonous as it is claustrophobic. For far too many, winning is all that matters. And everything that facilitates victory – cheating, bullying, poaching players from other teams – is not just tolerated, it is encouraged.

Oddly, the desperate urge for vicarious victory seems only to obtain in boys' football. The other day I refereed a game between two sets of 12-year-old girls and suddenly I felt as if I could breathe more easily. The girls played with smiles rather than snarls. On the touchline parents laughed and encouraged, their coaches were paragons of good cheer.

In its training courses, the FA preaches an enlightened doctrine of sportsmanship and relaxation. Professional clubs enforce strict codes of parental conduct. But that is at the top of the tree. For too many small boys their experience of the beautiful game will be limited to red-faced coaches and snarling parents. No wonder once they reach adulthood, they are giving up football in droves.

Our generation should be ashamed.

Club where the goal is enjoyment

By Ben Fenton

There may be no Maradonas on display at Cirencester Town FC's mini-football session, but there are no prima donnas either.

Under a cavernous green plastic roof, about 60 children aged between seven and 10 are just getting on with the boisterous fun of football.

The coaches stand among them, but offer little or no advice. The children largely police themselves and there are no whistles.

It is when they break up into groups of eight that the real change of mood takes place. This is what they come for every week.

Embracing the Give Us Back Our Game philosophy, they play simple football, just like most of the dads watching from the sidelines used to do on the streets of Cirencester 30 years ago.

Taking a breather between games, Jack Owen, nine, says: "Other teams have coaches who shout at them, but ours just encourage us. I'm glad I play here."

Daily Telegraph 9 January 2007
© Telegraph Group Limited 2007

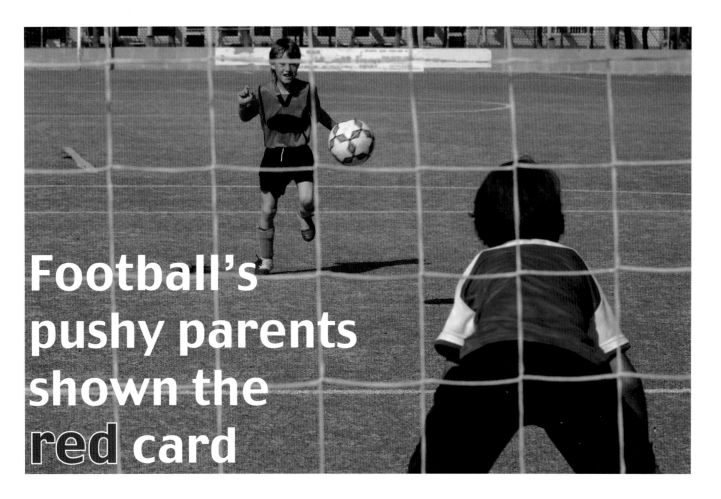

Football's pushy parents shown the red card

Campaign seeks to revive spirit of fun-filled games in the street

By Ben Fenton

A GRASSROOTS campaign to reclaim children's football from the tyranny of pushy parents and overbearing coaches is launched today.

The campaign, Give Us Back Our Game, which has already taken off by word of mouth, aims to revive the spirit of playing on the streets, now regarded as too dangerous, but which lay at the heart of football for earlier generations.

GUBOG began informally on the internet two months ago, but is now thought to have the support of at least 300 clubs across the country, a figure that grows every week.

The basic aim of the organisers, Paul Cooper, a coach based in Gloucestershire, and Rick Fenoglio, a sports scientist from Manchester, is to rid children's football of its rigid format of seven-against-seven games in smart kit, hectored by foul-mouthed parents and overseen by obsessive coaches and punctilious referees.

Instead they want children in the six- to 10-year-old age groups to play four against four, referee themselves and play almost entirely without the interference of adults.

"Football for children is now very different from earlier generations when the only adult involvement was a call from your mum that your tea was ready," Mr Cooper said yesterday. "Football is no longer beautiful for our kids: it's ugly."

The GUBOG campaigners have organised a mass day of protest for football clubs on June 4, when hundreds will play 4v4 unrefereed tournaments instead of the 7v7 or 8v8 favoured by the Football Association.

They hope it will force the FA to take action against the trends that more and more youth club organisers say are ruining the experience of the sport for children under 11.

Mr Fenoglio, a researcher at the Department of Exercise and Sports Science at Manchester Metropolitan University, said: "In a world where children can no longer play outside without supervision, parents and coaches have taken over. And the competitive drive adults bring to the game means youngsters no longer have time to fall in love with football, to play for fun and truly develop their skills."

He said studies had clearly shown that children who play in smaller, unsupervised games had so much more exposure to possession and to different roles on the pitch that they not only enjoyed it more, but their skills increased more quickly.

"Manchester United have been doing 4v4 for several years and their under-12 side, the first generation to have done the smaller scale matches, are regarded as the best in their age group," Mr Fenoglio added.

Daily Telegraph 9 January 2007
© Telegraph Group Limited 2007
www.giveusbackourgame.co.uk

Predicting the future: what to expect in the next 25 years

Each year since 1985, the editors of the American magazine THE FUTURIST have selected the most thought-provoking ideas and forecasts appearing in the magazine. Over the years, they have spotlighted the emergence of such epochal developments as the Internet, virtual reality, and the end of the Cold War. Although the predictions are based on the Unites States, they have implications for all of us.

Here are the editors' top 10 forecasts from 2007:

1 Generation Y will migrate heavily overseas. For the first time in its history, the United States will see a significant proportion of its population emigrate due to overseas opportunities. According to futurists Arnold Brown and Edie Weiner, Generation Y, the population segment born between 1978 and 1995, may be the first U.S. generation to have many of its members leave the country to pursue large portions of their lives, if not their entire adult lives, overseas. Brown and Weiner also predict that by 2025, 75% of Americans will live on the country's coasts.

2 Dwindling supplies of water in China will impact the global economy. With uneven development across China, the most water-intensive industries and densest population are in regions where water is scarcest. The result is higher prices for commodities and goods exported from China, so the costs of resource and environmental mismanagement are transferred to the rest of the world. As a nation, China already outconsumes the United States on basic commodities, such as food, energy, meat, grain, oil, coal, and steel.

3 Workers will increasingly choose more time over more money. The productivity boom in the U.S. economy during the twentieth century created a massive consumer culture – people made more money, so they bought more stuff. In the twenty-first century, however, workers will increasingly choose to trade higher salaries for more time with their families. Nearly a third of U.S. workers recently polled said they would prefer more time off rather than more hours of paid employment.

4 Outlook for Asia: China for the short term, India for the long term. By 2025, both countries will be stronger, wealthier, freer, and more stable than they are today, but India's unique assets such as widespread use of English, a democratic government, and relative transparency of its institutions make it more economically viable farther out.

5 Children's "nature deficit disorder" will grow as a health threat. Children today are spending less time in direct contact with nature than did previous generations. The impacts are showing up not only in their lack of physical fitness, but also in the growing prevalence of hyperactivity and attention deficit. Studies show that immersing children in outdoor settings – away from television and video games – fosters more creative mental activity and concentration.

6 We'll incorporate wireless technology into our thought processing by 2030. In the next 25 years, we'll learn how to augment our 100 trillion relatively slow inter-neuronal connections with high-speed virtual connections via nanorobotics. This will allow us to greatly boost our pattern-recognition abilities, memories, and overall thinking capacity, as well as to directly interface with powerful forms of computer intelligence and with each other. By the end of the 2030s, we will be able to move beyond the basic architecture of the brain's neural regions.

7 The robotic workforce will change how bosses value employees. As robots and intelligent software increasingly emulate the knowledge work that humans can do, businesses will "hire" whatever type of mind that can do the work – robotic or human. Future human workers may collaborate with robotic minds on projects for a variety of enterprises, rather than work for a single employer.

9 Companies will see the age range of their workers span four generations. Workers over the age of 55 are expected to grow from 14% of the labour force to 19% by 2012. In less than five years, 77 million baby boomers in the United States will begin reaching age 65, the traditional retirement age, but many are expected to continue working. As a result, the concept of "retirement" will change significantly.

8 The costs of global-warming-related disasters will reach $150 billion per year. The world's total economic loss from weather-related catastrophes has risen 25% in the last decade. According to the insurance firm Swiss Re, the overall economic cost of catastrophes related to climate change threatens to reach $150 billion per year in a decade or double the present level. The U.S. insurance industry's share would be $30–$40 billion annually. The size of these estimates also reflects increased growth and higher real-estate prices in coastal communities.

10 A rise of disabled Americans will strain public transportation systems. By the year 2025, the number of Americans aged 65 or older will expand from 35 million to more than 65 million, according to the U.S. Census Bureau. Individuals in that age group are more than twice as likely to have a disability as those aged 16 to 65. If that figure remains unchanged, the number of disabled people living in the United States will grow to 24 million over the course of the next 20 years. Rising rates of outpatient care and chronic illness point to an increased demand for public transportation as well as special public transportation services in the coming decades.

Source: World Future Society
http://www.wfs.org/

Code: 002681017714127770
Woman: 777120014XASC
Status: RST 645
State of health: 222 4 7714
Target group: B

Nr.o Identification accepted / person scanned

Total recall

Are you hopeless at putting names to faces? Or do you just wish you could remember what you got up to at your last birthday party? The solution could be to record your entire life digitally, **Ian Taylor** reports

You'll never forget another wedding anniversary. In fact, you'll never forget anything, ever again. That's because in the next few decades, you'll be able to store all your memories on a device which is small enough to wear around your neck.

A bit like a personal black box recorder, the gadget will remember anything you keep in digital form. It might carry the footage your father took on the day you were born. Your electronic school report. Your health records and your bank statements.

Every email you ever send can be archived alongside every digital photo you take. With the reality of cameras small enough to be wearable, your

whole life could be kept safe on a hard drive, ready to boot up whenever you feel like a stroll down memory lane,

This is not the future according to some starry-eyed science fiction writer. It's what a group of UK scientists realise has already begun. Memories for Life (M4L) is a network of researchers – computer scientists, psychologists, neuroscientists and sociologists – that

>> **Memories from the future 2009**
The MySpace and Second life websites go mobile as your profile and avatar is beamed to 'matches' in a pub or club, so you're more likely to meet a suitable date

have spent the last two years swapping notes on what to do with the growing bulk of information we keep in digital form.

From simple emails to every last byte contained on MySpace, Flickr and YouTube, it's all electronic. Web browsers keep track of where you go online, while gadgets built with GPS can trace your steps in the real world.

Shrinking memory
"This if all happening right now," says Prof Nigel Shadbolt, the M4L network's principal investigator. "There's more and more information going digital and the technology to store it is shrinking at the same time."

Moore's Law states that the number of transistors you can pack on a computer chip doubles every two years. It's held true for the last four decades and shows no sign of letting up. "In 20 years, a device the size of a sugar cube will be able to store a lifetime of video images," Shadbolt says.

Of course, people won't necessarily *want* to record every waking moment on video. But for the M4L crowd, the very prospect raises endless potential for other applications. The goal now is to develop actual products that make innovative use of our digital memories.

Imagine electronic teddy bears for children that get to know their owner via stored memories so they can chat with them about their interests. Or a fridge that remembers your diet and can write your shopping list for you. Theme parks could measure your heart rate on the rollercoaster and flog you a second-by-second, multimedia account to remind you of the nausea.

Oiling social cogs

There's also talk of innovative education tools and virtual reality replays of sporting events or birthday parties. Yet some of the most obvious ideas are those designed to give *real* memories a little electronic back-up.

"I want to build a memory aid," says Prof Wendy Hall, another M4L networker. "Something that will tell me who you are when I meet you. I might need a picture of you so the device can spot you via face-recognition technology. Or you might be carrying some kind of sensor that beams out what you want me to know."

>> **Memories from the future 2011**
Former PM Gordon Brown publishes his much-anticipated memoirs, they include MP3 files of key speeches and a searchable collection of his favourite emails to Tony Blair.

Similarly, elderly people suffering with short-term memory loss could have a device that remembers their daily routine and gives reminders whenever they're needed. Just like glasses help us to see, memory aids could help us to remember things. Although there will be limitations. "When someone's eyesight fails, you give them stronger and stronger glasses until they're virtually blind," Hall notes. "You've got the same discussion with dementia patients. There comes a point when technology

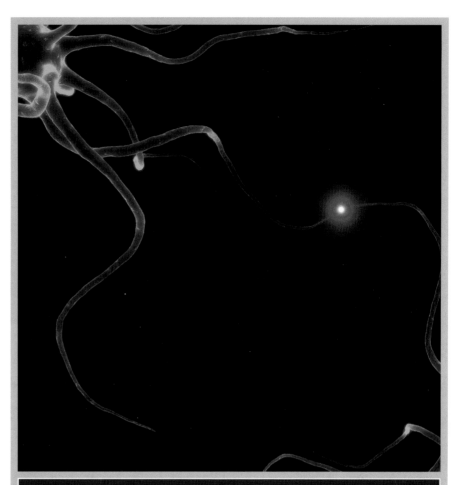

THE MEMORY MACHINE

Researchers in the US are developing brain implants to help people store memories

While the Memories for Life network contemplates how we record our lives as digital data, others are investigating a more direct fusion between memory and technology. Researchers in the US are developing a silicon chip designed to replace the region of the brain responsible for creating memories.

The implant would interact directly with neurons in the hippocampus, the part of the brain where short-term memories are reprogrammed for long-term storage. When the hippocampus is damaged, as in stroke cases or Alzheimer's disease, patients lose the ability to form long-term memories. The chip could bypass the damaged tissue, process the electrical signals itself and restore some long-term memory function.

That's the goal of Prof Theodore Berger working at the University of Southern California. By studying the neural circuitry in the hippocampus, he and his team have devised mathematical models for the way neurons process electrical signals. The models allow the chip implant to accept a signal and process it in the same way as healthy tissue.

Berger has already proved this can work. In 2004, his team used the chip with slices of rat brain kept alive in nutrients. The implant stimulated neurons in the tissue and electrical output patterns were then compared with the real thing. They were 95% accurate.

Now the plan is to replicate the results in live rats, and then in monkeys. Eventually, Berger believes it will be possible to replace damaged human hippocampus tissue with an implant. But he admits the process is complex: "[We will have to use] a chip small enough to be surgically and strategically placed in a particular location in the brain."

will not be able to help them." Artificial memory devices offer huge potential for the healthcare sector. Electronic diagnosis systems can already put human doctors to shame. All they need is enough data about a patient. "Clearly, we're moving into a world where health information and biosignals are being collected," Shadbolt says. "That's happening now for athletes in training, or people carrying certain medical risks. But in the future, we can imagine everyone routinely collecting a lifetime of biophysical data."

Collecting data, then, will not be a problem. Storing it should also be easy. But the way this information is used – whether it's medical, business-related or completely banal – raises a number of questions about managing such vast databanks. Copyright gets very murky when digital data is published en masse. And the dangers of identity theft are heightened when there's so much personal information out there.

There's also the issue of privacy. If everything's connected, just who will have access to your digital memories? And should you be allowed to keep digital memories of others? The police could even follow digital footprints when hunting criminals, presenting digital memories as evidence in court.

You're being watched
It's clearly a sensitive issue. In 2004 LifeLog, a US research project not dissimilar to Memories for Life, was shut down. It too had begun investigating the plausibility of recording everything about a person in digital format. But there was outrage. Civil liberty campaigners pounced on the project, claiming it toyed with technology that Big Brother could use to keep tabs on everyone. It didn't help matters that the project was run by DARPA, the research wing of the US defence department.

To ensure that M4L is not derailed by similar concerns, the network is actively discussing how privacy and rights can be protected. One theory is that management companies will emerge solely to control the flow and access of personal data. Whatever happens, Shadbolt believes that it is vital to continue reviewing the implication of the technology as it moves forward. "There has to be a conversation in society about who has this information," he says. "How can it be screened and how can we make it available on our terms?'

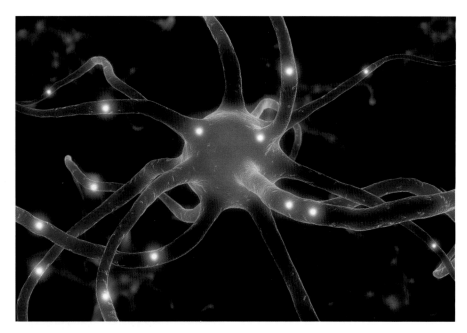

One man to ask would be Gordon Bell. He has more digital memories than anyone else on Earth. Since 1998, the senior Microsoft researcher has diligently recorded his entire life for a project called MyLifeBits. Designed to push the limits of life storage, the project keeps digital copies of pretty much everything.

All his photos and documents are scanned and saved, and conversations are taken down on a recorder. His

> **›› Memories from the future 2018**
> A cabbie is convicted of murdering a woman in London, after GPS data stored on his mobile phone pins him to the murder scene on the day in question

computer retains all emails, web pages and instant messages, and even his mouse and keyboard activity is remembered. Around his neck, Microsoft's prototype SenseCam automatically takes photos throughout the day to provide a visual record.

"We tend to want it all," Bell says "You never know what little barb will stick out that can help in providing a retrieval handle."

With nearly a decade of his life on a hard-drive, Bell sees his personal databank as an extension or even a surrogate of his very identity. And he is clear about what he wants to happen to it in the long term. "Only one thing – have it be accessible to my progeny in 10, 20 or 50 years."

The trouble is, when you've got that volume of information, how do you trawl through it and pick out what's useful?

Or sentimental? "We don't believe that anyone will use a system that requires a great deal of administration," he says.

So the biggest technical challenge for Bell – and the entire M4L movement – is management. Life would not be worth recording in the first place if you had to spend half of it tagging and archiving your data. There's a long way to go. Automatic systems are needed. Standardised storage formats and voice-activated software. And of course, we need tools to let us filter, or even *forget* the more banal information. Anything that will make our digital lives easier to organise, retrieve and re-present for ourselves and others.

Because, if nothing else, digital memories will give us the chance to leave a bit of ourselves behind. "I think people in the future will pass on these digital memories just like people today who put together photo albums," says Wendy Hall. "They're edited, of course, it's like an executive summary. Because there are still some things that you don't want people to know."

Find out more

www.memoriesforlife.org
Background info and papers from the M4L network

http://tinyurl.com/yuw2b4
Gordon Bell's MyLifeBits project

www.neural-prosthesis.com
Theodore Berger's research into brain implants

www.bbc.co.uk/radio4/memory
BBC's Memory Experience

BBC Focus March 2007

Ignored and neglected:

why did my sister have to die like this?

Janet Street-Porter
EDITOR -AT-LARGE

Patricia Balsom, who recorded her painful and frightening experiences in a diary

My sister died last Thursday, on the same day that *The Independent* published the shocking diaries Pat had written, chronicling the failings of the National Health Service during the last three weeks of her life. Unfortunately, she suffered a seizure in the early hours of Thursday, and by the time I had reached Hillingdon Hospital in west London and the ward she had made her family promise we would never let her return to, she was barely able to speak. We lay the printed pages on her bed, not sure whether she realised just what a blow they were striking for hospital patients. In any event, four pages laying bare the ghastly ineptitude of Hillingdon Primary Care Trust in a national newspaper could do little to ease her last hours.

When my sister was diagnosed with terminal cancer earlier this year, she was, as always, ruthlessly practical. Pat had smoked all her life. She was over 55, and when she was found to have tumours in her brain as well as her lungs, she knew that she would not be around for another decade. She had worked

"I watched helplessly as she was shunted around from carer to carer, sent home with the wrong drugs, breathing with an oxygen cylinder"

hard all her life, paid her tax and National Insurance, and had absolute faith that the NHS would provide her with all the treatment and nursing care that she needed.

How horribly over-optimistic that turned out to be. She had read about Hillingdon Hospital's cash crisis and massive debt in her local newspaper, but Pat never believed that these problems would end up ruining the short time she had left to live. And I was to watch helplessly as my sister was shunted around from carer to carer and from nurse to nurse, sent home from hospital with the wrong drugs, no diet sheet, no information about the effects of the medicines she was taking, compelled to sit at home breathing with an oxygen cylinder waiting for a doctor to visit her. No one came for two weeks, and her GP didn't visit her at all before her life ended.

After I could take no more, I ranted at someone in the anticoagulation unit. They said they had no records for my sister, even though she had been a patient at the hospital for seven months. Next day, I witnessed a visit from a lady from the complaints department, who turned up at my sister's bedside for a chat, leaving her notebook behind in the car. Pat had been sent home in an NHS delivery van, had suffered the indignity of a mixed ward (with a naked man masturbating in front of her at night), and was not allowed a second pillow "because we can't afford two". This complaints woman told us: "We value hearing patients' stories because it helps us fine-tune our standards of care." Hillingdon doesn't need to fine-tune. In Pat's experience it needed to go back to basics. After two weeks and much complaining, the hospital sent a doctor from the Palliative Care

Unit (jokily referred to as "Pals" in a letter from the chief executive, as if Pat needed another pal – what she needed was co-ordinated care and one person in charge of her case). This doctor told Pat not to ring 999 if she felt ill at night, but to call the "Harmony Out of Hours Doctors Service". Late last Wednesday, after I'd left, Pat felt nauseous. Mick, her husband, rang the Harmony number to be told they were very busy and that a doctor could not visit for at least two hours. After two hours Pat was starting to have a fit, so Mick rang again to be told the doctor would be at least another 45 minutes. He then disregarded Miss Pals' instructions and dialed 999. My sister suffered a seizure en route to Hillingdon A and E department and another when she got there. She was revived and placed back on Grange Ward, the mixed ward she had loathed so much before.

When I arrived nobody was in charge of her, the special needs nurse she had seen before was unavailable and the staff nurse told us the doctors would be around "later". I called Pat's oncologist on her mobile and demanded my sister was sent home to die as she had wished. The racket from the cluster of trainee doctors and nursing auxiliaries chatting and joking around the nurses' station made it impossible to rest, creating a totally unsuitable atmosphere for a terminally-ill patient with a distressed husband and son. I rang the chief executive's office and was told that "a great many of our operatives are off-site at present". When all else fails, jargon prevails. The acting head of nursing and the director of operations talked to me and seemed worried that we might take legal action against the trust. They also repeated the mantra about "valuing patients' stories".

Pat's oncologist, Miss Lemon, happened to be in the hospital – she is only based there one morning a week. After my desperate phone call, she popped up and saw Pat. Within 20 minutes a bed had been found for my sister in the Michael Sobell unit, an NHS hospice within Mount Vernon Hospital. In spite of it being categorised as an emergency, no one could find an ambulance. After an hour we were told by the staff nurse that another one would have to be booked and might be "another hour". I threatened to call a private ambulance service and use my credit card to get my sister out of this noisy, unsuitable environment straight away. Suddenly an ambulance materialised.

The hospice was welcoming, calm and exactly the right place for Pat, even though by now she was barely conscious. We were brought teas, given cards with 24-hour numbers to call, shown quiet rooms and easy chairs to doze in. My sister was visited by her specialist and received regular monitoring during the afternoon. The care she had never had during the past three weeks at home materialised, but it was too late. At least she died with dignity, and not in the hell of Grange Ward in Hillingdon Hospital, where she had been told to roll up her blanket herself in order to support her swollen legs. That's not any kind of care, is it?

The Independent on Sunday
19 November 2006

To read Patricia Balsom's diaries:
http://www.independent.co.uk/arts/books/features/article1988136.ece

Should NHS charge for 'doubtful' treatments?

Doctor triggers debate on future of health funding with a provocative question

Celia Hall reports

THE NHS should consider billing patients for ineffective treatments and drop all prescription charges, senior public health doctors said yesterday.

Spiralling health costs had to be controlled, said Dr Tim Crayford, the president of the Association of Directors of Public Health, and one way would be to charge patients for treatments for which there was not good evidence that they worked or when cheaper options were available.

Their list includes insertion of grommets, surgery for benign moles, varicose veins procedures, hysterectomy for heavy bleeding, carpel tunnel surgery for sore wrists, tonsils removal and homeopathy.

Dr Crayford also said not offering cataract or hip replacement surgery too early in the progression of the disease, could be added to the list.

He called for national standards to be set as to when NHS surgery should be offered for these complaints.

"I know this is controversial but we need to have this debate," he said.

"Medicines and treatments that people need for health reasons should be free. But where there's little proof of clinical benefit, the use of treatments would reduce more quickly if there was a price tag attached."

Waiting time targets had removed the traditional way that health service treatments had been rationed to contain costs and a new system had to be adopted, he said.

"The NHS has always struggled financially to meet public expectations and this proposal would help the NHS ensure that most people in most health need get the treatments they require," he said.

He said that 89 per cent of prescriptions were already free and it was not logical to charge patients for pills like statins to reduce cholesterol and prevent heart attacks, while providing free treatments that were not always effective.

"Taking children's tonsils out, for example, makes very little difference to how many days they have off school or how many sore throats they suffer from.

"The savings to the NHS by charging for doubtful procedures could easily compensate for the revenue lost by making most prescriptions free," he said.

Dr Crayford added that the NHS would save £1 billion a year by not offering "doubtful" surgery, around twice as much as the current NHS deficit.

The British Medical Association is drawing up its own document on what the NHS should provide and welcomed the call for a public debate. "We are already rationing procedures," said Dr Jonathan Fielden, the chairman of the BMA consultants' committee.

"Cosmetic surgery is not carried out on the NHS and the drugs that we use are restricted. There is scope to include other things like varicose veins and hernias. But how far do you go? If you include cataracts and hips I think you are breaking down the traditional values of the NHS," he said.

Prof John Appleby, the chief economist at the King's Fund, the independent health service analysts, told the BBC that he "did not buy into these doomsday scenarios".

He said it was likely that the public would want to increase spending to keep pace with increasing demand.

Norman Lamb, the health spokesman for the Liberal Democrats, said: "This statement highlights how charging has crept into a service that was originally designed to be free at the point of use.

"The system is confusing, outdated and unfair on people who rely on regular medication and tests. We urgently need an open and honest debate about how care should be rationed in an NHS with escalating costs and demands."

A Department of Health spokesman said: "The NHS budget has doubled since 1997 and will have tripled by 2008. This extra money has brought the fastest ever access to care and treatment, hundreds of new hospitals and GP surgeries, and 300,000 more staff.

"We continue to be fully committed to a publicly funded NHS which delivers health care according to clinical need, not ability to pay. Our current system reform programme means that by 2008 the NHS will have further cut its costs, become more efficient and productive, and will be squeezing better value out of every penny of taxpayer's money.

"A treatment carried out in a GP surgery costs a third of what it does in an acute hospital; fitting a £25 grab rail in an older person's home helps avoid a fall, and so saves the thousands of pounds that treating a broken hip costs."

Operations that could be at risk

Procedure	Cost*	Reason
Breast reduction	£4,000	For back pain but also cosmetic
Cataract (early)	£2,000	Cataracts take time to develop
Elective Caesarean	£3,000	Too posh to push, say critics
Gender reassignment	£9,600	Some say it's a lifestyle choice
Grommet insertion	£1,300	Not always effective
Hip replacement (early)	£9,000	Pain increases over time
Homeopathy	£40 consultation	Effectiveness is questioned
Hysterectomy for heavy bleeding	£5,000	Drugs usually work as an alternative
IVF	£2,599 per cycle	Not an illness
Mole removal	£150	Largely cosmetic
Tonsillectomy	£1,700	Can make little difference
Varicose veins	£1,500 (one leg)	For pain but also cosmetic
Vasectomy reversal	£600	Lifestyle choice - not always effective

*average costs for private treatment

Should NHS charge for 'doubtful' treatments?

Yes

Dr Jonathan Fielden, is chairman of the British Medical Association's consultants' committee

Although politicians are loath to admit it, there has always been some form of rationing in the NHS, whether in the form of waiting lists, or treatments being ruled out because the clinical case for them is insufficiently strong. Cosmetic surgery, for example, is rarely carried out on the NHS. We strongly believe in an NHS free at the point of delivery and funded from general taxation. However from 2008, the year-on-year funding increases which the NHS has seen in recent years will drop significantly.

Meanwhile, the population is ageing and expectations are rising. Hospitals are dealing with increasing volumes of patients, and the costs of drugs and new technologies continue to rise. NHS trusts are in deficit during this time of feast, let alone the coming famine.

The public should be trusted to debate what a comprehensive health service is and how much they are willing to pay. The result must be universal and equitable or the ethos of the NHS will be lost.

While this discussion needs to be professionally led, politicians must be honest about what funds are available, and the public must be allowed a real say. However, the debate on where NHS money goes should be about more than which treatments are available – it should also focus on who provides them.

While the NHS may be unable to meet all demand for services, it has historically provided excellent value for money – a claim which cannot be made about all the private firms currently profiting from the NHS.

No

Professor John Appleby is chief economist at the King's Fund

DOOMSDAY predictions about the inability of the NHS to cope with demand pressures have been made for decades – yet the NHS continues to cope.

Clearly, there is only so much money the NHS has to spend each year and decisions have to be made about what it spends its money on – crudely, who gets what and when. This has always been true and will remain so despite new costly drugs coming along.

The NHS is facing one of its most challenging periods. But there is nothing particularly special about the next few years that will reduce the NHS – as some claim – to a rump of a service, only able to provide a mere basic level of care.

We used to think that an ageing population would eventually lead to the NHS going bust, but as of yet this hasn't happened, although pressures on the health service from rising numbers of older people will increase over the next 20 years.

And there are always those who say that new, expensive drugs will mean that the NHS will find it difficult to afford everything that is medically possible. But again, this has always been the case. But further, many of the new cancer drugs, for example, are not just costly, but have marginal impacts on health. In other words, there will be serious doubt about whether they will be "good buys" for the NHS.

The debate about NHS rationing is not whether it should be done, but how it should be done given that as a society we have taken the decision not to ration access to health care on the basis of price and the individual's ability to pay.

Daily Telegraph 30 January 2007
© *Telegraph Group Limited 2007*

As the Prime Minister defends reforms in the health service, morale is at an all-time low. And yet more money has been poured in than ever before. So what has gone wrong? *Lucy Chapman* describes the ordeals of a modern hospital

A doctor's
scream

No one is at their best at the 5am trauma call. It is the sound everyone dreads. It is the hour of the night shift when doctors begin dying on their feet: and then the emergency bleep – the drunk driver who's in a coma after colliding with a lamp-post, the schizophrenic who has jumped from the seventh floor, the stabbing or the post-nightclub gunshot wound. "Trauma call ... trauma team to A&E resus," wail the pagers. Bleary-eyed, we assemble in casualty under the strip lights to wait for the ambulance to deliver the patient. We chat while we wait.

Today the subject is the overhaul of training and careers. The surgical registrar, an entertaining Irishman, is adamant that if he weren't at the end of his training, he would leave. Only a mortgage, a baby and a lack of suitable alternatives for a man with ten years' experience and a PhD cause him to hesitate. The patient arrives in cardiac arrest, having been shot through the stomach and chest with a single bullet. The crew are giving him chest compressions as he is wheeled in. I watch the same registrar slit open his abdomen and crack open his chest to stem the bleeding from his heart in less than three minutes. His skill, speed and dexterity are awe-inspiring, but they are no longer enough to make him want to continue. The patient dies an hour later anyway.

Morale in medicine is at an all-time low. Doctors of my generation have never worked harder, and yet their pay is being cut, while colleagues who leave are not replaced; they face an uncertain future and possible unemployment as hospital services are broken up and privatised. Most depressing of all is that our work is dictated by irrelevant and conflicting targets that render us impotent to deliver the care our patients need. This week, managers decided that 26 surgical beds must be closed to save money for the trust. This was implemented overnight and the beds physically removed from the ward.

These same people oversee the waiting lists. At no point did anyone see fit to inform the patients who had been asked to come in for surgery that there would be no beds for them. The patients duly turned up at an ungodly hour to have their blood taken and their consent forms filled in by me. They then had to wait for hours before being told that their operations had been cancelled because no beds could be found. Naturally, it is the doctors and nurses who have to explain and apologise. Managers are never on the wards and never take calls: "I'm sorry, she's in a meeting. Can I take a message for you?"

When I worked in neurosurgery, I had to clerk for cancer patients with brain tumours who were being admitted for scheduled surgery. The psychological build-up to something like this – having to sign a form acknowledging that you wish to proceed despite a substantial risk of dying on the table – is something that few can appreciate. Every week, one such patient would have their operation cancelled on the morning of surgery because their bed had been filled overnight by a drunk or by a nervous wreck with a headache admitted from A&E, courtesy of the priority given to admitting patients from casualty, however well, because they were in danger of breaching the government's four-hour-wait target.

It is doctors who have to apologise. Managers are never on the wards and never take calls

Undervalued and overworked

Doctors feel undervalued and overworked because they are. We are routinely coerced into submitting false time sheets to underpay ourselves, in order not to breach the legal limit for working hours on paper and so incur fines to the hospital. Trusts across the country, including my own hospital, have cancelled study leave and funding for training courses for medical staff. Whole wards are threatened with closure even though no bed is ever empty for more than a few hours.

It is not only doctors who are affected. Nurses on my ward are being made to reapply for their jobs. We have two excellent ward secretaries, both facing redundancy after 20 years of efficiency and goodwill. One of them arrives on the ward at six in the morning, so that the notes and scans can be put in order. Doubtless their places will be filled by new, temporary, expendable people, with no pension or rights attached.

In this strange new world we are also inundated with expensive and time-consuming private sector initiatives, imposed by the government with no thought for whether there is any need for them and any infrastructure in place to support them, or if there are any staff trained to implement them. One example is the electronic patient record, which must be used for requesting investigations. The forms still have to be printed, thereby using exactly the same amount of paper, but there are only two working printers in my hospital. This requires a doctor to make a six-flights-of-stairs round trip to collect the forms every time a patient needs a blood test.

Meanwhile, billions of pounds of taxpayers' money touted as funding is poured into the building of PFI hospitals, and diagnosis and treatment centres. Or it is spent on consultants. The money ends up in the hands of private firms by way of glistening new buildings and headlines about modernisation, but with no discernible improvement in the quality, or quantity, of healthcare provided.

Indeed, the only obvious effect, apart from the haemorrhage of money, is an increase in the waste of clinical time. To get anything done for our patients – a chest X-ray, let's say – doctors go to extreme lengths: they have to make phone calls, negotiate with people who couldn't care less, usually find and handwrite the forms because the printer doesn't work, and then wheel the patient to the X-ray department and back so that he or she doesn't die waiting for porters. My rage is not your concern: it becomes relevant only when you consider that sometimes my choice is between staying with a patient who is haemorrhaging, or going to another building to collect the blood they need, because no one else will go.

Protests start

Then there is the ludicrous débâcle of payment by results. The policy applies only to the remaining public hospitals, while contracts for elective operations are guaranteed to private treatment centres, regardless of work done. We audited our own performance managers and found that the figures they use to obtain funds from the government under the new system underestimated the medical treatment given by almost one-third. In any case, we have no need to advertise our wares, because, as hospitals around the region are scaled back, we are oversubscribed.

The first large protests came last month, as patients, nurses, doctors and members of the public gathered outside parliament to express their frustration. But the horse has already bolted: this government is ideologically committed to fragmenting and privatising the NHS. Poll after poll has shown that the public opposes private sector involvement. The British Medical Association has repeatedly stated its opposition. The Royal College of Nursing is against it. Who, except the CBI and private health corporations, supports it?

I started training the year Tony Blair took office, and I quickly became disillusioned. I could not understand how students could be so conservative. I wondered who was left to defend the blueprint for a comprehensive, tax-funded, health service. Last week, on my way home after my 17th consecutive 12-hour shift, I had cause to remember the answer I received back then as an undergraduate, when I typed the words "left" and "medicine" into Google and found more than 3,000 items themed "Why I left medicine".

The author is a junior doctor at an NHS hospital, writing under a pseudonym

New Statesman 11 December 2006

Senator Barack Obama, an early frontrunner in the 2008 presidential race, advocates something the US has never had – universal health care, but just how bad a state is America's health care service really in?

Caring for America's health

Justin Webb

It was the summer of 1981. Mrs Thatcher was only two years into her first term and Ronald Reagan only months into his.

I was starting out as well. Writing stories for the Beaver newspaper at the London School of Economics (LSE) about students throwing eggs at government ministers and the iniquities of low-cost coach travel to Greece.

I had arrived in London from a boarding school in the West Country and a black and white world had suddenly burst into colour.

My room mate in our hall of residence was a cheerful American with lively eyes and a vague resemblance to Bruce Springsteen (a resemblance of which he was enormously proud).

Bo Nora was exotic. My friends at school had been called Patrick or Adrian, and mostly hailed from Somerset.

Increasing numbers of Americans have reduced their health insurance to the barest minimum

Bo came from Chicago and studied at the University of California. He was at the LSE for only a few months.

Parting company

Bo and I never felt the slightest bit mortal. I remember us listening to a programme on the local London radio station where people with emotional problems would call in for counselling. We laughed. We had no problems.

I said goodbye to Bo on Great Portland Street tube station and we stayed in touch for a few years. And then life took over and Bo Nora became a memory. I moved to Northern Ireland, back to London, to Brussels and here to the US.

Insured but unwanted

A few months ago, 25 years after that central London goodbye, I tracked Bo down. I found his e-mail address and sent him a message.

His reply talked of marriage and career and children and then came these words: "After several years of increasing physical difficulties, I saw a doctor in 1991 and was diagnosed with multiple sclerosis. I retired due to further disability and incapacity. Presently, I am spastic quadriplegic."

I went to see Bo the other day in his home on the outskirts of Chicago. We had supper. Bo's eyes flashing with recognition as we talked about London and university and people we had known.

His wife fed him.

Bo is not a bitter person – funny how happiness is wired into some people whatever life brings – but one subject genuinely pained him.

Bo has health insurance, I presume provided by the law firm he worked for when he was diagnosed. This is good news for Bo – bad news for the insurance company. Bo is expensive and the insurers do not want him... and they make it obvious.

Bo is expensive and the insurers do not want him... and they make it obvious

'Cut no slack'

Every year Bo gets a letter asking him if he is still ill.

Someone has to fill in a form for him: "Yes, I am quadriplegic; no, no miracle appears to have happened."

He told me recently he had to have a minor procedure associated with the condition. The bill was $78,000 (£40,000).

In the end he paid only a small part of it himself but of the various entities that chipped in – the state, the insurer, the hospital – you can bet that no-one wanted to, and everyone would have got out of it if they could.

Americans who fall ill are cut no slack. A society which expects everyone to pay their way, expects it of them as well.

As a jolly man selling life insurance pointed out to me the other day, most personal bankruptcies in the US are the result of illness.

Endless letters

The story of American healthcare is one of huge expenditure for little obvious benefit. By head of population America spends twice the amount Britain does on health.

But life expectancy here is lower and infant mortality is higher, way higher in some ethnic groups.

Most of the money seems to go on overheads and on profits for the many private companies providing care, the hospital groups, the drug manufacturers, and above all the insurance companies which write letters to Bo inquiring about his MS and write incessantly to all their other customers as well, endlessly negotiating, fussing, harassing.

As the costs spiral upwards and private employers ditch their health care schemes to stave off bankruptcy, increasing numbers of Americans have reduced their health insurance to the barest minimum, and when something goes wrong they are dependent on the back-up provided by the state.

So in a nation where socialised medicine is a phrase to be spat out contemptuously, Americans are on course by the year 2050 to spend every cent the government takes in tax, on health-related claims. Nothing left even for the tiniest war.

For the time being, Bo Nora will go on getting his annual letter but all of America is cottoning on to what Bo has known for years: there must be a better way of looking after sick Americans.

If Iraq is eventually resolved, the issue waiting next in line for the president, or more likely for his successors, is restoring health to American health care.

From Our Own Correspondent
BBC Radio 4
27 January, 2007

If you're too famous for an ASBO, try rehab

By Jan Moir

Rehab must be tremendous fun, because everyone keeps going to it all the time; perhaps it now has the same kind of gritty, street cachet for singers and actors that Asbos have for some of the less affluent and gifted members of our society. At the moment, film star Lindsay Lohan is in, Jade Goody is in, Mel Gibson was in but now he's out, ditto Whitney Houston, while a late autumnal rush to the clinics last year saw Robin Williams, Ronnie Wood, Justin Hawkins, Keane singer Tom Chapman and party girl Meg Mathews among those who checked in to try to check out of their assorted addictions and waywardness. Some of them even jammed together in a little rehab band down at the Priory — isn't that cute?

Meanwhile, Pete Doherty and Kate Moss remain rehab royalty, with Doherty being particularly keen to sandwich clinic trips between birthday parties, holidays, Cotswold weekends, setting his hat on fire and being arrested in a stolen car in the early hours of the morning. Devoted Moss has paid for some of her boyfriend's rehab sojourns, and was by his side on another visit to a facility this week.

While some, if indeed not all, of these stars have genuine health problems that need addressing, it is

The Observer 25 February 2007

also true that, for others, going to rehab has become a useful modern cipher; a way that troubled celebs can semaphore the contrite message out to their fans — and any future employers — that they are suffering for their sins and determined to get well, even if they have no intention of doing any such thing.

With big money and deals at stake, many performers are booted into facilities by publicists or management, less keen for rehabilitation than for penance to be seen to be done. In more genteel times, a quiet bit of charity work among the poor was deemed a suitable atonement, whereas today, a trumpeted spell in rehab is deemed an effective admission of showbiz guilt and regret, whether the rehabitees believe it themselves or not.

The Daily Telegraph 31 January 2007

Back from the dead

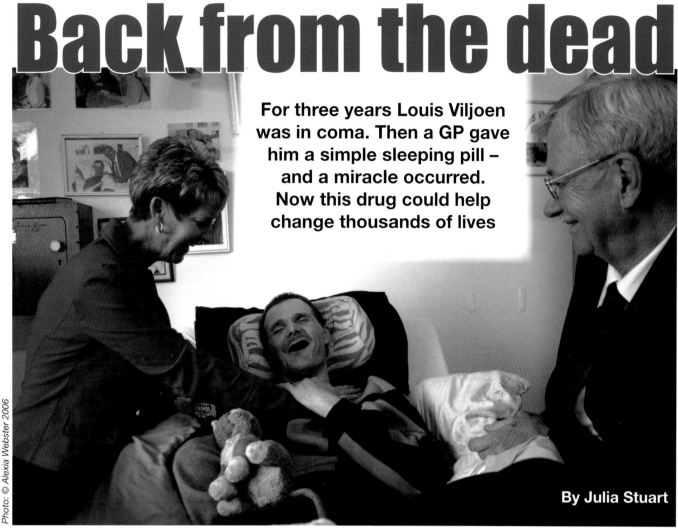

For three years Louis Viljoen was in coma. Then a GP gave him a simple sleeping pill – and a miracle occurred. Now this drug could help change thousands of lives

By Julia Stuart

Photo: © Alexia Webster 2006

Dr Wally Nel with Louis Viljoen and his mother Sienie Engelbrecht

There were times when Sienie Engelbrecht wondered whether her only child would be better off dead. Louis Viljoen had been in a persistent vegetative state since 1996, when he was hit by a lorry while cycling to work as a hospital switchboard operator. He was 25 and engaged to be married.

Sienie, a 58-year-old sales consultant, visited him every evening in a rehabilitation centre near his home in South Africa. She always talked to him, but he never responded. "For me it was a very heartfelt story because he was very sporty. He used to play soccer and was a very good swimmer. To see him lying like that in a coma not doing anything was terrible. I couldn't stand it. He couldn't talk, he didn't do anything. He was just looking at you all the time. I don't know whether he realised it was me. Sometimes I thought why didn't God take him away. It would have been better," says Sienie, who lives in Springs, about 40 miles from Johannesburg.

One day, in 1999, one of the ward sisters told Sienie that Louis had been restless and was pulling at his mattress. Sienie spoke to her GP, Dr Wally Nel, who suggested that she gave him one of the sleeping pills he had just prescribed for her. She duly crushed it, put it in a drink and gave it to him. She was astounded by what happened next.

"After about 20 minutes I heard Louis make a sound like 'mmm'. I thought, am I dreaming? He didn't make any sound usually. I looked at his eyes and they were sparkling. He turned his head to me and I said: 'Louis, can you hear me?' And then all of a sudden he said 'yes'. I couldn't believe it. I just cried. I said 'say hello to me' and then he said 'hello, Mummy' and started talking. I was so heartsore I couldn't talk."

After about two hours, Louis slipped back into a semi-conscious state. His mother gave him the drug for the following few nights and each time the reaction was the same. Convinced that Zolpidem was the cause, she told Dr Nel. He came to the rehabilitation centre and watched as Louis became fully conscious again about 20 minutes after taking the drug. It was the world's first reported case of a Zolpidem-induced awakening.

"There was definitely a tear in my eye," says the GP, who has worked at the same practice in Springs for 35 years. Dr Ralf Clauss, a nuclear medicine physician at the Royal Surrey County Hospital in the UK, who at the time was working in the Medical University of

Southern Africa, performed a brain scan on Louis before and after taking Zolpidem. Before taking the sleeping tablet, about 30 per cent of his brain was in darkness, which is abnormal. After taking the drug, it lit up. "We were elated to see it and really surprised. At that point we didn't know what we were dealing with," says Dr Clauss.

Since then, another South African and an American, both classified as being in a permanently vegetative state, have also been roused to full consciousness by the drug. There have also been reports that about 10 to 15 patients in a minimally conscious state have been awakened. One of them was seen coming out of her partial coma for the first time on My Shocking Story: Coma Miracle on the Discovery Channel. Dianne Katz, 51, had been in a semi-conscious state since she had two brain aneurysms and three strokes two years ago. The book-keeper from Kenilworth, Johannesburg, couldn't talk, eat or wash unaided. She is seen coming round and talking shortly after taking the drug, while her family looks on in amazement.

But it is not only those with impaired consciousness who have been helped by the sleeping pill. Those brain damaged by trauma and strokes have also significantly improved. Dr Clauss says Zolpidem seems to help between 30 to 60 per cent of patients with less severe injury, such as a small stroke.

For those with serious impairment of consciousness the figure is around 15 per cent. Dr Nel also has a small number of patients with spinal injuries, which have had some response. One quadriplegic patient is now able to hold his torso upright in his wheelchair. Some patients can talk again, hear and move their limbs.

One of his patients, Paul Ras, 70, who also lives in Springs, was in a head-on car accident in 1995. His jaw was broken, he suffered five broken ribs and a crushed pelvis. He spent three weeks in a coma. After the same hip was replaced twice, the runner, who was used to competing in 50km races, finally had it removed altogether in 1999. With one leg shorter than the other, he had to wear a built- up shoe and was told he would never be able to do sports again. That year he was prescribed Zolpidem for sleep problems. "When I woke up in the morning I was a different man," he says. "It's changed me completely. I can do my gardening myself. I've built a double garage all on my own. I carry my

own bricks. People can't believe it with no hip."

The drug, which is also available in the UK, is still only under licence as a sleeping pill. "We are not experimenting," insists Dr Nel, 65. "We can give it to people as a sleeping tablet and then I follow it up on the clinical picture. At the end of the day my ear is red from people phoning me. We get so many queries because with a brain injury that was the end of the road. Nobody said that a brain could ever recover and now we say there is hope. It's a whole new world opening for brain injury."

It has taken eight years of research for Dr Clauss to reach his hypothesis of how Zolpidem affects brain injury. "The drug is a GABA agonist, which means in normal tissue it stimulates GABA receptors and normally they put you to sleep," he explains. "But in Louis's brain, for example, these GABA receptors are abnormal and overactive. They keep Louis's brain in a sleeping or dormant state all the time. The drug distorts these abnormal receptors which put Louis to sleep, dormancy is switched off and the brain returns back to normal."

So why does it help some patients and not others? "Some people have dormancy – inactive brain tissue which is functioning, but not functioning correctly, and others have dead tissue. It doesn't do anything to the dead tissue, but it reverses the dormant tissue, and the response depends on how big the dormancy part is."

The British firm ReGen Therapeutics is carrying out a trial on 20 patients in South Africa already on the drug. Percy Lomax, the firm's chairman, says: "Stroke is the third biggest cause of death in the United Kingdom. Around 450,000 people in the UK are currently suffering from some form of disability from a stroke. If we can reduce that disability that would seem to me to be an important step forward." It is not expected that Zolpidem will be licensed for use for brain injury for several years.

Meanwhile, Dianne Katz, who "woke" last November, can now walk on her own, talk and eat unaided. And Louis, now 36, is going from strength to strength. He is now fully conscious. "He still talks and has got such a good sense of humour and he remembers everything before the accident: his birthday, my birthday, where he went to school and work," says his mother. "I'm so glad, I can't describe it to anyone. Nobody could believe that a sleeping tablet would get someone out of his coma."

The Independent 27 March 2007

COMA: THE FACTS

☐ Coma is the most severe of impaired consciousness states. There is no reaction from the person and the eyes are closed.

☐ Vegetative state is like coma, except the eyes are open.

☐ The minimally conscious state is like the vegetative state, but there is some response.

☐ Causes of brain damage that can result in a coma or vegetative state are either traumatic, such as a blow to the head, or non-traumatic such as stroke, brain disease and severe infection of the nervous system such as rabies.

☐ Vegetative state occurs when the upper brain is damaged so the ability to think is lost while the lower part of the brain continues to function.

☐ A vegetative state often develops when a person comes out of a coma.

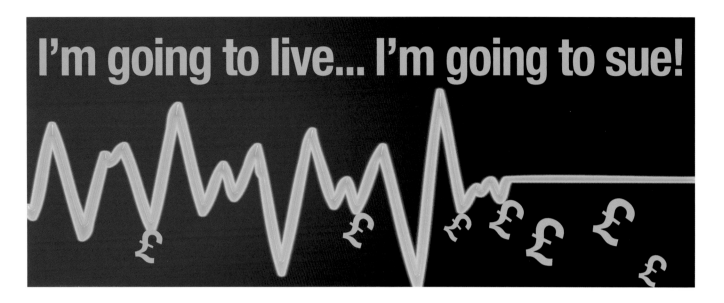

I'm going to live... I'm going to sue!

To discover that you have less than a year to live must be every person's worst nightmare. But when John Brandrick, 62, was told that he wasn't, in fact, going to die of cancer, that's when the trouble started.

The ordeal began in February 2005 when father of two, John Brandrick, was struck by acute abdominal pain. Within days his skin had turned yellow and blood tests confirmed he had jaundice. The pain continued to intensify and John was rushed into hospital where an ultrasound scan showed a 7cm tumour on his pancreas. John and his family were totally devastated when experts at the Royal Cornwall Hospital, Treliske, explained that this pancreatic cancer was incurable and that John only had approximately six months left to live.

> **John had only 6 months to live.**

A letter in April confirmed the diagnosis. Knowing this was indeed his fate John threw caution to the wind and decided to live what was left of his life to the absolute full. John explained, "It's not something any of us think we'll hear. We all hope to die of old age. But I had to come to terms with it quickly. I wanted quality time with Sally."

John's partner Sally Laskey, 55, was given time off work as a receptionist to be with him. John went ahead and quit his £13,000-a-year council job, sold or gave away most of his possessions, including his clothes and even his car and stopped paying his mortgage. Keeping just a suit, shirt and tie which he planned to be buried in, and enough clothes to keep him going, John, along with his partner, set about enjoying the time he had left in style.

> **"That wrong diagnosis has left me in financial ruin."**

Too concerned about his health to travel abroad, they explored Cornwall where John has lived since 1999, dined in swish restaurants around Padstow, Mevagissey, Fowey, Falmouth and Newquay. Day by day John's life savings went on luxuries such as expensive meals, wine and hotels. As he explained, "We paid £80 for meals, things Sally and I were unable to afford normally." The divorced father also spent time with his children, son Andrew, 18, and daughter Kerri, 34, who live in the Midlands.

As his six month deadline drew closer, John planned his funeral and along with his family, prepared as much as he could for the inevitable. But then something happened, or rather didn't happen. Twelve months after his diagnosis John still hadn't died, in fact his symptoms had actually started to fade. Doctors scanned John to investigate the situation only to discover that the tumour had disappeared.

So how had John managed to get rid of the tumour? He hadn't. Further tests revealed that the "cancer" in the original diagnosis, was in fact pancreatitis, a non life-threatening inflammation. It also transpired that a biopsy taken only weeks after John's initial diagnosis had given him the all-clear. However, a spokesman for the Royal Cornwall Hospital's NHS Trust said that the diagnosis of pancreatic cancer, given to John, was not only based on the symptoms Mr Brandrick was experiencing in 2005, but also on the results of a series of investigations.

But what seems like good news is a double edged sword for John who said, "It was such a relief. But that wrong diagnosis has left me in financial ruin." Having discovered the good but shocking news that he will live, John, who is now penniless, is considering suing the hospital for the wrong diagnosis. In a struggle to get some money together he is also having to sell the £280,000 house he shares with partner Sally, as he spent almost everything else he had. "I'm really pleased that I've got a second chance in life... but if you haven't got no money after all this, which is my fault... I spent it all... they should pay something back."

The Royal Cornwall Hospital is denying that its staff are to blame and a spokesman said, "While we do sympathise with Mr Brandrick's position, a clinical review of his case has not revealed that any different diagnosis would have been made at the time, based on the same evidence."

John Brandrick explained, "It's put me and my family through hell, we have nothing at all." Except his life that is. But although his body is healthy, it seems his bank balance is definitely not.

Source: Various

"YOU WOULDN'T LOOK AT MUM AND THINK SHE'S DYING"

When breast-cancer sufferer Jane Tomlinson was given just six months to live, her daughters Suzanne, 21, and Rebecca, 18, were devastated. Six years on, Jane has competed in marathons around the world and raised more that £1million for charity

Jane and family with her MBE in October 2003

Photo: Kirsty Wigglesworth PA Archive/PA Photos

Most women, when diagnosed with terminal breast cancer, would spend every moment with their families and prepare to say their goodbyes. But when *Cosmo* Fun Fearless Female nominee Jane Tomlinson, 42, from Leeds, was given six months to live back in 2000, she made a different choice. She transformed herself from a gardening, needlework-loving mum into a sportswoman, and has raised more that £1.2 million for cancer and children's charities.

She has competed in some of the toughest endurance events, including three London marathons, the New York marathon, several triathlons and the gruelling Iron Man challenge (a four kilometre swim, 180 kilometre bike ride and a full marathon within 17 hours). Her most recent challenge was 4,200-mile bike ride across America. She achieved all this in addition to having five courses of chemotherapy and developing chronic heart disease as a result of her medication. And her 'six months to live' has so far spun out into six years.

But although Jane's ordeal has been tough, it can be tougher still for her family at home, worrying about her. Her daughters Suzanne and Rebecca have grown up knowing that their mother's time is running out, and watching her test her body to its limits and beyond. Here, for the first time, they tell *Cosmo* how it feels to have a miracle woman for a mum.

Suzanne Tomlinson, 21, is an IT helpdesk analyst, she and her partner, Tom Waldron, 19, a bricklayer, are expecting their first baby in September
"You always imagine that big moment when you tell you mother she's going to be a grandmother. But for me there was a difference, I didn't know whether Mum would ever hear me say those words. Now, fingers crossed, she'll get to hold her first grandchild.

Photo: Martin Rickett PA Archive/PA Photos

Jane and her daughters competing in the 'People's Race' in the Salford Triathlon World Cup, July 2004

"Fingers crossed is an expression I've come to use often. In 2000, Mum was told she had incurable breast cancer that had spread to her lungs and bones. She was given just six months to live. But life went on – hers and ours. Milestones I thought she would miss have come and gone: my little brother Steven's first day at school, my 21st birthday, my graduation and now my first baby. After six years of not knowing if Mum would be here in a year or six months or less, you adjust; it becomes part of life.

"My 21st birthday back in June was a special moment, though. Mum and Dad gave me a photograph of Ayres Rock they'd bought in Australia five years ago on a 'last chance' holiday. Mum had put it away, assuming she wouldn't be there when I turned 21. She handed it to me and said, 'I didn't think I'd get to give you this.' I'm grateful for times like that.

"Mum was 26 (just five years older than I am now) when she was first diagnosed with breast cancer. Rebecca and I were very young, but we knew Mum was ill; there were stays with Grandma and hospital visits. Mum had a mastectomy and everything seemed OK. In retrospect, though, she was never 100% well again.

"We knew there was a risk the

It sometimes feels like we have a different mum to the one we grew up with

cancer would return and, 10 years later when I was 15, it did. Mum and Dad were honest from the very beginning about her prognosis. We'd been staying with our grandmother while Mum was having tests when they sat us down and told us all together that the disease was incurable. It's the kind of thing you think you're taking on board but it doesn't hit you fully. Instead, we all focused on the present, which was Mum getting through her intensive chemotherapy.

"Naturally, life changed at home. Dad was ironing school shirts and making dinner, while we tiptoed around the house, trying not to disturb Mum. At first we were overly nice and helpful but it drove Mum round the bend. So we just reverted to living a normal life. But there were certainly times as a teenager when I resisted being difficult and thought before I spoke. Her first challenge was the five-kilometre Race For Life in 2001 and after that things just snowballed. She'd get an idea to do something and that would be it.

"That's been the most amazing change in Mum – not her illness but what she's achieved. I'd never have imagined she could do what she's done. Before, I don't think she even owned at a pair of trainers, except perhaps on old pair she wore to do gardening. Now the house is full of trainers; different types for cycling and running.

"The publicity she attracted was a bit overwhelming at first. Even today I don't think we realise how many people know who Jane Tomlinson is – to us, she's Mum. There are times when it would be nicer to be private but the reason Mum started all this was to raise money, and the media coverage is important for that, so you can't say that you want to be left alone.

"If someone has a limited time left to live, you might assume they'd want to spend every waking moment of it with their family, but you need to do your own thing and live life as normally as possible. That's what Mum has done – and urged us to do, too.

"When I was at university I wouldn't necessarily phone home every day, so I'd often find out what Mum was up to from newspaper interviews, which was a bit strange. But Mum didn't want me to drop everything and come home every weekend or miss out on seeing my friends. She wanted me to go away to university and enjoy it, which I did. But there are times when I wonder if I've done the right thing. Will I regret spending so much time away from her?

"Of course, I do miss Mum when she's away, but I always try to go along and support her whenever I can. And she's shared her time with us equally. We've all done things with her separately, like gone away for weekends. She wants us to have those memories.

"When Mum planned her ride across America she made sure Steven, who's now nine, could go for the full nine weeks and Rebecca could go for a month. I was upset to be left behind, but I couldn't go because of my pregnancy.

"As far as I know, the ride across America was to be Mum's last challenge. We've always had an inkling in the past when she's been tempted to do something else, but not this time. She realises this is the last big challenge and that she needs to spend some time with her family now.

"Every time there's more bad news you get upset, but then you forget about it. Because of what Mum's like. Sometimes she's very weak and it's difficult to see her struggling. You offer to help and she says "No. I'm fine.' I don't know whether that's because she feels

she has to or because she doesn't want someone else to do it for her. A lot of the time, though, she looks fine and that makes it harder. You wouldn't look at her and think she's dying, especially when she's running a marathon or competing in a triathlon. I do get anxious about her health but you can't ask her to stop – she'll know herself when it's time.

"Mum and I haven't had a talk about the time when she won't be there. She'll know eventually when the time has come to say anything she wants to say. In the meantime, my

That's been the most amazing change in Mum – not her illness but what she's achieved

fingers are crossed in the hope that Mum can stay as well as she possibly can and that cycling across America doesn't take too much out of her. And obviously being there when my child is born. I need her around to answer all my baby questions after all!"

Rebecca Tomlinson, 18, is a student
"I was in Boots recently waiting for a prescription, when the chemist looked at my name and said, 'Oh! Are you related to the sports personality?' I didn't know what she was talking about at first. Then she said 'You know, the woman who does all the running for charity.' Then it dawned on me she that she meant Mum!

"It sometimes feels as though we have a different mum to the one we grew up with. There was the mum who went to work, sat down to do her tapestry or pottered in the garden. Now there's the mum who'll cycle 70 miles a day across America. We used to go for family walks, now we compete in triathlons together.

"Mum has such amazing stamina; her illness is not something you can see when you look at her, when she has chemotherapy, it's the physical effects – her face becoming puffy and losing her hair – that reminds you of how ill she really is. I remember Mum getting very upset once when she had to shave all her hair off. It's weird seeing your mum upset. It was so unlike her.

"She gets very weak after chemo, though, and changes completely. Dad has to take charge. One time, when I was about 12, he totally ruined dinner. He burnt the fish fingers on the outside and they were still frozen inside. I ran to tell Mum. She was in bed, but she got up and cooked tea, even though she was supposed to be resting. We laugh about things like that – you have to. When Mum was losing her hair, we'd joke that she and Dad (whose hair is thinning) were starting to look the same. But we knew how far to take the joke and when to leave her alone.

"Early on, I didn't know how to tell my friends that Mum was ill, so I didn't confide in many people. There's still a part of me that wants to keep her health a private thing, but she's so well known now that you can't really hide it. At the same time, I've found the buzz around Mum's sporting challenges exciting. She got a Sports Personality of the Year award, received an MBE from the Queen and we've been invited to Downing Street.

"I get very annoyed if people are critical of Mum, saying she's selfish and should be spending time with her family. I don't resent what Mum does. She told us she wouldn't go to America if we wanted her around. But I've got used to it, I know she'd just get restless at home. Life has been like this for so long – six years – that thinking that way would be a waste of time. Mum always made it clear that she wanted to see Steven on his first day of school, which she managed to do. She realises that out of the three of us, when it comes to memories she needs to spend more time with him.

"My wish would be that Mum could be at my graduation, but that's too far ahead to think about. For now, I just look forward to spending time with Mum and competing in more events with her. Mum and I run together – that's our thing."

Cosmopolitan October 2006
© *The National Magazine Company Ltd*
www.janesappeal.com

Blogger is jailed for four years

**By Hugh Miles
in Cairo**

An Egyptian who enraged his government with outspoken views on Islam and politics expressed in his internet diary was jailed yesterday amid an international outcry.

The 22-year-old former law student, whose own father has disowned him and called for his execution under Islamic law, was sentenced to four years by a court in Alexandria.

The convictions resulting from the views published on his weblog, sandmonkey, included counts for "spreading information disruptive of public order and damaging to the country's reputation"; "incitement to hate Islam" and "defaming the President of the Republic".

Abdelkareem Suleiman was also found guilty of criticising Al-Azhar University. He was expelled from the university last March after writing in his blog that the "professors and sheikhs at Al-Azhar who ... stand against anyone who thinks freely" would "end up in the dustbin of history".

The sentence, which was condemned by human rights groups, is widely seen as the latest attempt by the government to punish internet activism. The interior ministry recently established a new intelligence unit, called the department for confronting computer and internet crime, and new laws have made it easier for the police to shut websites deemed subversive.

Identification is now a requirement to use the internet in public places and state security issues proprietors with black lists of those forbidden from going online. The state-controlled press often accuses bloggers of defaming Egypt's reputation abroad or of being in the pay of foreign powers.

Seven bloggers were among dozens of people arrested last year during student demonstrations, but Suleiman was the first to be convicted. Blogging about Muslim-Christian riots that took place in Alexandria in October 2005, Suleiman wrote in typically provocative fashion: "Muslims have taken the mask off to show their true hateful face, and they have shown that they are at the top of their brutality and inhumanity."

Until two years ago there were still only about 30 blogs written in Egypt, which has a population of 80 million. Now more than 3,000 men and women can be found blogging in every major town and city.

Abdelkareen Suleiman, 22. His sentence has provoked international outrage.

Photo: American Islamic Congress

Governments battle against internet tide

Governments across the world strive to control their people's access to the internet, but with mixed success.

The Chinese are reported to employ thousands of computer experts to monitor, block and shut critical internet sites. Western search engines have been co-opted into the system, with Google, Yahoo and others agreeing to block access to politically sensitive pages in return for access to the lucrative Chinese market.

Only the Saudis have developed a more successful system, funnelling all internet traffic through a single state-owned service provider which blocks all content deemed un-Islamic.

But elsewhere attempts to stem the online tide have proved largely ineffective. While President Robert Mugabe regularly shuts down opposition sites in Zimbabwe, and the regimes in Tunisia, Vietnam and Burma have attempted to build their own filter systems, the internet remains one of the most powerful tools for debate.

Matthew Moore

The Daily Telegraph 23 February 2007 © Telegraph Group Ltd

Open to all?

Pressure is mounting to curb the prevalence
of internet censorship across the globe

Matthew Richards

Welcome to Cuba, where free computer clubs are thriving, the smallest backwater schools have PCs and thousands are in training at a new IT college in Havana.

PCs are also filling the shelves of shops, apparently available for the buying public – but there's a catch. Cubans are not allowed to buy a computer without government approval, which is flatly denied in most cases. Similarly, web access is strictly monitored, with access being forbidden to American-based sites that play host to Cuban dissidents.

Meanwhile, in the United Arab Emirates, the monopoly internet provider, Etisilat, blocks access to any site if it deems the content to be "inconsistent with the religious, cultural, political and moral values of the UAE." This can mean any site which questions the power of the Gulf states' ruling families. Recent reports also suggest that internet café users in Dubai are having their personal details recorded and kept on file, raising further concerns over privacy.

Extreme internet censorship is now a trait of many nations including Burma, Iran, Libya, Nepal, North Korea, Saudi Arabia, Syria, Turkmenistan and Vietnam. Worse still, internet users have been imprisoned in Egypt, Iran, Libya, the Maldives, Syria, Tunisia and Vietnam, as have more than 60 people in China. Sadly, it seems to be a growing trend, with Zimbabwe the latest reported applicant to buy internet censorship technology direct from China.

Fighting back

In a concerted drive to stop internet repression, Amnesty International (www.amnesty.org.uk) has launched a new online campaign at http://irrepressible.info, focusing opinion on cases where, it says, chat rooms are monitored, blogs deleted, websites blocked, search engines restricted and people imprisoned for simply posting and sharing information. Site visitors are encouraged to get involved, signing an online pledge calling on governments and companies to ensure that the internet is a force for political freedom, not repression.

Companies under the spotlight include Google and Microsoft, which are alleged to have supplied internet software to China that allows censorship of its users. The pledge itself was presented to the UN's Internet Governance Forum's (www.intgovforum.org) first meeting in November 2006, where member states began a global discourse on best web practices for issues such as access, security and diversity.

On a more individual level, one recent case concerns Chinese journalist Shi Tao, who is serving a 10-year jail sentence for nothing more than sending an email. The email outlined the restrictions that the Chinese government was seeking to impose on journalists reporting the 15th anniversary of the Tiananmen Square massacre. None other than Yahoo! assisted Chinese authorities in identifying Shi Tao, and a spokeswoman told the BBC that Yahoo! had "received a valid and legal demand for information and responded to it as required by the law."

While to some extent the damage has already been done, you can still get involved in the fight to free Shi Tao at Amnesty.org by signing the pledge or posting censored material on your own site. With internet censorship rife in other parts of the world, it's a relief to be allowed to do even that much.

BBC Focus September 2006

Preserve of the rich?

James Eagle examines the reach of the world wide web and concludes that it's far from a global affair

If you believe the wilder-eyed zealots of the technological revolution, the internet is transforming politics, the media and the entertainment industry, sweeping away the old top-down structures and replacing them with a new order based on grass-roots participation and giving a voice to the voiceless. And they have a point – to an extent.

Legions of political bloggers are already speaking truth to power, highlighting gross errors or flat-out lies in mainstream reporting (**nielsenhayden.com/makinglight/ archives/008078.html**) or covering stories that would otherwise be ignored (**leninology.blogspot.com/2006/09/ blair-protest-report.html**).

Left-wing politicians can speak to the public without the sneers of the cosy middle class media (**www. john4leader.org.uk**). The likes of YouTube (**www.youtube.com**) throw open broadcasting to the masses and PledgeBank (**www.pledgebank.com**) offers a way to mobilize thousands of strangers in support of a cause.

Technological advances over the last two or three years have opened up whole new vistas of possibilities, fundamentally changing notions of what a website is and does (**en.wikipedia.org/wiki/Web_2**).

But technological advances are only half the story – although, given that those wild-eyed zealots that I mentioned tend to be techies themselves, this is the half that you'll hear the most.

The other, overlooked, half involves people. Who is actually joining this brave new world of democracy, mass participation and bottom-up creativity?

Make no mistake – Britain's internet users are barely any more representative of the country at large than new Labour's cosy little clique is representative of the British working class.

The government's own statistics (**tinyurl.com/2n7lxr**) show that, in the first quarter of last year 57 per cent of British households had internet access. Or, to put it another way, more than two in five did not. And there's a heavy bias towards the prosperous south, with fewer than half of Scottish households connected.

The poor, the elderly, people in northern England and Scotland – all are badly under-represented on the net. And the "digital divide" is far worse in the developing world.

Just 3.5 per cent of Africans are on the net and only 10.5 per cent of Asians, despite the march of technology in countries such as Japan and South Korea (**www.internetworldstats. com**).

In India, for instance, the urban middle classes enjoy a Western standard of living, including their own PCs and broadband access. Cheap internet cafes offer a way onto the net for those a rung or two below on the economic ladder, but that still leaves vast swathes of the country's poor – 96.5 per cent, to be precise – disconnected.

One plus point of the otherwise misguided One Laptop Per Child project (**www.laptop.org**) is that it could bring some of these voices into the global conversation. Here, too, there are measures afoot to bring the net to Britain's poor (**www.egovmonitor. com/node/9130**).

But, for now, the online world is dominated by the same people who have a stanglehold on politicians and conventional media – the white, the wealthy and, predominantly, the male.

At least the marginalized can't be forced off the net in the same way that they can be forced from politics and the media. But, so long as the net remains dominated by the same old voices of the powerful, be wary of overstating its effects.

It can be revolutionary – but not until the poor, the old, the disenfranchised and dispossessed can make themselves heard in overwhelming numbers.

Morning Star 3 February 2007

A few years ago no-one had heard of a podcast – now we are creating our own websites and blogs

Welcome to the Digi:Nation

In May 2006, a Harris poll, on behalf of *The Guardian* looked at how the online population – nicknamed Digi:zens by the researchers – uses digital media. They found that internet users are no longer passive consumers but are actively generating their own content.

The majority of the UK online population (67%) has tried some sort of digital activity such as downloading music, reading blogs, creating their own websites, listening to podcasts and downloading TV programmes.

But we are not merely consumers of digital information. User-generated content is gradually becoming mainstream, with over a third having read a blog and nearly 10% having created their own. A further 17% have created their own website.

Like any society, the Digi:Nation can be divided into groups:

Digi:scenti – These are at the top of the Digi:zen hierarchy, making up 4% of the internet population. They are aged between 25 and 44 with a bias towards the younger male population. Members of this group have owned their MP3 player or iPod for at least two years, and 44% own more than one digital music player. They create their own media – nearly half have their own website, nearly a quarter have a blog. This group are early adopters of new technology, 85% of them can imagine using one portable device for all information and entertainment needs.

Early Digitizers – these make up 11% of the onlin population. 92% download music, 30% have downloaded podcast and just over half have downloaded a film and ove two thirds can imagine using one device for all informatio and entertainment needs.

Digi Joe Public – these are the largest group of a making up 53% of the online population. They have done least one digital activity and largely embrace user generate content. 40% have read blogs,18% have created their ow website and 9% have their own blog. They are aged betwee 25-45 and there is a slight female bias in this group.

Digi:phobes make up 11% of the online community Most would like to engage in some digital activity but woul need someone to help them, for instance by showing ther where they can download music.

Digi:refuseniks – These are generally 50+, wit a female bias, and belong to the online population but ar much slower and less inclined to participate – digital activit holds no appeal for them.

In the next few years technologies will continue to converg – one device can be your radio, tv and computer; you mobile phone is probably already your MP3 player, camero address book and personal assistant. The Digi:Nation i bound to have a population explosion – and, with mor users and more user-generated content, its voice will b both louder and more diverse.

Source: variou
www.adinfo-guardian.co.uk/display/dignation/dignation.shtm

RUINING INNOCENT LIVES

Ordinary citizens can be stripped of their property, deprived of their home and livelihood without a criminal trial.
Graham Campbell reports

When police officers discovered a small quantity of cannabis at the home of John Reid, (then Defence Secretary, later Home Secretary) this April, the police immediately concluded that neither Dr Reid nor any member of his family was involved in any wrong doing. The possibility that there was anything amiss was considered too preposterous, too unlikely to be taken seriously. Thus as far as John Reid was concerned the matter ended there.

Dr Reid is luckier than he may know. Innocence is no longer a protection from punishment. As Home Secretary he should have taken a fresh look at the laws enacted by the government of which he was a member. He would have discovered that an ordinary citizen can, without a criminal trial, be:

■ stripped of their property;
■ deprived of their home;
■ deprived of their livelihood.

Once, the state could only punish a citizen of this country if a criminal offence had been proven in a criminal court. Criminal courts could only convict on evidence that reached the criminal standard of proof. Serious offences were tried by juries. Most importantly, citizens were innocent unless found guilty.

Recent legislation has made huge inroads into these principles. Safeguards against arbitrary power have gone. A citizen who is no more than suspected of a crime can be punished.

Recovery Orders

We are all familiar with orders that the courts can make confiscating property from convicted drug offenders. The Proceeds of Crime Act 2002 introduced a legal device which allows the state to seize the property of a citizen who has not been convicted of any offence.

This device is called the "recovery order". The Assets Recovery Agency can apply to the High Court for a recovery order to obtain "property obtained through unlawful conduct". This section is deliberately aimed at the innocent. There is no need for any criminal trial. These powers can be exercised "... whether or not any proceedings have been brought for an offence in connection with the property ".

The High Court can only make a recovery order if it is satisfied that property has been obtained through unlawful conduct. That issue is decided to the civil standard of proof; on a balance of probabilities.

So here we have the government seizing the property of the individual, after a finding of unlawful conduct. All that is missing are the safeguards of trial by jury and proof beyond reasonable doubt. The state has the power to punish the innocent.

However it does not end there. The statute has given wide ancillary powers that are, in themselves, oppressive.

Interim Receivers

Before the High Court has made any finding of unlawfulness, The Asset Recovery Agency can apply for the appointment of a receiver to take possession of all or part of the property of the suspected person. All that is required is a "good arguable case" that property will be made the subject of a recovery order.

The powers of the receiver, which are in Schedule 6 of The Proceeds of Crime Act, are very wide. He or she can seize the property, ask questions, enter premises to search and seize property, sell any perishable assets, appoint someone to manage any business seized, or incur capital expenditure.

There is no need for any criminal prosecution, trial or conviction. The order is made by the High Court. The innocent citizen (innocent because unconvicted of any offence) is deprived of control of his or her own property.

Freezing Orders

The Serious Organised Crime Act 2005 has introduced a new power to be used in conjunction with recovery orders. In advance of any finding, even in advance of issue of any application, the court can freeze all the assets of the citizen.

As with interim receivers, an arguable case that the property will be "recoverable" is enough. The court can allow the citizen access to funds and property for the purpose of financing legal representation and cost of living. But, again, an innocent citizen is deprived of his or her property, without prosecution, trial or conviction.

Production Orders

Where a recovery order is contemplated, the courts can now make a 'production' order requiring a citizen to grant access to private property and hand over or give access to property set out in the production order.

No-one would complain about the police having the power to search private property and to seize

anything found there as part of a criminal investigation. But these powers can be granted by the court even when there is no intention to prosecute anyone. The essential safeguards against state oppression (trial by peers and conviction only where there is no reasonable doubt), have gone.

Customer Information Orders & Account Monitoring Orders

If a recovery order is contemplated against a citizen, the courts have the power to make a "Customer Information Order" and an "Account Monitoring Order". The first of these requires any financial institution to disclose details of any bank account held by a named person. Again, criminal proceedings need not even be contemplated.

"Account Monitoring Orders" require the financial institution to provide 'any information' including details of transactions, about any account that the suspect has.

All these powers can be exercised against a citizen who has not been convicted of any offence. He might have been acquitted or it may be that there is no intention to prosecute him. Innocence under the criminal law is irrelevant.

Closure Notices and Closure Orders

Introduced by the Anti-Social Behaviour Act 2003 these give the police power, if they consider premises have been used for use, production or supply of Class A drugs, to forbid access to premises by anyone other than the habitual resident. This may seem to make sense for a drug den on an inner city estate. But the language of the section applies equally to shops, offices and homes (even those belonging to Cabinet Ministers).

It matters not that the owner of the building, or anyone resident there, was unaware of the criminal activity. If a Police Superintendent or above has reasonable grounds for believing that premises have been used in connection with unlawful

use, production or supply of a Class A drug and that the use of the premises is connected with disorder or serious nuisance to members of the public, a closure order can be issued.

This section can be used to close down shops and businesses, depriving people of their livelihood. The ordinary citizen is prevented from inviting family and friends to his or her home. No court order is needed. Police suspicion is enough.

This power is aimed at the innocent. Section 1(8) of the Anti-Social Behaviour Act 2003 states "It is immaterial whether any person has been convicted of an offence relating to the use, production or supply of a controlled drug." The owner of the premises need not have done anything unlawful. Suspicion that the premises have been used by someone for use, production or supply of a Class A drug is enough.

The police must apply to the magistrate's court for a "closure order", and this application must be heard within 48 hours. Closure orders can forbid anyone (including habitual residents) from going to the premises. Again, this power is aimed at the innocent. Conviction of an offence is immaterial. The owner, occupier or any resident of the premises need not be guilty of anything.

Again, this may sound OK if you are thinking of a person who knowingly turns a blind eye to what is going on in their property, but what of the person who genuinely doesn't know? And remember, no jury will ever be invited to decide this point.

All these provisions are an unjustified encroachment on the rights of ordinary citizens. They are aimed at people who have been convicted of nothing. The law has dispensed with the need for a tiresome and expensive criminal trial. We all want to see criminals deprived of the profits of their crimes; but this is not the way. If the state cannot prove guilt beyond reasonable doubt, the citizen should not be punished.

Counsel August 2006

Prison doesn't work – but there is another way to tackle criminals

An answer to the lock 'em up brigade?

It was Michael Howard who famously proclaimed that "prison works." He was wrong and he probably knew it at the time, but it played well to the mob at the 1993 Tory Party conference.

by ADAM TAYLOR

The phrase "restorative justice works" does not play so well to the crowds, but that doesn't mean that it isn't true.

The UK prison population is now at a record high and the public, led by the media and the shadow home secretary, want more prison places.

At 146 prisoners in every 100,000 citizens, the UK incarceration rate is now almost 50 per cent greater than the 106 per 100,000 average of the 15 states of the pre-enlargement European Union. Among the newest members in eastern Europe, the rate is above 150 per 100,000.

These are dwarfed by figures for police states such as Russia or the US, where almost 1,000 in 100,000 residents is incarcerated. Significantly, this has still not stopped chronic levels of crime.

Concepts of criminal justice tend to be stereotyped into two, mutually exclusive, models. On the one hand, there is the "hanging's too good for 'em, lock 'em up and throw away the key" brigade. On the other, there is the "criminals are victims of society" line.

Even the more sensible voices on the left may be partly missing the point. Getting "tough on crime, tough on the causes of crime" smacks of a macro versus micro approach, with a progressive attitude on wider social cohesion issues, but leaving criminal justice itself to tough-talking populism, "zero-tolerance" policing and a burgeoning prison population.

But it is possible to be tough on crime without having to revert to the expensive populism of reliance on prisons and "law enforcement" alone. Restorative justice aims to ensure that the victim feels that the injustice done to them has been redressed, while at the same time, engaging with the offender.

This is achieved by bringing an offender and his victim together in a managed environment and forcing the offender to face the harm that he has done to another person.

According to Thames Valley Police Chief Constable Sir Charles Pollard, who is a pioneer of restorative justice in the British criminal justice system, many offenders are ignorant, rather than indifferent to the

'It's possible to be tough on crime without reverting to prisons and enforcement alone.'

harm they are causing. Restorative justice, he argues, can be something of a revelation for offenders who have never really realized the human cost of their actions, reducing the likelihood of reoffending among habitual criminals.

Recent research from Cambridge University has suggested that this effect is particularly powerful with adult offenders.

Independent research by the Justice Research Consortium published by the Home Office in 2006 has shown generally positive results in both terms of victim participation and offender outcomes.

The JRC research revealed that, despite the vengeful emphasis of the media, victim participation in the scheme is high, particularly with young offenders. In the 217 conferences observed, 60 per cent of offenders showed remorse for their action's, while only 11 per cent admitted little or no responsibility.

Critics of restorative justice argue that it is a potentially soft option for intelligent criminals able to feign remorse in front of the victim as an easy alternative to prison. Davis, just such a critic, has argued that the restorative justice system is administered by "middle-class girls in their early twenties," who, he implied, are too naïve to be able to spot real remorse or implement the restorative system effectively.

While Davis's potentially sexist remarks may be dismissed as polemic, it must be accepted that poorly managed restorative justice could be abused by some offenders.

The JRC pilot incorporated "outcome agreements," lists of two to six measures to rehabilitate the offender such as bringing drug or alcohol addiction under control, to get a job or gain qualifications. These lists were agreed by the offender, the victim and other people involved and, six months later it was found that 88 per cent of these agreements had been completely or partly implemented.

These results suggest that the potential for "getting tough of the causes of crime" within the criminal justice system itself should not by dismissed lightly, especially when extrapolated and compared with the reoffending rates of Davis's preferred populist option – long prison sentences.

Unlike building prisons, restorative justice is an evidence-based policy. The Home Office is, theoretically, committed to it. However, the government continues to drift toward ever more popularist authoritarian criminal justice polices, with Home Secretary John Reid playing to the mob in a way that would make David Blunkett blush.

If the phrase hadn't already been taken, we could expect a Labour home secretary to be bellowing "prison works" at this year's party conference.

Adam Taylor is a political commentator affiliated to the University of Warwick and the European University Institute, Florence

Morning Star 15 February 2007

The Observer 11 March 2007

Free after 36 years:

the man who was left to rot in Broadmoor

Bill Collins tells the *Independent on Sunday* how his four-year prison sentence for assault turned into a life wasted in a secure hospital

By David Cohen and Sophie Goodchild

At the age of 19, Bill Collins attacked his girlfriend. He was found guilty of wounding her and sent to prison. It was 1962. He should have been out after four years. Instead he ended up in Broadmoor, where he spent 36 years of his life.

He never denied hurting his girlfriend or complained about being punished. "I was completely miserable," he says now, "but what I did was terrible." What happened to him after he was sent from prison to Britain's most notorious mental hospital was even more terrible. "In Broadmoor I was bashed and tortured, and wasted so much of my life."

He now fears others may be locked up for long periods in secure hospitals for lesser offences than he committed under mental health legislation that is expected to get a savaging in the House of Lords tomorrow.

A series of amendments has been put forward by peers who are furious that ministers have failed to heed their warnings that the Bill will stop people seeking help. The nine changes tabled include the stipulation that patients should be forced into treatment only if they do not have the mental ability to make a decision for themselves and that people suffering from autism should not be targeted.

The strong cross-party support for the changes means that ministers may be forced either to rethink or discard many of their more draconian measures. The Mental Health Alliance, whose members include the Law Society and Mind, said the Government must listen to the concerns of peers, psychiatrists and patients.

> **"In Broadmoor I was bashed and tortured, and wasted so much of my life."**

Broadmoor has housed many of the most difficult and dangerous people in the UK

"What was laid before Parliament last month is not, in our view, a truly balanced Bill. It will neither promote civil rights nor make the public safer," said Andy Bell, chair of the Alliance.

Bill Collins was first sent to Wakefield Prison, where he studied botany and biology. "But I messed up." He attacked a civilian instructor. A few weeks later, Mr Collins was driven to Broadmoor. And the system forgot he had been sentenced to only four years. He recalls: "The nurses asked me if I wanted to do it the hard way or the easy way. I asked if doing it the easy way would mean compromising my integrity. They replied: 'We know which way you want to do it.'"

Broadmoor has housed many of the most difficult and dangerous people in the UK, including the serial killers Peter Sutcliffe or Dennis Nilsen. But in the 1960s not all of the most violent people were inmates. In the 1970s news leaked of nurses assaulting patients – a practice nicknamed the "boot treatment". The "wet towel"

treatment was worse; patients were strangled almost to death with a wet towel. A few sex offenders were given female hormones and developed breasts. One man had to have a breast removed because the treatment went badly wrong.

Mr Collins admits he could be difficult sometimes. So he often got kicked and beaten by nurses. In 1967, three of them broke his arm deliberately.

For many years, Mr Collins's responsible medical officer was Broadmoor's boss, the medical superintendent Dr Patrick McGrath, father of the novelist, also called Patrick, who wrote Asylum. "I often asked him to take me off my medication because it caused me so much pain and so many side effects," Mr Collins said. He has lost most of his teeth, for example. "Don't nag me, Bill," Dr McGrath replied. "I'll take you off when you're ready." It took more than 35 years for psychiatrists to decide Mr Collins could do without the drugs.

In 2000 Mr Collins was released to

Thornford Park, a medium-and low-secure unit in Thatcham, Berkshire. There, in one of the unit's flats, he learned to live on his own. Since leaving nine months ago, he has tried to get work but he was always turned down. He passed the tests to be a postman but was asked to provide employers' references for the past five years.

He now chairs a self-help group called *Survivors Speak Out*. While in Broadmoor, he won three Koestler prizes for performance of the spoken word. One was a 15-minute show about Isambard Kingdom Brunel. Today he works one day a week at the Brunel Museum.

Speaking from his flat in Clapham, south London, surrounded by a mass of books, Victorian prints, files, general mess and two birdcages, Mr Collins is remarkably sanguine. "The British mental health system is crap," he says. "If I hadn't been behind bars, I'd have been a collector."

The Independent on Sunday 7 January 2007

The war on youth

Crime rates are falling throughout Britain, yet the number of children being prosecuted just keeps on rising. Why are we turning so many young people into criminals?

By *Alice O'Keeffe*

"The police have always been on my case, always stopping and searching me… they lost me a job as well": Jason, 17

"I admit that I recklessly ripped Linda's bra strap, causing damage." Fourteen-year-old Musa writes the sentence out painstakingly, signs it and hands it to his solicitor. The atmosphere in the dingy side room at Brent Youth Court is tense: Musa is awaiting a hearing on charges of criminal damage. His offence was to rip the lacy strap of a family friend's £20 bra accidentally during an altercation.

It would be laughable if it weren't so serious. Musa has not had an easy childhood – his father was a drug addict; his parents had an acrimonious divorce. He suffers anxiety attacks, and was crying with worry before coming to court, explains his mother. That's why he decided to confess rather than plead not guilty; anything to avoid the long and stressful wait for another court appearance. He'll get a reprimand, which stays on his police file for life, but as long as he doesn't get arrested again, that will be the end of it. If he does, no matter how small the incident, he'll get his final warning before a mandatory court appearance.

"I do worry that something else will happen," she says. "I've told him: 'Now you know to watch yourself. The smallest thing and you could end up in big trouble.'"

Musa had never been arrested before. He did not injure anyone, and he did not steal anything. In fact, the woman whose bra strap he ripped still stops and chats to Musa's mother in the street. In a more innocent age, he might have been grounded at home, or perhaps ticked off informally by a policeman. But in 21st-century Britain, the behaviour of children – or, more accurately, of working-class children such as Musa – is a criminal matter. As his youth worker observes wryly after we leave the court: "The attitude towards young people seems to be: get them!"

Just for Kids Law, which represents Musa, spends much of its time dealing with cases as petty as his: a 15-year-old arrested for carrying a toy gun home from the shop in a plastic bag; a 12-year-old put through the courts because his friend gave him a copy of the school master key. Another 15-year-old who was caught with a mobile phone that his adult friend had stolen had to make five court appearances, one of which was at an adult court alongside a man being given bail for child pornography offences.

"We are teaching these kids a complete lack of respect for the adult world, because we are treating them so frequently with no respect," says Shauneen Lambe, director of Just for Kids Law. "Police will bang them up against walls as they might with prolific adult offenders. We had one child who was chased down the road with no shoes on until he wore through his socks, and then beaten by the police. What is the point of criminalising all of our young people, so that when they grow up they can't even get a job in the Post Office because they've all got criminal records?"

"I've been in so many children's homes, I've lost count..."

Thomas Pulhofer, 18, is serving a sentence for robbery

Thomas is currently in Norwich Prison. He was in care from the age of eight, in 30 different homes. When he is out of jail he is given £45 a week to live on; in custody, he costs the taxpayer £40,000 a year. He got four GCSEs when he was 14 in a secure unit. He wrote the following while detained at Warren Hill Prison in Suffolk.

"My life has been a struggle from the start I haven't had it easy in any area of life I've got five sisters who I don't really see that much I haven't seen my dad in over 16 years and I've never had a stable relationship with my mum full stop.

"I've been in so many children's homes that I have lost count I've been every corner of the country one time or another jail has been like a second home for me I've been seven times my first sentence was 18 months and my second sentence was 18 months I was only 11 when I first went to jail orchard lodge was my first destination.

"After a while I got institutionalised and didn't care if I got sent back to prison I took it as a joke there was know way you could punish me I ended up liking prison even when it come to my release date I didn't want to leave certain people would call me a jail cat but I'm not there was just nothing on the other side of those gates that I wanted I can remember the first time I was released from prison I nearly got run over I forgot how to cross the road properly as they had these new trains that went on the same road as what cars went on with know wheels I shit myself I've been Feltham three times Huntercombe twice and orchard lodge twice and now I'm in some prison called Warren Hill it's in Suffolk. I can see the sea out of my cell window that's why it gets too cold at night on the way to the prison there's know street lights all you can see is trees it's right out in the sticks.

"When you're in prison you have a lot of time to think about what your going to do when you get out but when you do get released you forget about that most of the time and go back to your old life you can't help it. I'm not preaching to you because who am I to give advice but if you've been jail before and you come out to the same people you did crime with you will be dragged back into criminal activities I know they're your boys but they're not the one who will be getting sent back to prison you will be I hope [this] helped you understand more about prisons and maybe answered some of your questions it's not a holiday camp in prison it's a ten foot by eight foot wide cell that you spend 23 hours a day of your life in it's not a joke." ●

Crime rates have fallen drastically in Britain over the past ten years, but the number of children going through the criminal justice system just keeps on growing: it stands at 210,000 annually, up from 185,000 in the mid-1990s. In the past, most of those who come into contact with the system were given cautions. Now, half are prosecuted. With more than 3,000 under-18s in prison and juvenile detention centres bursting at the seams, Britain has one of the most punitive youth criminal justice systems of any democratic country.

Rod Morgan, chair of the Youth Justice Board, the government body that oversees the juvenile system in England and Wales, is "very preoccupied" with the situation, which he says needs "urgent attention". He has been lobbying the Home Office, but his criticisms are falling on deaf ears. "There is a good deal of political pressure to stick with the tough talk," he says. "The government has nailed its colours to the mast." John Reid has not met with Morgan since becoming Home Secretary; with terrorists to catch and immigrants to deport, child welfare seems low on his list of priorities.

Anxiety about the behaviour of young people is nothing new. According to Barry Goldson, professor of criminology at Liverpool University, children have always occupied an uneasy place in British culture. "The Jamie Bulger case was a very significant turning point in our view of young people – it came to represent all kinds of concerns about childhood being in crisis, and the moral health of the nation," he says. "But if you look deeper, you see that children have a troubled role in the British psyche. In continental Europe, young people are welcome to join in adult social life; they fit comfortably into society. That is not the case here."

Under new Labour, however, this anxiety has become institutional. Amid the rhetoric of "tackling social exclusion", ever greater emphasis has been placed upon early intervention in the lives of "problem" children. As a result of reforms introduced since 1997, the criminal justice system deals with young people more punitively than it does with adults. The police have no discretion in dealing with juvenile cases: an adult who offends can be cautioned an indefinite number of times; a child is allowed only two reprimands (the juvenile equivalent of a caution) before prosecution. If an adult is caught with cannabis, he or she will be dealt with informally; a child committing the same offence will be arrested. In effect, children are expected to be better behaved and more responsible than their parents.

In a more innocent age they might have been ticked off informally by a policeman

The imbalance has been compounded by the introduction of government targets for "offences brought to justice". The police are expected to bring 1.25 million cases to justice every year. So far they are well ahead of their target – and not because the number of adult convictions has increased. Children are easy to catch, because their crimes are generally committed in the streets and other public places, and their cases are easy to process. Morgan says that, for the police, arresting children is like "picking low-hanging fruit".

I talked to several teenagers in Kent, London and Essex and all of them were used to being stopped and searched by the police. "I can't remember how many times it has happened. It started when I was about 14," said one 16-year-old. "They make you empty your pockets. They check to see if your phone is stolen. Sometimes they're polite, but sometimes they're pretty rough. Of course you get pissed off, but what are you going to do? You can't make a fuss because you'll get nicked." Another boy told me that a common where teenagers congregate in his town is constantly monitored by policemen in plain clothes. "They come over and search us all the time. We made the front page of the paper when we left a few beer bottles lying on the grass." The Home Office compiles exhaustive statistics on the ethnicity of people who are stopped and searched, but it does not keep any record of the number of children.

Politics of prison

So, will this new punitiveness create a generation of well-behaved, law-abiding citizens? The evidence is that it is likely to have quite the reverse effect. The most wide-ranging study of the effectiveness of early intervention by the criminal justice system, the Edinburgh Study of Youth Transitions and Crime, has tracked 4,300 children over eight years. It has come up with two main findings: first, that working-class children are more likely to come into contact with the criminal justice system regardless of whether or not they actually offend more; and second, that those who do have contact with the criminal justice system are less likely to stop offending than those who do not.

"The message is that doing nothing is often the most effective way to prevent reoffending," says Lesley McAra, who is conducting the study. "But politically, that is obviously a very difficult message."

Politically, it is easier to carry on filling up Britain's jails with young people who will come out more likely to reoffend than they were before they went in. The Home Office would not arrange a visit to a juvenile centre

"If they could put me in prison, they would"

Jason, 17, was arrested for using the word "nigga"

Jason is one of only a few mixed-race kids in his area, a sleepy market town in Essex. On his 16th birthday, he and a friend were stopped and searched by the police on their way home. He said to the policeman, "Let's get on with it, nigga." He was arrested for a public order offence (using the word "nigga"), despite the fact that he was the only black person present. At a court hearing he was found guilty and sentenced to community service. He later appealed, and the conviction was overturned.

"It was my first time in court, but I was feeling confident. The whole way through I thought I was going to win, because the whole thing seemed so ridiculous. Then they found me guilty. I couldn't believe it.

"Since I won the appeal, the police don't hassle me as much as they did. They don't talk to me like I'm a piece of scum because they know that I can put forth an argument, and they don't expect that of someone like me. But I have to watch myself, because I know that if they've got the smallest chance to put me in prison, they will do it. I haven't got white skin, blue eyes, blonde hair. I haven't got a stiff back and stiff upper lip. I'm different, and they don't like it.

"They've always been on my case, always stopping and searching me. They drag you off to Braintree, or to Stansted Airport, and put you in the cells, and then give you a lift home. Once I borrowed my friend's BMX. The cops pulled me over and the next thing I know I'm sitting in the cells in Stansted accused of stealing it.

"But I've learned my rights now, so I send them running for my paper and pen, or a cup of water.

"They lost me a job as well. The police kept coming into the restaurant, saying they wanted to talk to me – they came in three, four, five times and eventually the manager didn't give me any more work.

"I was bad for business." ●

 for me, but organised instead for me to go to Rochester Young Offenders' Institution, which houses 392 prisoners between the ages of 18 and 21.

As these places go, Rochester is a model institution: the imposing former borstal is not overcrowded, and on the day of my visit, the sun is shining on the pleasant Kent countryside beyond the barbed-wire fence. The governor, John Wilson, greets me genially with a volley of information about "action plans", "access to employment" courses and "prisoner management guidelines". He is more reticent about the wider implications of his work. "The responsibility of a prison is to take into custody those who are sent to us by the courts. Taking a view on whether or not they should be here in the first place is a political issue."

I am taken to meet a classroom of young men learning how to "disclose" their criminal records to employers. "We try to teach them how to talk about their time in prison in a positive way," explains the teacher. "So instead of trying to cover it up or lie about it, you talk about the courses you have been on, and how much you've changed from since you started offending." One boy shows me the statement he has prepared for his first job interview: "I have a conviction for robbery. I was homeless and had problems with drugs and alcohol at the time. I am confident that my life has moved on..."

Those selected for the class are nearing the end of their sentences, thinking about getting their lives back together. "It's very, very hard to break out of the cycle if you've been here for a long time," says Imani, a bright, highly motivated 19-year-old. "You have to be very strong to leave jail and not be tempted. You meet so many connections, people who could easily smuggle drugs ... It's very hard – that's why so many people here come back to jail."

The atmosphere is quite different on E-Wing, where those with less freedom of association spend their days. The long, straight corridor with cell doors evenly spaced along its length is a sight familiar from the television news. The eerie thing is the silence: there are more than a hundred young people in here, but there is no talking, no shouting, no laughter. The sound of muffled R'n'B emanates from one or two of the cells, but other than that the only evidence of life is a photograph stuck to each door: young faces, unsmiling, mostly black.

I am shown into a cell, which is only a few centimetres wider than the thin, single bed. This cramped space seems to sum up something about being young in 21st-century Britain: no room to move or grow; no room to be naughty, or to be forgiven.

Names have been changed.
www.justforkidslaw.org
New Statesman 16 October 2006

UNDER AGE SEX

or RAPE?

Sex education takes on a new meaning when a young man is faced with a Crown Court Trial for rape of his girlfriend after her parents discover they have had under age sex, says **Felicity Gerry**

No-one condones young children having sexual intercourse with each other but when a mother discovers her 15 year old son has had consensual sexual intercourse with his 12 year old (but more mature) girlfriend at the girlfriend's house with her positive encouragement (and using a condom) the mother might be concerned, angry and disappointed. She would consider her son to have been stupid. She would not think him a rapist and would not imagine that his name could be added to what has become known as the "Sex Offenders Register".

Should there be a prosecution?

Section 5 of the Sexual Offences Act 2003 makes it an offence of **rape** to have sexual intercourse with a girl under the age of 13, **regardless** of consent. The boy finds himself before the Crown Court. The girl suffers no more than a parental reaction and a trip to the video interviewing suite. The boy might well be guilty in law but should he be prosecuted?

The answer to this question depends on the approach of the individual Crown Prosecutor and whether all parties have all the

The boy's name will be added to the Sex Offenders Register

relevant background information on the children involved. In the brave new world of "CPS Direct" where the police seek advice on charge from an absent Crown Prosecution Service lawyer, by telephone who may not even be in the county, the chances of an informed decision are extremely limited and anecdotal evidence suggests that the charging of young people for having underage sex is on the increase (other criminal charges exist where the sexual partner is over 13).

Consider all the circumstances

Crown Prosecutors should consider all the circumstances surrounding the offence and the circumstances of the youth **before** reaching a decision to prosecute. Factors include the home and social circumstances of the alleged offender, the manner in which matters were brought to the attention of the police and the views of the "victim" involved. These factors determine how the public interest is satisfied.

In a recent decision the Court of Appeal held that to prosecute a 15 year old boy for section 5 rape (even though it was accepted that he believed the girl to be 13 at the time) was not a breach of Article 6 of the European Convention on Human Rights. His initial 12 month sentence was varied to a conditional discharge. He had been in custody for five months awaiting his appeal hearing.

However, in the same case, the Court of Appeal did not rule out that the prosecution of a child could, on other particular facts, produce consequences that amounted to an interference with the child's rights that were not justified. Short of both children being under 13 one wonders what those circumstance would be?

Sex and Alcopops

How much worse does the situation get for a boy when a girl lies about her age and fills herself up with alcopops?

There may be compelling reasons not to blight the lives of either child involved in the act of what amounts to under age sex. If there are such reasons but the Crown continues to pursue the matter, an application for judicial review of the decision can be made.

In a similar case in which I defended, the defendant might well have been guilty in law but, after leave was given by the High Court on an application for judicial review, the Crown took the sensible decision to offer no evidence on the basis that it was not in the public interest to pursue the matter. This decision was plainly in accordance with the CPS legal guidance, published on their website www.cps.gov.uk which declared that prosecutors may exercise more discretion where the defendant is a child and that the overriding public concern is to protect children. "It was not parliament's intention to punish children unnecessarily or for the criminal law to intervene where it is wholly inappropriate." It may well also have been dictated by the willingness or otherwise of the girl to give evidence against someone who was hitherto her boyfriend.

As to what is or is not appropriate sexual conduct between children seems to be no longer just a question for parents but has become an integral decision in the youth justice system.

Counsel November 2006

The rise and rise of the single woman...

MARRIED AT 25

Chloe Rhodes
Aged 27
Rhodes had known her boyfriend for 11 years before they married: she knew he was Mr Right

AS OF yesterday, I am officially part of a minority group: married women. And, as my wedding took place three months after my 25th birthday, it seems I am even more of an oddity, because for twentysomethings, marriage is apparently going out of fashion.

But though this survey has me down as a bit of a freak, yesterday's statistics are not as clear cut as they look – the numbers of "single" women include divorcées, widows and those who may be planning to marry, as well as those who never have. What is clear though is that women are waiting longer before they make that step. In the early Seventies, 85 per cent of women were married by the time they were 30, now, fewer than one woman in three is married by that age.

And yet, I can't think of a single friend who would choose to remain unmarried once they had found the right partner. My girlfriends were thrilled when I told them I was engaged and when we talk about the prospect of their getting married, they unfalteringly use the word when, not if.

In my experience, women in their twenties are just as eager to get down the aisle as their grandmothers were – and because we are so utterly free from the

As new statistics show that there are fewer married women than singles, one of our writers explains why marriage is right for her, while another reveals why she won't be 'married alive' again as she approaches her forties

social pressures that forced them into marriage, we often do it for better reasons.

When I decided to get married there had been no disapproving relatives muttering about the perils of living in sin. In fact, our parents thought we'd been sensible to wait until we'd lived together before we tied the knot. I'm not religious so I didn't have to worry about being made an honest woman and I certainly didn't marry to guarantee financial security. I loved the idea of getting married partly because I knew I didn't have to.

In fact, social expectations seem to have swung so far away from tradition that when I tell people in their thirties that I'm married, they seem to find it as shocking as their

great-grandparents would have found an illegitimate child. But my friends have watched the Bridget Jones generation stay single – and we've decided we don't need to do the same.

The fact is – for me, being married is wonderful. I had been with my boyfriend for 11 years by the time we made our vows; I knew, absolutely, that he was the man for me and marrying him felt like a natural rite of passage.

I have given away none of my freedoms in exchange for the ring on my finger, I am financially independent (though he does tend to buy the drinks), I have a career that I love and I have just as many girly nights out as I always have done.

Had I been born in a time when marriage would have made me the property of my husband, or diminished my status as an individual, I would certainly have felt compelled to take a stand against it – and I like to think I would have remained a spinster as a gesture of defiance.

There are plenty of institutions that are still bastions of male privilege, but marriage isn't one of them. And when you strip away all the outdated bad bits, all that's left is a celebration of love between two people and a declaration of devotion to each other.

I didn't get married for security or a sign of commitment, I had those things already. My husband and I don't need to be married at all, the beauty of it is – we just want to be.

SINGLE AT 39

Julia Stephenson
Aged 39
Married in haste at 24, Stephenson yearned to escape and now revels in her freedom

I'VE BEEN married and I've been single – and I know which side of the fence I'd rather be on.

It's no surprise to me that the Office for National Statistics has revealed that there are more single, divorced and widowed women than wives in England and Wales. But how times have changed since I got married at the age of 24. That was 15 years ago. I was longing for a ring on my finger, and most of my girlfriends were gasping to wed, too. We believed marriage would be a guarantee of security, commitment and unconditional love. How wrong we were! Let my tale be a warning to any Bridget Jones pining for Mr Right.

I married my first boyfriend, a steady, dependable accountant, and moved out of the chaotic London home I shared with two girlfriends, to a large house in the countryside. I'm a city girl, but for some bizarre reason I thought it would be great to move to the middle of a dank wood and grow vegetables. As my vegetables wilted and died in the acid soil, so did my marriage.

Yet I felt compelled to become a domestic goddess – and was sucked into the competitive dinner party circuit with my husband's golfing cronies and their gym-honed wives. I would spend days preparing these feasts. Most people think that the Galloping Gourmet – the Seventies cookery writer famous for his extravagant creamy recipes – is dead, but let me tell you, his candle was still burning brightly in the Surrey suburbs then.

As it was, I very soon realised I was Married Alive.

I really tried to make it work for, um, six months. Then I went blonde with grief and bolted back to the big smoke. My thwarted husband was enraged but finally (oh bliss!) the decree nisi was signed and I was free.

There followed a wonderful time of excitable and highly unsuitable living. If you don't get all this out of your system before you marry – which I didn't – you'll spend your days at the kitchen sink fantasising about what you're missing out on. This is why girls must wait until they are very old before they settle down, so they are sure of what they want. After all, who in their right mind wants security in their twenties? This is a time for feckless fun, binge drinking and unsuitable boyfriends. As for commitment, what a terrible word it is – she was committed to the lunatic asylum; she committed murder. (And if you're gasping for unconditional love buy a dog.)

I don't regret being married. If I hadn't experienced it, I would still be dreaming of my big day, the hideous meringue I was going to wear – and no doubt scaring all the single men in the vicinity to death with my longing to settle down.

My life since my divorce has had its ups and downs, but barely a day goes by without me relishing my freedom. I have no desire for children, or to marry again. Instead I'm free to write novels and articles and pursue my environmental interests.

I'm dating a wonderful man who has no interest in getting married. And having no legal tie makes us behave better and not take one another for granted (well, in theory anyway).

It's wonderful to have love, satisfaction and security in your life – but you don't need to be married for that. We have the zing without the ring.

The Daily Telegraph 20 December 2006
© Telegraph Group Ltd

Paula Hall, a relationship psycho-therapist with Relate, examines the pros and cons of marriage

Good reasons to tie the knot

Bad reasons to tie the knot

❑ Because you're in love. Although love shouldn't be the only reason to marry, it's an important ingredient in the most successful relationships.

❑ To make a commitment. You've decided that you want to be together forever, knowing each other's faults and failings.

❑ It's part of your culture. The ceremony of marriage is an integral part of your cultural or religious beliefs and an essential part of your core value system.

❑ To start a family. You've both enjoyed a secure and committed relationship for some time and feel marriage is the best environment in which to bring up children.

❑ To celebrate. Because you want your family and friends to share in your happiness and commitment as a couple.

❑ It's the right time. You have a solid and secure relationship and it feels like the logical next step.

❑ You may have many more reasons why you want to marry. The most important thing is that you and your partner have fully discussed your reasons and that you're both confident you share the same intentions.

❑ To make your relationship secure. If your relationship isn't secure before you marry, there's no reason to think it will be afterwards. It may be harder for you to separate after marriage, but that doesn't mean you'll be happy.

❑ Fear of being alone. Some people marry because they're scared that no one else will have them. Remember, it's better to be left on the shelf than spend your whole life in the wrong cupboard.

❑ For the children. It's true that, on the whole, children benefit from living with two parents, but marrying purely for your child is unlikely to create a happy home environment.

❑ You want a big wedding. The big white wedding may seem like a fairy tale come true, but it only lasts a day. Marriage is (supposed to be) for life.

❑ To recover from divorce. Some people want a second marriage to help them to get over the first — to prove that they're OK. But those feelings must come from within.

Source: Relate

Japanese men take marriage lessons

By Chris Hogg   BBC Tokyo Correspondent

Japanese men are learning to be better husbands amid speculation that a new law allowing wives to keep half of their partner's pensions if they divorce will spark a rash of marital splits.

It is a cold Saturday evening and I am standing in the rain in Tokyo's entertainment district. Glamorous girls in thigh high boots strut past with barely a backwards glance at the men who cannot take their eyes off them. This is not what I have come to see though.

Instead, I climb the steep stairs to the top floor of a small Izakaya or Japanese pub. Here, a group of 10 men have gathered, to drink, to smoke, to eat and, most importantly, to learn how to save their marriages.

This is the Tokyo chapter of what might best be described as the 'National Chauvinistic Husbands Association'. Its founder, Shuichi Amano, made the long journey up from the southern island of Kyushu for tonight's meeting. He is a large, self-confident man who sits, as befits his status, at the centre of the long table. This is a man comfortable with being the centre of attention.

They begin with a declaration of their three basic rules for love. They chant in unison.

Say thank you without hesitation.
Say sorry without fear.
Say I love you without being ashamed.

People sitting at nearby tables go quiet but then the women give them a round of applause.

The chants begin again. The three basic rules for not winning.

We do not win.
We cannot win.
We do not want to win.

In the battle of the sexes these men are waving a white flag. But are they wimps? The man in charge, Mr Amano, does not think so.

He started the group eight years ago after finding out that three or four of his friends had been told by their wives that they wanted a divorce. When he mentioned this to his wife she told him he might be next. He was shocked.

"I started doing the household chores right away," he told me. This was a new experience for both of them.

At first, his wife was suspicious.

"What have you done wrong?" she said.

But then gradually their relationship improved. He started to share his techniques with other people. Word spread and today he says he has more than 1,200 members across Japan.

Mr Amano says he has created a network where for the first time men can share their problems and advise each other how to solve them. Women

'Gengo is mixing his group therapy with his Samurai work a bit too much for my liking.'

can always find a couple of friends to talk to when things are going wrong, he says. But men, Japanese men especially, find it harder to share their emotional concerns.

Listening to him talk was 28-year-old Yohei Takayama. He has been married just six months, but he told me he had joined the group because he was worried already that his wife might try to divorce him.

'Smileage' points

Why were Japanese men such bad husbands I asked him.

"It's the way of the Samurai," he replied without a smirk or a grin. Traditionally he said, men went out to work, the women stayed at home and kept house. Even today, for many, that is still true. That is a pretty fair description of a lot of Japanese marriages, particularly among the older generations.

But now Yohei, like the others gathered around the table, is employing some of Mr Amano's techniques in a bid to save his marriage.

> ## In the battle of the sexes these men are waving a white flag

He tries to win smileage – one point for every time he makes his wife smile – by doing a good deed, or even cracking a joke with her.

Mr Amano believes if you can build up a smileage total of around forty a month you will have enough credit for coming home drunk once a fortnight, for example.

Towards the end of the evening certificates were presented. The association has 10 levels of attainment, and much like in Sumo wrestling very few reach the highest levels.

The criteria for the different ranks were written out on cards displayed at the end of the table. To be recognised at the lowest rank you have to love your wife after three years of marriage and help with the household chores.

'Earnest efforts'

Mr Amano himself has only reached the fifth level, which you attain when you can hold hands with your wife in public.

The highest or tenth level is reserved for those members who can say *I love you* without embarrassment. It is an accolade many strive for but so far only a tiny proportion of the members has achieved.

It would be easy to poke fun at their earnest efforts to learn behaviour that many others find natural. But the men who had gathered here to learn from their guru seemed as thirsty for his wisdom as they were for the beers.

By nine o'clock though it was time to pack up and go home. When you are out drinking, and learning how to treat your wife well, it does not do to keep her up waiting.

From Our Own Correspondent, BBC Radio 4
31 March 2007

A Childless Future?

A future without children is a prospect that looms so large in Japan that they have invented a word for it – Shoshika.

Japan has one of the lowest birthrates in the world at 1.29 per woman, well below replacement level. The women born during Japan's last baby boom are now in their twenties and thirties, their prime child bearing years, but a record number of them are unmarried and childless. As a consequence, the population of 128 million could drop by 20% by 2050. With people also living longer, one third of that population of 100 million would be over 65, an imbalance which could lead to economic collapse. The fact that every year fewer couples are choosing to marry suggests that measures to slow this decline are not working.

Most developed countries have a declining birthrate, but this is a uniquely Japanese crisis. Japanese women do not feel that their government supports child rearing – 70% want more financial support for education – and they find it especially difficult to combine child rearing with work. Japan spends less than 2% of its GDP on supporting those with children and the expense of bringing up children is quoted as one reason why young people do not marry.

Young women also want to work and enjoy independence but cultural attitudes, which still expect men to work long hours and spend little time at home, mean that there is pressure on women to become full-time mothers. They already face discrimination in the workplace. Many Japanese companies have a policy of hiring women as part time workers, saving money on bonuses and paid holidays, and this is unlikely to change in the face of competition from lower cost countries.

The government has tried, and so far failed, to reverse this trend with 'Angel Plans' which vastly increased the number of nursery places. Now they are prepared to go further, doubling the current child allowance and encouraging companies to decrease working hours for both men and women.

But there may be a more fundamental reason for the absence of children, and one which no government ruling is likely to change: more than a third of Japanese couples do not have sex. Some of the reasons relate to lifestyle – long working hours, long commutes and 'compulsory' socialising with colleagues leave men longing for nothing more than sleep. Women, too, have little leisure time and small, thin-walled apartments mean a lack of privacy which inhibits passion. Poor communication between spouses is also blamed.

Other sources confirm the findings of this government sponsored survey. One survey, found that the Japanese had sex only 45 times a year, less than half the world average, and in an American survey of sexual satisfaction they came last.

The problem may be very deep rooted. A website (http://japanese.about.com/blpod.htm) offering a Japanese phrase to learn every day chose 'marriage and arguments' as the theme for May 2007.

Things start well:

May 1st

" I should start thinking seriously about marriage"

but soon there is disillusion:

May 5th

" This is not what I was led to believe before we got married."

May 7th

" You always use work as an excuse"

May 10th

" I have a right to stay out late once in a while."

Later in the month things have deteriorated badly:

May 22nd

" Leave me alone"

May 24th

" Stop bothering me"

May 26th

" I can't even stand the sight of you!"

It continues despairingly:

May 27th

" Why did we ever get married?"

Yet there is still hope:

May 28th

" He/she is not such a bad person after all."

And by the end of the month there is reconciliation:

May 31st

" I'm really glad I chose him/her as my husband/wife."

Perhaps the childless future – Shoshika – can be averted after all!

*"It's such a shame that **ALL** Keiko's friends are imaginary."*

Sources: various

Can you imagine trusting your parents to find you a partner for life? That's exactly what Rita Zaccarelli, 23, did – and then she fell in love with the man they chose for her

Photo: KEN CEDENO AP/PA Photos

"I MARRIED A VIRTUAL STRANGER"

"Ask my friends to describe me and the word 'shopaholic' may come up. I hope they'd also say 'kind' or 'caring', that I'm good fun on a night out and that they can turn to me when they're in trouble. In short, when you first meet me, I seem like pretty much any other 23-year-old – so you'd probably be surprised to hear that I let my parents choose my husband for me.

"It's not so strange for me, though, as I've grown up with the idea. My mother and father had an arranged marriage. So although they'd never met before they were matched, and come from different countries (Britain and Italy), they've been happy together for 36 years.

"When I was a teenager, my school friends thought the idea was crazy. Although they'd accepted that my family and I were part of the Unification Church, commonly known as Moonies, they couldn't get their heads around the idea that the Reverend Moon, the religion's founder and spiritual leader, could match me with someone I didn't know, who might not even speak the same language.

"They weren't the only ones. My eldest brother and sister had both made it clear that nobody was going to pick their partners, especially after my other sister's arranged marriage had broken down after just four years. We were all upset for her, but I still believed Reverend Moon would do a better job of picking a husband for me than I would myself.

"We were taught that marriage was supposed to be for life, but having experienced crushes on boys that had

"A huge ceremony is held in Korea, where the religion was established"

petered out after a couple of months or even weeks, I had no idea how I'd know for sure when I'd met Mr Right. We saw our match as literally made in heaven, by God, and having someone I trusted make the decision took away a lot of the uncertainty.

"In order to be matched, prospective brides and grooms fill out a questionnaire about themselves and then, depending on age and previous marital status, are put on a particular list. The lists are made available to members in other countries, so there was a real chance I'd end up marrying someone from abroad. Although photos are attached to the forms, matching isn't supposed to be based on looks.

"After I finished my A-levels, I decided to take some time out and travel around Europe, doing charity work with other church members from different countries. There were several groups on the road and everyone was around the same age, so it was a really amazing experience.

"We were travelling through Norway when my mother called to tell me that another set of parents had enquired about me. They were from Spain and their son was called Juan Piqué. She had a good feeling about it and had agreed to meet them in Poland, where a big church event was taking place. She didn't know it, but it turns out we'd already met each other – he was travelling with another group! I'd spoken to him a couple of times and thought he was attractive, but it was strange to think I could be spending the rest of my life with him.

"All the volunteer groups converged in Poland, where my family and Juan's family met. There's only one way to describe the experience – awkward! I was so nervous that I couldn't eat a thing. My mother and his parents chatted away about us while Juan and I stared at the floor. Afterwards, all the parents were really enthusiastic but I just felt confused. My mother said that as far as she was concerned, I was matched. In other words, Juan and I were engaged. Hearing her say that ended my confusion and, even though I was only 19, I felt relieved.

"I'd concentrated so hard on this moment that I hadn't really thought about who I'd be matched with. I felt huge relief that my destiny, as I saw it, had been sorted out. But I still didn't know much about Juan. I knew I had plenty of time to get to know him, though. And, if it turned out that I hated him, I could always back out."

A perfect match

"Before our blessing, we spent a year learning more about each other. We talked on the phone and met whenever our travelling groups were in the same area – about once a month. One of the first things that struck me was his sense of humour, but then I also realized that underneath he was a devoted, loyal person. I knew once we were married he'd be completely committed to making the relationship work. While I get easily stressed, he's very laid-back – definitely a good thing. Our religion meant we couldn't kiss or even hold hands before we were married. It may seem strange to some people but it was actually a huge relief,

as it meant we could get to know each other without intimacy being an issue.

"Even though I really started to like Juan, I still needed time to make sure I knew what I was getting into. Juan, on the other hand, was completely comfortable about it and was more than ready to get married straightaway.

"By the time we actually got a date for our wedding (about a year after we'd been matched), I knew I was doing the right thing. In our church, thousands of couples get married at the same time. A huge ceremony is held in Korea, where the religion was established, and other weddings feed into it via satellite link-up.

"Our blessing was to be held in July 2003. The moment I saw Juan on my wedding day, any lingering doubts disappeared in a flash. It was as if that cheesy thunderbolt had struck us – he looked gorgeous in his suit and, for the first time, I realized I totally fancied him. He couldn't stop saying how beautiful I looked in my dress. It was a very special moment when, after a year, we finally held hands for the first time.

"The ceremony was held in a stadium and tens of thousand of brides and grooms were blessed at the same time. It sounds impersonal but we were so focused on our own marriage that it was actually very romantic. During each blessing, three couples are chosen to go up on the stage with Reverend Moon and be given rings by him. I couldn't believe it when Juan and I were chosen. It made the whole experience extra special."

"Our match has worked better than I ever could have expected"

Falling in love

"Just as our wedding had been a bit different by many people's standards, the start of our married life was hardly traditional, either. Our wedding night was far from the norm – we'd only just held hands, so it would have been a

huge step to suddenly leap into bed together! We stayed up late talking in our hotel, and I felt very close to him, but then I went to my room and Juan went to his.

"We were both still very much involved with our church volunteer work and, for a few months, we had to go our separate ways. Finally, though, we were reunited in Venice and that's when we really fell for each other. Not long after that, we shared our first kiss, although we still agreed not to rush into sleeping together.

"After I spent a holiday with his family in Spain, we decided that Juan would move to London. We'd talked about having separate rooms at my parents' house but after the romantic holiday in Spain, it just didn't work out that way. By then I knew I loved him and he loved me. We slept together about three months after he arrived in London and now we have a great sex life.

"It wasn't all plain sailing, though. I started my degree in psychology at University College London, and was enjoying student life, but Juan wasn't so happy with his course at Goldsmiths, another London college. It was a tough time for both of us and, eventually, Juan decided to take time off from studying and work for the church in Germany. I felt torn; I wanted him to be happy but needed to finish my own degree, so I stayed in the UK.

"We've just celebrated our third anniversary and, although our love is long distance, we feel totally as one. We have a house in London together, which we share with friends, we speak on the phone every day and we see each other as often as possible. Our match has worked better than I ever could have expected – we're very happy.

"There's only one more thing I need to do – as our blessing wasn't legally binding, we need to seal it with a registry office ceremony in this country. We've wanted to do this for ages, but we'd like to have a big party and can't afford it at the moment. So I can't truly, legally describe Juan as my husband, but our blessing is more binding than any contract – we intend to be together forever".

Cosmopolitan October 2006
© The National Magazine Company Ltd

Inspiration or affliction?

Award-winning pianist Nick van Bloss suffers from Tourette's syndrome. Music was his only release from the debilitating symptoms. But when they struck mid-performance at a competition in 1993, he walked off stage and has never played in public since. Ironically, Tourette's may have been the root of his talent in the first place, as he tells **Sally Palmer**

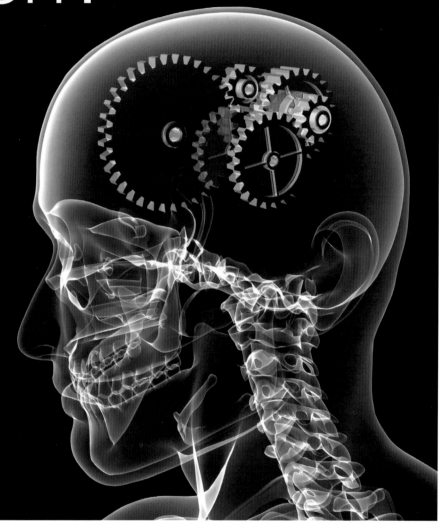

How does Tourette's affect your daily life?

I've had to adopt Tourette's as being a lifestyle in itself. Tourette's *is* me, it defines me. Everything I do is in a sense fuelled by and geared towards Tourette's. Some of it comes out in very positive ways and motivates me, gives me a sense of humour and a bursting personality. It's as if things are being thrust out of me; thoughts and ideas which other people often find a bit difficult to handle. On the other hand, there's a very negative side; while I'm functioning perfectly normally in the world, I'm in inner turmoil because all my muscles are attacking me, all the time – even now as we speak.

Is it more painful when you control the symptoms or when you tic?

It's a double-edged sword, because it's painful to control and it's very painful to tic as well. If I let go and tic as I want to if I am on my own, it's exhausting. It's like doing aerobic activity all the time, and I really think that's why I'm trim, because I eat like an absolute pig. Day-to-day, I'm living life to the Tourette's rhythm. It dictates very much what it wants, when it wants it and I have to obey.

■ WHAT IS TOURETTE'S

It's not all about swearing

Tourette's syndrome is a neurological disorder named after 19th century French neurologist Gilles de la Tourette. Symptoms include muscular tics, grunts and yelps. Coprolalia, the compulsion to swear, is present in fewer than fifteen per cent of sufferers. Tourette's is hereditary, although environmental factors are also involved.

■ TOURETTE'S AND CREATIVITY

Are Tourette's sufferers more creative? Does their brain's chemical make-up influence their abilities?

Most of us feel curious when we experience anything new for the first time. We explore it, assessing it for potential danger or use. If it's neither dangerous nor useful, we ignore it, which is how we stop ourselves from becoming overwhelmed with new information.

"The learned irrelevancy of things is called 'latent inhibition'," says Jordan Peterson, a clinical psychologist at the University of Toronto in Canada. Peterson says there's a link between latent inhibition and creativity. "Artists have low latent inhibition, so all things are new for them," he says. "Artists strip off the latent inhibition from familiar objects and remind you what something was like the first time you encountered it".

He also sees a connection between low latent inhibition and brain levels of the chemical dopamine, which makes people feel exploratory and energetic. Dopamine levels are heightened in people with disorders such as schizophrenia. Tourette's has also been linked to dopamine levels in the brain.

Current research puts Tourette's syndrome down to brain abnormalities in the frontal lobes and the cortex, in circuits that connect these regions and in some of the chemical signals, particularly dopamine.

Some research suggest that Tourette's brain may be super sensitive to normal levels of dopamine, others that it may produce extra dopamine.

Peterson adds: "You can't say creativity comes as a consequence of low latent inhibition. It's just that low inhibition allows for an increased inflow of information. It's the mapping of the inflow, the adapting to it, that is really the creative part."

What forms do your tics take?

All the ranges of flexing, contorting, pulling, pushing, shaking and almost putting my neck out of joint – I often wear a neck collar just to hold my head up. It really hurts, but I have to do it. I hit myself on the forehead with my knuckle and count how many times I do it. Last night was about 2000 times, very hard, while I was doing Su Doku. I also have vocal tics which are usually nonsensical utterances. The sounds I make vary. They could be oohs, aahs, grunts or shrieks, but my Tourette's doesn't make me swear. I try my best to keep the verbal tics as soft as possible, as they do shock people, but I always have to let some run their natural course at some point and explode loudly – sometimes very loudly.

Does your Tourette's have any other mental or emotional effects?

I see and hear much more detail than most people. Most people have filters, but with me, unfortunately, it's the opposite. As we sit in this coffee shop talking, I'm cataloguing and counting all the details of everyone who is in here. I know the people in the corner are speaking about someone who had an illicit affair, because every word is shrieking out. I also have this phenomenal memory. In a year's time, I'll still remember where they were sitting and what they were doing, it's total recall. So that's the thing about Tourette's – it gifts you and it also afflicts you, I can't work out whether it's a good or bad thing.

Have you always had Tourette's?

It began when I was seven [he's now 39]. Even though it is genetic, it generally comes out between about age seven and 11. I do remember being this normal boy who didn't have it, because the contrast was so sudden. One day I was fine and the next I wasn't. And of course, no one knew what it was, and I didn't know what it was. I wanted it to go away.

When did you first realise that the piano could help you?

The piano came into my life at twelve, which is late – most pianists start aged three or four. I went to the piano because I love touching and counting, and saw a number of keys, black and white, which are evenly spaced and I found them very touchable. I developed rapidly, and it was my haven, my solace. It was somewhere I could escape, because not only was I getting constant touch, chemicals were also being released in my brain to stop the tics while I played. That is really common with Tourette's. When you use 100 per cent concentration, the tics stop. Mind you, it's exhausting to keep up that level of concentration. But I could do it for 14 hours at one go.

Do you get the same release from typing at a computer, or playing other instruments?

No. But maybe that's because I can never write creatively at a computer, although I do type very fast. The blank screen always stares defiantly back and I have to fill it. I tried other instruments at music college, but nothing gave me the satisfaction of the piano.

What happened when your Tourette's came out at a competition in 1993?

It was a big international piano competition in Spain, with a huge panel of judges. I was through to the third round and I was playing marvellously. But suddenly I was aware of all the lights on me, and I felt the tic energy coming. I wanted to jerk my head and to tense my arms, and you can't do that and coordinate a musical passage. I was fumbling around on the piano, panicking. I could feel something that I had never felt when I played the piano. My hands flew up and stayed flexed. And my head spun round. I remember I froze because it was the last thing I had expected and the most unwelcome. I heard a gasp through the auditorium – it was very dramatic – and I just stood up and walked off.

How did it affect you?

The fact that Tourette's entered my performing world shattered my confidence, not only because I was hoping to develop an international career, but also because the piano was my safe haven, it was something I could do. At the piano, I wasn't the self-conscious, ugly, bullied boy with an affliction. People liked my playing, I knew I could do it well. And I thought, now I can't even do this. Other people said, we understand, we all forget a piece. But I hadn't forgotten, I don't forget because of the wonderful memory. I remember just saying, "OK, Tourette's, you win" It was the dirtiest trick I think a neurological complaint could play.

How do you feel about your Tourette's now?

Tourette's gifted me with a tremendous talent for music, but it also hindered and utterly broke me at the same time. It took years – until I wrote my book [*Busy Body: my life with Tourette's* Fusion, 2006] – for me to finally accept myself as a person with Tourette's and to turn the tables so my Tourette's now works for me again and not against me.

Do you think you will ever play in public again?

The harsh reality is that I probably won't. But I'd like to record. Now that time has passed, I feel I've still got something in me to give. Especially Bach. I adore Bach. It sings to me at a level that stimulates almost every cell in my body.

Focus March 2007

■ TREATING TOURETTE'S

Electrodes have been implanted into the brains of sufferers with some surprising effects.

William (whose name has been changed to maintain patient confidentiality) has severe Tourette's syndrome. He has fractured his foot from stamping repeatedly on the floor and injured his wrist from hitting it against his computer keyboard. He is blind in one eye because he has jerked his head so hard he has detached his retina.

Sufferers can suppress tics, but only temporarily. After a period of suppression, the tics are usually worse when they return. Medication can help, though some people prefer not to take it because some drugs can produce side effects.

In 2002, William had a revolutionary treatment to try and alleviate some of his symptoms: two electrodes were implanted into his brain. In 2006, he had two more.

Deep brain stimulation from electrodes has previously been used on patients with Parkinson's disease to help reduce the shaking. Just 30 Tourette's sufferers have had the treatment to date. The electrodes are placed deep inside the brain beside the thalamus, which controls movement. They send high-frequency electrical signals through the brain in an attempt to control the spasmodic movements.

The electrodes have helped William's symptoms, but there has been an added unusual side effect. When current is applied from the electrodes to particular points in his brain, he finds himself more irritable and hyperactive, but also awash with creative ideas.

William was already a creative person before the electrodes, but the change has been dramatic. His neurologist, Alice Flaherty from Harvard University, thinks the extra creativity stems from increased activity in the brain's frontal lobes. "The frontal lobes are very important for producing language, action and ideas," she says. "Brain imaging studies show more activity in the frontal lobes of highly creative people than non-creative people."

A Pool of Ignorance

Georgina Wakefield's son has schizophrenia and attracts unwelcome attention even in the swimming pool

One afternoon my son, Christian said to me: "Mum, while I was swimming today one of the lifeguards called me over and said, 'You're in here a lot, mate.' I told him the truth and said, 'I'm recovering from a mental illness'. I explained I'd stayed in bed all day for a year, but was feeling better now and wanted to build up my muscles". Alarm bells went off in my head, when I voiced my concerns to his father he assured me the lifeguard was just being friendly.

The following morning, Chris went swimming while I was a work. My phone rang. When I answered, the line was silent. Then I heard heavy sobs. It was hard to understand what Chris was saying because his teeth were chattering. "The police were asking horrible questions. I was so cold – they called me out of the pool in front of everybody. They asked me why I was in there while there were children in there, but I didn't understand what they meant. Do you know what they meant?"

I was enraged because of the injustice, and repulsed by the fact that anyone would suggest such a thing. I couldn't believe this had happened. But most of all, I was sad because my son was so shocked and upset.

His father and I went straight to the pool and spoke to the manager, who appeared to have no idea what all the fuss was about.

I'll never forget the tears on my husband's face as he spoke: "I would trust my son with children more than I would trust myself, and I can assure you I would never harm a child. How dare you suggest that my son had an ulterior motive! Chris's only mistake was telling a member of your staff that he was recovering from a mental illness."

Next stop was the police station. The young sergeant seemed genuinely sorry, and told us that he didn't know anything about schizophrenia. Unbelievable, considering these are the people who look into incidents and deal with young people who are having psychotic episodes.

Despite our problems, compared with another carer we met recently, we know we are lucky. After being sectioned and spending two years in rehab, her son moved into his own flat. That same week, while he was out buying a pizza, someone put a lighted torch through the letter box. He came home to a flat that was burned and gutted. He ended up back in hospital.

A few weeks after the swimming pool incident, my son received a letter of apology and two free swimming vouchers, which the people at the pool seemed to think made everything OK. It was nine months before Chris plucked up the courage to go swimming again. He kept saying that he felt ashamed. His shame was born out of their ignorance. Having been raised to be open and honest, Chris will have to learn to change his ways and tell lies due to the lack of education and understanding of others. And the hardest part for us as his parents? The injustice of it all.

Georgina Wakefield is a carer for her son who is in his 30s and is diagnosed with schizophrenia

Community Care 18-24 January 2007
www.communitycare.co.uk

"When does thrill-seeking cross over into mental illness?" Alison Gadsby

So, Steve Irwin is dead. I'm hoping you've all finished mourning. If you haven't, maybe now is not a good time to read this. Yes, the man affectionately known as 'Stevo' will no longer grace our screens, due to an unfortunate incident with a stingray. My sons were fans of the legend that was Steve, but even at their young age they are astute enough to know that if you play with fire, sooner or later the singeing begins.

"Dangling his child in front of crocodiles was frankly irresponsible"

As I'm in the fortunate position of not being Australian, I have been able to view this story with some objectivity. Not that I'm saying I wouldn't like to be Australian – I'd like nothing more than spending every day on the beach drinking Fosters and cheerily saying 'G'day mate' to passing strangers – but back to the point. Within this generalised outpouring of grief, why, I'm wondering, has no one thought to say, 'Hang on a minute, is it not slightly odd to wrestle crocodiles, kiss poisonous snakes, and swim close to fish whose sting is fatal?' Not to mention the climbing-into-crocodile-enclosure-with-newborn-baby-incident. Some people would be sectioned for this sort of behaviour.

So I am left asking myself, when does thrill-seeking, living-on-the-edge behaviour cross over into mental illness? I am sure many of you remember the incident some years back when a young man being treated for psychosis by mental health services climbed into the lion enclosure at a zoo and was mauled. This was seen as a tragic manifestation of his mental health problems, which I'm sure it was. But now imagine replacing this man with Steve Irwin, or a similar person who does life-threatening things for our enjoyment. I know he wasn't being treated for a serious mental health problem but was his behaviour any more rational than that of the man who was? Maybe he was used to being around dangerous animals, but they are unpredictable, which Steve found out to his cost. So should he have been saved from himself? Should someone have had a friendly word along the lines of 'Listen Steve, I know you love all this dangerous stuff, but quite frankly I'm starting to think you're a bit unhinged, mate'. Much of his behaviour wasn't entirely rational, and dangling his child in front of crocodiles was frankly reckless.

So why is it that weird and dangerous behaviour is acceptable in some people but not in others? I think if he hadn't been the rich and entertaining owner of a zoo, his outlandish stunts wouldn't have fooled anyone and he would have been carted off to hospital years ago. Maybe our society is prepared to tolerate mental illness if it comes in a showbiz wrapper but not if it is poor and lonely and can only communicate its distress in 'unacceptable' ways.

Alison Gadsby is a mental health nurse in Cambridge

Nursing Times 17 October 2006
© Emap Healthcare 2006
Reproduced by permission of Nursing Times
www.nursingtimes.net

'I've never met Steve Irwin but I've dined out on many who thought they were him.'

A duty to integrate?

Photo: Rui Vieira PA Wire/PA Photos

Sparkbrook, Birmingham 2007. Muslim women respond to being photographed in the street

By conflating multiculturalism with religion, Tony Blair is betraying Britain's history of diversity

CHITRA RAMASWAMY

My nickname at school was Bounty Bar. It was a throwaway, childish dig, but a racist one nonetheless, because it referred to the fact that my classmates saw me as brown on the outside, white on the inside.

What they were alluding to was that although I looked like the many other Asians in our school (because, you know, we all look the same) I was different as I didn't hang out with my own kind: I watched *Neighbours*, wasn't religious and liked fish fingers as much as mutter paneer.

It wasn't until years later that I asked my parents why I mainly had white friends, why I didn't speak Kannada, their language, and why I didn't know more about Bangalore in south India, where they are both from or, for that matter, their religion Hinduism.

The answer was interesting and came back to me in light of the latest debate over the issue of multiculturalism and integration – two terms which have bizarrely become so at odds with one another in the past couple of years – following Tony Blair's speech on the subject on Friday.*

My parents explained that after arriving in Britain in the early 1970s, a much more racist Britain than it is today, they decided that they wanted their children to be as British as possible so that our lives would be easier and we would have greater opportunities than they had.

How could I argue? It seemed to me a bold decision and one that worked out for the best, although as a result I do feel more estranged from my parents' home country and their culture than I would like, and I regularly kick myself for passing up the chance of being bilingual. Unsurprisingly, integration had both positive and negative sides.

'I watched Neighbours, wasn't religious and liked fish fingers as much as mutter paneer'

But does any of this mean that Blair is right to argue, as Trevor Phillips, Ruth Kelly and so many others also have, that we all have "a duty to integrate", or that multicultural Britain has been thrown "into sharp relief" by last year's London bombings? In my view, no; just as has happened every time this debate has reared its head, most recently with all the attendant trappings of faith schools, the veil and terrorism, the blame has been landed squarely at multiculturalism's door.

Is anyone else starting to forget what multiculturalism actually means? A year ago Blair said he never quite knew what people meant by the term, which is pretty much the only time I've ever agreed with him.

I used to think it meant that I could live, work and hang out in the same places, the same cities, towns, offices, galleries and bars, as everyone else – that I was entitled to the same opportunities and quality of life, and that diversity was more than merely welcome in Britain, it was something to be celebrated, and perhaps, dare I say it, was part of being British itself.

Sure, adapting to British life – whatever that happened to be – was part of it, especially if, as with my parents, you wanted to further yourself as much as possible. But it also went the other way. Communities were supposedly enriched by rubbing up against each other's cultures and traditions.

Now, however, rather than standing for a rich diversity of cultures, multiculturalism has somehow become synonymous with separateness. It has become associated with fearful, isolated and inward-looking communities. It has been identified as the enemy of integration or, as New Labour terms it, "community cohesion". And when the Prime Minister pledged to crack down on funding for religious and racial groups, he once again conflated multiculturalism with religion.

Quite how multiculturalism has also been tangled up with terrorism is beyond me, when the majority of those among ethnic minorities who have not been integrated are mothers and grandmothers who have been unable to learn English; these are hardly the type prone to terrorism. Even looking at the backgrounds of the London bombers, one of the most striking things is just how integrated they were in their younger lives before they were seduced by fundamentalism.

In communities where racial tensions are high and people are consequently suspicious or scared of one another, levels of opportunity tend to be low. It's the deprivation that we should be addressing, rather than trying to force communities where trust has already broken down to just get out and mix more.

None of this is helped by the fact that whenever the debate comes around, the "other" voices we get to hear consist in the main of either Muslim Association of Britain spokespeople or self-appointed first-generation community leaders. These voices are pretty much exclusively male.

How could they possibly represent the 1.8 million population of

'Well, the Britishness classes seem to be working'

Muslims, especially second and third generations, let alone the millions of other ethnic minorities in Britain?

I, for one, am getting a little fed up of unrepresentative people speaking for me.

Blair is right, however, to call on mosques that exclude women's voices to "look again at their practices" and to rule out the possibility of introducing Islamic sharia law into the country. If tolerance and equality are what make Britain, which is the Prime Minister's claim, this is an important part of ensuring their protection, but again it is largely a matter of religion, not culture.

A study last week showed just how sidelined Muslim women are feeling, particularly in relation to such debates as the veil issue, both within and outside of their communities. It's time we got to hear some of these voices. After all, isn't that the point of a tolerant society?

Scotland on Sunday 10 December 2006

*Our Nation's Future – multiculturalism and integration – A speech by Tony Blair 8/12/06. For full text go to the 10 Downing Street website **www.number-10.gov.uk***

Forced out, looking inwards: Britain's Bangladeshis

By Ayub Korom Ali

On Christmas Day in Bangla Town, at the heart of London's Bangladeshi community in Spitalfields, more than 200 people gathered for an impromptu celebration at a well-known eatery, the Dilshad restaurant. News had come in that Shafiqur Rahman Chowdhury, a long-standing community leader in Tower Hamlets, had been nominated as the opposition party candidate for Sylhet, a district in north-eastern Bangladesh, in the forthcoming elections.

By five o'clock the restaurant was packed with people who turned up from all over London to lend their support. The meeting went on for well over four hours, with speaker after speaker pledging support. Many even volunteered to go out to Bangladesh to help. The atmosphere was electric.

It is not unusual for Bangladeshis to get excited about politics "back home", especially those of the first generation who came here as adults and have strong ties with the country. What was unusual was the large number of second – and third-generation – Bangladeshis present. Of the 200-plus people, well over half were under 30, and a good number even younger. So what is drawing these young people to the politics of Bangladesh, and why do they rarely show similar enthusiasm for politics here?

The key is social exclusion. Unemployment and educational underachievement are widespread among British Bangladeshi youth. Although things are improving, the dominant picture is one of failure: even those who achieve educationally often find themselves on the dole. In Tower Hamlets, the London borough with the largest concentration of Bangladeshis, 32 per cent of 18- to 25-year-olds are unemployed. When people are excluded, there is a natural tendency to turn inward, to look for recognition and excitement from within.

The Prime Minister talked recently about the "duty to integrate". What Tony Blair doesn't appreciate is that integration cannot be achieved by imposing a set of values from the top. Integration is a process achieved through real and lived experiences. The most important of such experiences are provided by the education system and the workplace.

The sad fact is that a large number of British Bangladeshis find themselves poorly educated and with no job. It is this group that is turning to politics elsewhere. It is also the same group that is being targeted by extremist groups and being radicalised. During canvassing in last May's local election, I was stopped many times by young Bangladeshis and challenged about why I was standing for the Labour Party. Clearly, they felt that by being a Labour candidate, I was betraying my religion and my community. These were ordinary local lads, born and brought up here. It left me wondering where these young people were getting their political education from.

Unless social exclusion is tackled, disenchantment with the political process, especially among young people in our community, can only grow stronger.

Ayub Korom Ali is a Labour councillor in the London Borough of Newham

New Statesman 22 January 2007

Two communities

IN BANGLADESH

147.4 million:
total population

88% are Muslim

£4.60:
weekly average income

50% of males and **69%** of females aged over 15 are unable to read and write

45% of the population live below the poverty line

62:
average life expectancy

22:
average age

250,000 Bangladeshis leave their country each year

84% of the population live in rural areas

2/3 of the country is flooded each year in the monsoon rains

500,000 Bangladeshis were killed in 1970 by a tidal wave caused by a cyclone

138,000 were killed in 1991 by a tidal wave caused by a cyclone

1 metre:
the rise in sea level that would inundate more than 15% of Bangladesh

60 million Bangladeshis are ingesting arsenic by drinking contaminated groundwater, a newly discovered threat

8,500 Bangladeshis have been diagnosed with chronic arsenic poisoning from drinking unsafe water

IN BRITAIN

238,000:
Bangladeshi population of Britain

154,000 live in London, **15,000** in Birmingham, **10,000** in Greater Manchester

1/3 of Britain's Bangladeshi population was born in the UK

90% are Muslim

£182:
average weekly income

45% of the Bangladeshi community have no qualifications

68% live in low-income households

78:
average life expectancy

21:
average age

2/3 of all immigrants entering the UK are from the Indian subcontinent

3% marry non-Asians

£80m:
value of UK exports to Bangladesh in 2005

80% of all "Indian" restaurants in Britain are run by Bangladeshis

18% of Bangladeshis are self-employed

25% of the men work in restaurants

44% of Bangladeshi men smoke, the highest proportion among all ethnic groups

Research: Mosarrof Hussain

New Statesman 22 January 2007

This isn't about guns

The traditional Caribbean family no longer works here, and black youngsters are paying the price

Joseph Harker

As officers investigate the third teenage killing in 12 days, and within five miles, no doubt many will be commending yesterday's Metropolitan police decision to set up armed patrols on south London's most notorious estates. But this is a false dawn: it would take an armed officer in every home to have any lasting impact.

This is not about guns. And we will never defeat murderous inner-city youth crime through the actions of the police alone. Nor will the answer come through stiffer sentences, though that would be equally popular. Sadly, we're beyond all that: the teenagers who take to guns are just the tip of the iceberg.

Much attention has focused on the fact that many victims, and their killers, are black – which is impossible to ignore, though it makes many people uncomfortable. But though this is not an issue entirely about race – the latest victim was half white, half Thai – we need to quickly find answers as to why urban youth culture, as also witnessed in Manchester and Nottingham, has become so violent.

What is it that makes one youngster want, and then decide, to kill another, by whatever weapon? Yes, many of them grow up in poverty, and on crime-ridden estates, but there's little doubt that the glorification of gang culture through the multibillion entertainment industry – "Get rich or die tryin'", as 50 Cent says – is a factor. However, whereas politicians are happy to clamp down on the junk food industry for luring kids towards burgers, they seem to be less keen on fighting those who lure them towards guns. Is it because they see the latter as just a black problem, which won't affect swing voters?

We can't, though, entirely pass the buck to politicians. In the week when Britain's failures towards its children have been exposed by a devastating Unicef report, much has been made of the need to listen to children. But more crucial is the need to lead children: to combat the "bling" culture and ground our kids in what is really important.

In Caribbean history, a central role is taken by the heroic mother who raised her family while the father literally slaved in the fields, and support came from the extended family. This ideal was popularised by Hillary Clinton, in her book named after the claimed African proverb: "It takes a village to raise a child".

But in today's overdeveloped world, where status is gained either through jobs or money, and where community bonds have grown ever weaker, the notion of the backup

Steve Martin, the father of 2004 murder victim Solomon Martin wears a shirt showing his son's picture. Hundreds of South London residents took part in a 'Peace March' on the streets of Peckham to show the capital will not tolerate gun crime.

Photo: Jeff Moore/EMPICS Entertainment

"village" has become irrelevant. Fathers have continued to abandon mothers, who feel they have to cope even though they've lost their traditional support. Children have often been the ones to suffer, growing up in a moral vacuum where they make their own rules, in a society that's too complex for them to understand.

This is not to blame single parents for their circumstances. But society can't afford to worsen the problem by making it appear there's no advantage in a child having two participating parents. It takes a mother and a father to raise a child. We can't give men an excuse to go awol.

Twenty years ago, as a journalist in the black press, I was optimistic about the future for black Britons, assuming as our presence here grew stronger we'd see our people prosper. Today, though, despite the progress of many, we have seen the growth of an underclass; and without breaking the cycle, it will become more entrenched and more desperate, with teenage pregnancies and ruined life chances becoming the norm.

Our schools throw information about sex and drugs at children from as young as seven. Isn't it time a greater priority was given to teaching youngsters about parenting, about families, and about making sure the next generation doesn't suffer the same traumas as this?

© *The Guardian 16 February 2007*

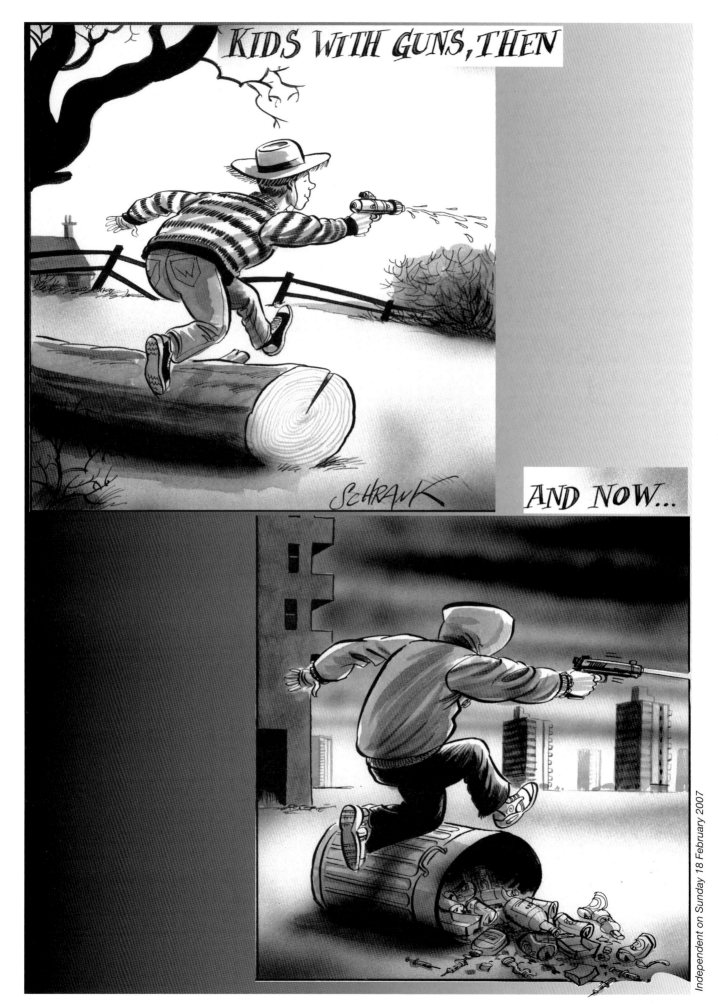

Independent on Sunday 18 February 2007

The mean streets of Britain

The shootings in a Brixton McDonald's were a terrible metaphor for the way we live now, writes **Allister Heath**. A whole section of society, raised on violence and fast food, is drifting away from the rest of the nation: nutrition is destiny

Instead of the heavy police presence I had expected to find at Brixton's underground station, I was greeted by a canned rendition of Beethoven's 5th Symphony. To cool tempers in the notoriously volatile south London hotspot, classical music is being pumped through the ticket hall's sound system; unfortunately, like the flower power 'make love, not war' ideology of the 1960s, this latest gimmick is straight out of the politically correct rulebook.

Graffiti already disfigures the huge glass sign outside the newly refurbished station and dubious characters continue to congregate, oblivious to the banks of CCTV cameras. I turned left after leaving the station; it was the middle of the day but the air was already thick with menace. I had walked barely a dozen yards towards the Coldharbour Lane, now more closely associated with Yardie gangs than John Major, before being accosted by my first drug-dealer of the day: 'skunk, crack, weed,' he muttered under his breath. Seconds later, two more approached me.

I studiously avoided making eye contact. Instead, I looked over Brixton Road to the local branch of McDonald's, where two youngsters were shot at point-blank range last week. Across Acre Lane, next to the Town Hall, is the Fridge, the nightclub outside which two men were sprayed with bullets last week and which was raided by 200 police officers in April. But it was the scene of the first shooting I had come to see: with its lurid combination of gun crime and seemingly random use of extreme violence, served up with huge helpings of unhealthy food, it epitomises everything that distinguishes today's underclass from the rest; it illustrates how in our inner cities the devaluation of life has gone hand in hand with the devaluation of eating habits — even though McDonald's is an honest company and is itself a victim of this trend.

Fortunately, nobody died in those shootings; and in terms of pure evil none of these attacks can match the horrendous massacres in America over the past few days, especially at the Amish school in Pennsylvania on Monday, when a deranged lone gunman sought out young girls from a classroom and killed them one after the other. There is outrage in the US, and the Bush administration will hold a school violence summit within days. The reaction in Britain has been quite different; the sense of shock so obvious on the other side of the Atlantic is palpably missing here, where nobody can even be bothered to call for yet another anti-crime conference.

On the face of it, this lack of urgency is bizarre. In the UK in recent days we have suffered from an epidemic of gun and knife crime of such intensity that one murder or attempted killing simply melts into another. But while the violence still makes the headlines in newspapers and prominent slots in the TV bulletins, it no longer shocks a public numbed by the regularity of it all, and disillusioned by the apparent powerlessness of the authorities to do anything about it.

Americans know that crime can be tackled and they expect their politicians to do so. We don't, and

A police officer stands guard outside McDonalds restaurant in Brixton, south London, after a 17 year old and his friend were shot as they queued at the restaurant

Photo: ANE MINGAY/PA Archive/PA Photos

as a result Britain is suffering from an almost unprecedented outbreak of mindless violence. First of the latest batch of victims was a man shot in the stomach near the Old Kent Road in London; then Jason Gayle-Bent was pursued and stabbed in New Cross by a gang of 40 youths roaming the streets on bikes and firing shots into the air; 2,000 pupils in Peckham and East Dulwich were sent home because of a looming gang war between the Peckham Boys and the Ghetto Boys; a man was left paralysed after a shooting in Kennington; Carley Furness, 17, was stabbed in the neck in Orpington on Saturday; and on Sunday Stevens Nyembo-Ya-Muteba was stabbed to death in the stairwell of his Hackney flat after asking a group of youths to be quiet. In Nottingham, Nathan Williams, 17, was shot dead in a shopping centre. In Manchester, where an average of more than two firearm offences are committed by 15- to 20-year-olds every day, 15-year-old Jessie James was recently shot dead in Moss Side and, in a separate attack, 25-year-old Mark Daniels suffered the same fate.

The sheer volume of these crimes guarantees that most will soon be forgotten by all but the victims' loved ones. The public is frustrated and angry but also strangely resigned. The political classes, police and judiciary have failed to tackle the upsurge in lawlessness, which means that they are increasingly held in contempt by the public, who no longer believe that crime will ever be brought under control, regardless of who is in Downing Street.

The British underclass exists in a world of sink estates where welfare benefits, crime and the black market have become the settled lifestyle, providing a better standard of living than toiling in a minimum-wage job ever could. The problem here, therefore, is not principally material poverty: it is a lack of moral values and a rejection not only of work but also of family, marriage, manners, smart appearance and self-improvement. Millions now live in a cultural void, speaking their own private language, eating greasy fast food, watching trash TV, and listening to increasingly destructive music. These people are frighteningly uneducated and would never even dream of voting.

Young men have been robbed of their male role models as a result of broken homes. Their condition is made worse by permissive attitudes to crime, an unquestioning welfare state and an anti-family ideology. Instead of emerging as noble savages, freed from the shackles of civilisation, as followers of Jean-Jacques Rousseau would have predicted, younger residents of our inner cities have ended up fuelling an explosion in crime, gang rule and a barbaric, Hobbesian war of all against all.

The victims of this terrible social experiment are living a life that in many respects is nasty, brutish and short. In Calton, a district of east Glasgow which epitomises the worst of underclass Britain, a boy born today can expect to live just 53.9 years, at least three decades less than someone born in London's Kensington. In Glasgow as a whole, probably the worst affected city in the UK, life expectancy is 69, lower than that of Bosnia, Libya, Puerto Rico or even the Gaza Strip.

Calton residents are seven times more likely to die a drugs-related death than the rest of the country, 61 per cent have no qualifications and 37 per cent of children grow up in workless households. Around 57 per cent of adults do not work — and with only 8 per cent registered as unemployed, most are clearly content to live on benefits.

Because of their appalling diet, which often consists exclusively of crisps, chocolate and fizzy drinks, a quarter of Calton children are already obese before they reach school age. In west Glasgow, breastfeeding levels are 78 per cent in the most affluent areas, compared with 8.5 per cent in the most deprived areas. Hospital admissions for deliberate self-harm are ten times higher in the underclass areas than in the most affluent neighbourhoods. Close to 62 per cent of those in the most deprived areas of west Glasgow smoke, compared with 9.3 per cent in the richer parts; in poor parts of east Glasgow, 35 per cent of pregnant women smoke, with devastating effects on their unborn children. Rates of coronary heart disease, stroke and lung cancer are also much higher among the underclass.

Of all the shootings of the past few days, those in the Brixton McDonald's were the most significant because they highlighted this dramatic divergence between the habits and values of the modern, health-obsessed, metropolitan middle classes and those of the underclass. The two groups now live in

> **A generation of gun-toting, trigger-happy, amoral burger-and-fries-munching yobs select their victims in the same mindless way as they stuff their faces**

completely different worlds. The two young victims apparently had a minor disagreement with another youngster, perhaps merely because they had trodden on his toes; he felt 'disrespected', it seems, and responded with his semi-automatic weapon — presumably in the way he imagined his television or gangsta rap role model would have done. That the restaurant was packed with local teenagers and families at the time didn't bother the gunman, who evidently did not consider that others may be equally deserving of the 'respect' he so craves.

The setting of the attack is also deeply symbolic. When McDonald's was booming in Britain in the 1980s, despite a residual anti-American snootiness, many younger middle-class people saw it as a cheeky, naughty indulgence to which they would happily take their children. Eating at McDonald's soon became a classless phenomenon — rich and poor kids alike happily tucked into their Happy Meals and collected their plastic toys.

This picture has changed drastically during the past few years, as increased affluence, the emergence of obesity as a major health problem, the cult of Jamie Oliver and shifting political values have driven a middle-class eating revolution. Organic food, once the preserve of bearded eco-warriors, has gone mainstream; the better-off began to turn their backs on fast food and flocked instead to Waitrose to buy smoothies and sushi. One might call this David Cameron's Britain.

The tipping point came with Morgan Spurlock's influential propaganda film, Super Size Me, which, it must be said, unfairly demonised McDonald's. Eating habits went from being a matter of taste to a question of morality, a shift reinforced by Jamie Oliver's campaign against the dreadful diet in state schools. Despite its healthier menus, McDonald's has increasingly become a no-go area for the middle classes, a trend that started long before last week's gun attack in Brixton. But now the rise of a generation of gun-toting, trigger-happy, amoral burger-and-fries-munching yobs who select their victims in the same mindless way as they stuff their faces will only reinforce this exodus.

In today's Britain, where eating habits are taking over from accents as a sign of class, the combination of bad food and violence is proving a troubling and toxic one. The problems of the underclass, while monumental, are not intractable, but would require extraordinary political will to put right, including a market-led revolution in education, a dramatic reform in welfare to make work pay, the removal of the incentives for family breakdown, a much tougher 'broken windows' strategy for policing, and a changed cultural message that promotes decency and respect. The tragedy is that as long as the Cameron generation continue to congratulate themselves over their organic food and holier-than-thou smoothies, the chances of them ever doing anything about the catastrophic conditions endured by the other half are extremely slim. But if they insulate themselves further from the reality of life in the inner cities, while continuing to tolerate the failings of the welfare state, it is the middle class that will deserve the blame for the disaster on their doorsteps.

Allister Heath is associate editor of The Spectator and deputy editor of The Business.

The Spectator 28 October 2006

I mourn the days when the 'F' word really meant something

Paul Stokes

Pardon my French, but what the feck is going on with swearing these days? Is there any social situation now at which it is considered acceptable to refrain from using the real F word in polite conversation?

It's a genuine question. I'm a well brought up fellow. I don't tend to curse in front of strangers. As a result I am constantly in fear of offending some new acquaintance by not swearing in their company when I should.

I went to see the hot new British film London To Brighton this week. It was shown at the Glasgow Film Theatre, and the screening was followed by a Q&A session with its hot new British director, Paul Andrew Williams.

You would think a man with that many names would be well spoken, and he was, quite. He had much of interest to say. He was personable, enthusiastic and genuinely taken aback at the critical acclaim heaped upon his debut feature. And he could not go a single sentence without using the F word at least once. It was not to provide major emphasis,

it was just part of normal speech. So he thanked us for effing turning up, talked a bit about the various effing problems of making his effing film, said again how effing grateful he was that we turned up, and how effing taken a-effing-back he was at the effing response to his effing film, thanked us again for effing coming, and then bid us a good effing night. It really was odd.

I suppose the celebrity swearer, and part-time chef, Gordon Ramsay must take some responsibility for the increasing acceptance of the F word in popular society. It was even claimed recently that he goaded Sir Cliff Richard so much that even the saintly Sir Cliff told him, sotto voce, to go eff himself. Astonishing.

But it goes on at the highest echelons. We are constantly regaled with tales of Tony Blair's potty tongue. And Margaret Beckett's response on being offered the post of Foreign Secretary? One word, beginning with F.

At this rate it will not be long before really important and influential people,

like Parky, start swearing in public. Nor would it be entirely shocking if the Queen was to drop in a few F words in this year's Christmas message, especially now she is supposedly talking as common as what we do.

Now, I don't wish to appear prudish. I am actually a fan of swearing. I like to do a bit of it myself, it helps lower the blood pressure and I think I am quite good at it. But all this constant effing by everyone is ruining it for me. What is the point of us swearing if the Prime Minister, the Foreign Secretary and Sir Cliff are at it too?

I am not much of a golden ager but it does seem to me as if the great days of cursing are now behind us. It is all very sad. Frankly, the liberal use of the F word by our elders and betters means it is losing its value. If this carries on much longer, I reckon, as a swear word, it's f*cked.

Scotland on Sunday 10 December 2006

Possible great swear moments of the past. 1: The Rokeby Venus

You're really effing gorgeous, Miss!

You're so effing right, cherub.

Apologies to Velàzquez

**Tens of millions of people in Britain have no interest at all in football.
So, amid fresh allegations about bungs, international corporate crime and
sexual excess, should we call time on our obsession with the once beautiful game?**

By *Emma John*

Photo: Ian West/PA Archive/PA Photos

Footie as soap opera Ashley Cole and Cheryl Tweedy at a photocall to launch the National Lottery Dream Number

How football hijacked our culture

Another month, another football scandal. It said something about the nation that a TV programme revealing little more than we knew already – that there's corruption in football – made headline news the following day. After all the hype, the content of *Panorama's* bung exposé seemed thin fare. But then, football no longer has to justify its place after the pips. Even in the dead two months after the World Cup, stories such as Ashley Cole's transfer and book serialisation, Sven's pay-off and the Italian match-fixing scandal dominated the public consciousness. There is an assumption, tacitly accepted, that these stories are as significant a national concern as the war in Iraq or the state of the NHS. We live in an age that screams from every billboard that football matters.

Is it true? No one seems to know, or even cares to question it. There are football research institutes all over the country, but, on contacting them, I learn that none seems to be investigating the possibility that the game's vaunted position in our everyday culture is wildly out of proportion with levels of genuine interest. The UK home viewing figures for England's last World Cup knockout match were 16 million. Even if you agree with the wild guesstimates that suggest the actual number of viewers was 30 million – and this is publicity-led, remember – that still leaves more than half the country not watching. There are tens of millions of people in Britain who have no interest in the game.

Of course, that doesn't matter, because the money has spoken. The Premier League recently became the most highly valued sports league in the world, thanks to a £2.5bn deal for Premiership TV rights. Barclays has re-signed as the tournament's title sponsor for £21.9m per year over three years (to demonstrate how quickly the value of football has grown: in 1993, Carling got the gig for £3m). Newspapers have had their say, too. "The general view of sports editors is that football is 50 per cent of the pages and everything else is 50 per cent," says the *Observer's* sports editor, Brian Oliver. "That's what they think is a true reflection of what readers want."

Everyone agrees that the game's explosion owes a huge debt to the advent of all-seater stadiums, and the corresponding drop in violence. The end of standing terraces did for football what the end of the Blitz did for London. Oliver believes it also owes a big thank you to Paul Gascoigne, and that it was England's emotional World Cup exit from the Italia '90 semi-finals "wot won it for football". "Before 1990 there was no such thing as a sports supplement," says Oliver. "Gazza crying was worth hundreds of millions of pounds for football."

Dr Hilary Matheson, a lecturer at the University of Wales who specialises in the media representation of sport, has discovered that, since 1984, football coverage in newspapers has increased by up to 45 per cent, with a corresponding decrease in the amount of coverage for all other sports. "With the rise in the number of games shown on TV," she says, "the newsprint media have needed to focus on other aspects of the game, which has resulted in sports journalists writing about players' lives, contracts and other related topics which eight or so years ago would not have taken on the same level of importance." No wonder the sports pages alone are not enough for Rupert Murdoch's titles, which carry special pull-out supplements, from the *Sun's* Supergoals to The Game in the *Times*.

Football by numbers

£2.5bn
will be paid this year for Premier League TV rights

£30.8m
biggest transfer fee in English football history – agreed in summer 2006 by Chelsea for the striker Andriy Shevchenko

£640,000
average annual salary of Premiership footballers

£100,000
average amount spent by a season ticket holder on supporting a football team for 52 years

Research by Sam Alexandron

Anglers outnumber soccer fans

And all this despite football attendances actually going down. Soccer may be invading every part of our lives, but gates in the top four leagues have dropped steadily over the past four years. Only about 700,000 people actually pay to see a team play each weekend. Anglers outnumber them six to one. If our fishing fans were equally well represented in the media, you'd be reading about very different kinds of tackle.

There has been nothing comparable to football's sudden and rapacious takeover of public life. Less than 20 years ago the game was an almost exclusively male pastime with an unsavoury reputation for thuggery. Now it's one of the mainstays of the entertainment industry and a catwalk trendsetter. It has gained its place on the high altar of consumer culture so rapidly that we just nod at the obscenely inflated wages, the ludicrous transfer values set on players, as if these things had always been.

Dr Rogan Taylor leads the Football Industry Group at Liverpool University. The success of the sport, he says, has been in selling itself as a global language. "Globalisation has transferred tremendous value to a game that was always there," he enthuses (even academics can be in love with football). "Flies are attracted to a honey pot but they don't make the honey." For the record, Taylor doesn't think that football's domination of our culture is out of proportion. "We read quite blithely that 1.2 billion people watched the World Cup Final. We need to realise what that actually means. Nothing else comes close."

You can't argue with figures which tell you that almost one in five people in a world of six billion is watching football. But let's not forget, too, that football has an unparalleled talent for self-aggrandisement. English football's romance with adland is one that other sports can only dream of. The advent of the Premiership and silly money coincided perfectly with the rise of celebrity culture: a triumph of marketing and good old-fashioned voyeurism.

With its unstoppable advance from the back pages to the front pages to the glossy pages, football has been able to conquer its last frontier – women. Fashion brands, gossip magazines and TV soap operas have been able to do what the Football Association alone could not, hooking millions of women into a sport they conventionally cared little about. Victoria Beckham has clued more of the sisterhood into the game than any outreach strategy. And it was *Grazia* magazine which, by christening the Wags at this year's World Cup, defined England's 2006 campaign.

> **With this unstoppable advance, football has conquered its last frontier – women**

The beautiful game?

Ashley Cole, Chelsea
"When I heard my agent repeat the figure of £55,000 I nearly swerved off the road. 'He's taking the piss, Jonathan!' I yelled down the phone. I was trembling with anger."

David Beckham
"I have come to accept that if I have a new haircut it is front-page news."

Graham Bean, FA compliance unit
"The world of agents is a murky one – there's no getting away from it."

Chelsea statement on William Gallas
"Having failed to secure his demands, his position became increasingly intransigent. He refused to join the team during pre-season and went on to threaten that if he was forced to play, or financially punished for his breach of the rules, he could score an own goal."

Mike Newell, Luton manager
"It's about greed, bad economics and football's unique business model. But agents would not demand payments from clubs if players were happy to pay them for their work. Players are complicit, as are the clubs."

Colin Gordon, Steve McClaren's agent
"We pretend we are holier-than-thou. But the English game is considered the dirty man of Europe. We are the worst."

Coleen McLoughlin, girlfriend of Wayne Rooney
"Apparently, young women are getting into debt because they try to shop and party like a footballer's wife. If I heard of anyone doing that I'd tell them to get a grip."

Charles Collymore, agent
"There are managers out there who take bungs all day long."

Shocking brand values

"Football is no longer about 90 minutes," says Tony Quinn, head of strategic planning at the advertising agency Leagas Delaney, which counts Reebok among its clients. "It's about celebrity far more than it is about sport. The more lavish footballers' lifestyles become, the more we've been seduced by them. It's self-perpetuating." Yet if football is a brand, its brand values are shocking. Galloping self-interest, greed, squabbling, dodgy dealing: these are the themes that permeate media coverage of the sport every day. Yet we scarcely notice them. It takes something as truly blundering as Ashley Cole's woefully misjudged book – in which he claimed that a £55,000-a-week salary was "taking the piss" – to provoke any real debate about the game's appropriation of our culture.

David Goldblatt, who has just published a definitive history of global football called *The Ball Is Round*, believes strongly that football needs a more scrutinising press, but argues that we "get the football we deserve". "Football doesn't lead society, it reflects it," he says. "If we're going to complain about its conspicuous consumption, its anti-intellectualism – well, I can think of other places you see that. Yes, the game has reached unprecedented heights of significance. But I tend to think, 'Why not?'"

Politicians, too, are keen to play down any disparity. The sports minister Richard Caborn says that although he has concerns about the game's governance, he has none about the scale of its influence. "You can say the dominance of football is part of the problem, but I see it as part of the solution," says Caborn, who thinks it can persuade people to take up all sorts of sports. Hugh Robertson, Caborn's Tory opposite number, has a similar line. "If extensive football coverage encourages people to be more active I'm all for it," he says – though he admits that there is "no direct link between the number of people who follow sport and who take up activity". Quinn sees the distance between "real" football and the glamour machine increasing. "Umbro has taken pride in being real, in being about football in the park. And who buys Umbro?"

Still, it's possible to detect a backlash in people's personal experiences with the game. A lifelong West Bromwich fan recently told me he was giving up football. "I've decided to start following Rugby League instead," he said. "I don't know the rules, but it's got to be better than this. I can't stand reading about those idiots and paying for their luxury watches any longer." The "was Sven worth it?" lament, following the realisation that £25m had been lavished on a coach with more notches on his bedpost than on his team's record sheet, was the wounded cry of a cheated nation. It could be time to stop feeding the beast.

Emma John is associate editor of Observer Sport Monthly

New Statesman 9 October 2006

Photo posed by model

Poverty: the cost to families

Many families struggle to survive below the Government's deprivation thresholds, with consequences for children's education

Paul Nicolson

Most children love "Mufti Days" at school when they wear their own clothes instead of school uniform in return for a donation to charity. But some pupils dread these days and choose to stay at home rather than face the scorn of their fellow pupils for not wearing the latest clothes.

Such embarrassment is one of the milder consequences of the poverty suffered by children in Britain today. Even the Conservative leadership now believes that the ever-widening gap between the poorest and the most affluent in our society needs to be addressed. I welcome the sea-change in the Conservatives' thinking but they are wrong to describe the worst poverty in the United Kingdom as relative.

To have no money anywhere is absolute poverty. To have far too little money in a very expensive developed economy also threatens survival and is also absolute poverty. According to the charity End Child Poverty, 3.4 million children live in poverty in the UK, a shocking figure

for such a wealthy country. Their parents' incomes are all below the poverty line and sometimes a long way below due to overpayments and other debts. We have one of the worst rates of child poverty in the industrialised world.

The poorest children in the UK are more likely to be ill, to die younger and to be disadvantaged in our schools. The latter is especially worrying as education is key if children are to avoid the poverty suffered by their parents. One teacher, who has spent eight years teaching in two inner London comprehensives, told me that homework for some children is a virtual impossibility. Overcrowded homes with no table to work at and the television blaring constantly are not conducive to rote learning or coursework. The teacher tells of one boy who fainted at school because he had not eaten for 24 hours. There was no food at home and no money for school dinner. Another was persistently late, caused by broken nights because he had to sleep in an armchair under a coat.

Some children have onerous tasks to perform when hard-pressed parents are at work. One particular girl begged the teacher not to refer to her poor punctuality on her college application reference because she frequently had to negotiate public transport with her school bag, PE kit and a pushchair, as she had to drop her little brother off at the childminder's before going to school.

I have witnessed vulnerable families struggling to survive on inadequate unemployment benefits, then move over the line of legality into desperate but illegal attempts to beat poverty and assist the education of their children. One such case in the 1990s was a single father with three sons. He had gained legal custody of the children after his wife left him. His unemployment benefit was being taxed with 20 per cent of the poll tax. We have since discovered that, before it was taxed, the benefit was already at least £40 below barest minimum needed for healthy living, after commissioning research from the Family Budget Unit.

The family were most embarrassed by their poverty when they were unable to find the money for summer holidays, decent school clothes, birthdays and Christmas. Very few families were poor in their wealthy town, so the boys had to suffer listening to the tales of summer holidays, seeing the better clothes at the beginning of the school year and the yield of expensive Christmas presents shown off at school. Their father was humiliated by the family poverty and set about trying to help his children hold their own in the playground. When they were young, just starting school full time, work was impossible.

His first step was to borrow £500 from a high-street lender to which they added £274 interest to be paid off over 31 weeks. Other similar loans followed. The interest deepened the family poverty below the inadequate, and already taxed, benefits. He was still desperate when a friend suggested he could earn £50 a time carrying "parcels" in a plastic bag from Person A to Person B. Then A suggested he moved from carrying drugs to selling £700 worth for £800 making £100 a parcel instead of £50. My friend delivered one parcel to sell but the buyer disappeared without paying and was never seen again. He paid off A in small amounts while a third party paid for him and his boys to eat. He has never carried such parcels again.

Town Hall bureaucracy also has much to answer for. Jane was living in a two-bedroomed, damp flat with five children and pregnant with the sixth. The council refused to move the family of seven to a larger house because there were rent arrears, which would have been covered by housing benefit had she filled in an annual form at the right time, but she is epileptic and semi-literate. Social Services said it was the responsibility of the Housing Department and vice versa. I suggested to the chairmen of both county and district councils that the

matter should be decided by judicial review. I argued that the overriding consideration should be the needs of the children whose education and health were being damaged by overcrowded, damp housing. Social Services paid off the arrears and the family was moved, but to a three-bedroomed house far from the shops and the school, so huge problems remain.

Hillary Fisher, campaign director of End Child Poverty, emphasises that it is important that poor children are able to go to good schools and can participate in the relevant activities and trips as well as afford uniforms and equipment. It is also essential that they are able to come to school ready and able to learn, not worrying about what is happening at home, how safe it is to go to and from school, and eat nutritious food, including breakfast.

Housing is another fundamental issue. Shelter estimates that 55 days a year of schooling are missed by homeless children. If housing is inadequate children are also unable to study at home, and also suffer from ill health which affects their learning.

The true definition of poverty is in the level of the income remaining after all taxation and housing costs have been paid for – officially known as After Housing Costs [AHC]. It is

on that AHC share of total income that urban survival depends in the UK; it pays for food, fuel, clothing, transport, school trips, holidays, birthdays, Christmas, all other necessities and the ravages of the interest charged by home credit companies.

According to the Government's criteria, a family is living in poverty if its income – after housing and taxation costs have been paid for – is less than 60 per cent of the equivalent median income. Answers to parliamentary questions show that Income Support and Jobseekers Allowance paid to the unemployed after all taxation and housing costs have been met, are below the poverty threshold.

If income in work is to be the route out of poverty, as it is measured by government, it must rise above 60 per cent of the median income after housing and tax. That is becoming increasingly difficult as the cost of housing, transport to work and utilities rise and squeeze the income that remains to pay for food, fuel, clothing and parental support for education, both in and out of work. The rising cost of rented accommodation, particularly in London, is resulting in parents, who are above the income threshold for receiving housing benefit, and who therefore pay their own rent and council tax, finding that they are left with a lower AHC income in work than when they were unemployed.

We need macro-economic answers to poverty that include more vigorous housing policies that address buy-to-let, the flood of lending and the supply of housing, and that deal with the grotesque inequality in the distribution of incomes and wealth. The pips are squeaking in the poorest households in the UK. Talk of relative poverty should be replaced by a debate that faces the facts.

The Revd Paul Nicolson is chairman of the Zacchaeus 2000 Trust

The Tablet 2 December 2006
www.z2k.org
www.thetablet.co.uk

'I have never had a pay rise or been promoted in four years'

■ **Maria, 54, was a financial adviser in Bolivia but came to the UK four years ago to improve her qualifications and her English. She works in London as a cleaner.**

When I arrived I had some savings but the exchange rate was very bad and after a month they were all gone. I started working as a cleaner in the morning and studying in the afternoon, but this wasn't enough to live on, so I also started a job caring for the elderly in the evenings. At one stage I had to go to three jobs every day. Before 1 October 2006 [when the minimum wage was set at £5.35] I was on £5.05 an hour. I am now on £5.35 an hour, but I have never had a pay rise or been promoted in four years. I get up at 4a.m. every day and will get maybe one afternoon off a week. Our employers say we are not entitled to holidays because we are part-time workers. I do not get paid on bank holidays or if I am ill. Sometimes I am very miserable, I have no social life and it can be very lonely. But I know the money I send home to my daughter is so important, and I hope that by the end of this year I will have enough to start a part-time economics course.

I have no social life and it can be very lonely

■ **Laura, 34, is a single mother from Newcastle. She has one daughter aged 15, but no longer has any contact with her daughter's father.**

I work part-time in a newsagent for £5.35 an hour, but I'm paying £200 a month rent, so that uses up most of it. And all my gas and electric comes from the meters, which cost three times the usual rate, so by the end of the month I've got nothing left. I also get £17.45 a week child support, £43 a week child tax credit and £46 a week working tax credit and I know it sounds like a lot, but it isn't by the time you've paid for everything. Being paid monthly is also a problem – it would be easier to manage my money if I was paid weekly because I'm taxed weekly. I don't get any money from my daughter's father and I wouldn't want it anyway. I also volunteer here at the Cedarwood Project [a drop-in centre in North Shields] when I can, chatting to people, helping in the office – I've been doing it for years.

I don't get any money from my daughter's father

■ **After stepping in to break up an incident, Lee, 43, found himself the target of local gang violence which eventually forced him to abandon his Margate bedsit. He has been sleeping rough in London.**

When I first came to London, I sat in Hyde Park for three days just watching the planes go over. I didn't know who to approach – my mum's dead and I haven't seen my dad or my brother for about 10 years. In the end I went to the job centre, and found out about the Manna centre, and it's been a godsend. I'll come here at 8.30a.m. every day and have a shower and a shave, a couple of cups of tea and then a bit of dinner before it closes at 1.30p.m. I refuse to beg – that would be like going down another level. I'm still homeless now, but because I don't have a drink or drug or mental-health problem, I'm at the bottom of the ladder when it comes to receiving help. I'm looking for labouring work but it's all CSCS stuff [requiring a construction certificate]. The crazy thing is, when it comes to Jobseekers Allowance, which is about £57 a week, you actually get about £8 or £9 less if you are homeless, because they calculate that you won't need any money for gas and electric. When I first became homeless, I applied for a crisis loan, which came through nearly a month later – it was £31.

I'm at the bottom of the ladder when it comes to receiving help

■ All interviews by Alice Lascelles, a freelance journalist. Some of the names have been changed

The Tablet 2 December 2006

Neither a borrower nor a spender be?

Compulsive spending and debt in 21st-century Britain

Photo: Fred Goldstein

There was a time when shopping was regarded as a basic chore, something that had to be done to ensure adequate provisions within a home and a reasonably comfortable life. In modern times, however, the act of shopping has taken on a whole new role in our lives, with many people viewing it as a pastime, a pleasure, an addiction and even therapy! Germaine Greer has suggested that, for many women, shopping is an alternative to sex (which is absent or unfulfilling in their lives), while others claim that shopping has replaced religion and even culture in many people's lives, so that given any spare time they are more likely to go out and shop till they drop than read a book or take in a play or film.

Two particular modern traits that this fetishising of shopping and consumer goods has led to are shopaholics and so-called retail therapy.

Shopaholics are those people who simply live to shop. For them the buzz gained from going out and spending money is akin to a drug, and many claim to be unable to live without it. One European Union survey found that 33% of people are addicted to 'rash or unnecessary consumption' or, put more simply, going out and buying stuff we neither need nor, in the cold light of day, want. Young people in Scotland, apparently, are the worst affected according to the EU.

Of course, not many of us can match Elton John's reported shopping spree in which he spent £40 million in one 20-month period (of which £293,000 was on flowers alone), but for many people there is a danger that being addicted to shopping can cause severe strain on their bank balance and even put them into debt (of which more later).

One particular but rapidly increasing subset of shopaholics is those who claim to indulge in 'retail therapy' or 'shopping to make

one feel better'. In recent years this trait has seen an alarming increase as unhappy consumers splash the cash in a bid to treat and comfort themselves. One survey found that 55% of Britons claim to be unhappy with life or depressed and that among those people the tendency to try and feel better by spending money is twice as likely as normal.

Unfortunately, in many cases, retail therapy does not work and one finds oneself as unhappy as before only with a larger credit card bill and some possibly unwanted new clothes or products in the house.

Although most experts regard retail therapy and addictive shopping as symptoms of wider disorders such as depression or self-esteem issues, one group of psychology researchers in Melbourne have coined a new term, oniomania (compulsive shopping syndrome) to describe what they see as a distinct condition. It is still unclear whether oniomania is a genuine medical condition or simply a symptom of a society that puts undue emphasis on shopping, as entertainment and choice, as a form of self-definition, not to mention pushing the alleged palliative qualities of splashing the cash.

For shopaholics there is one small crumb of good news, however, as studies have shown that regular, compulsive shopping can actually have some health benefits. Apparently, most British women cover an estimated 133 miles a year by going to the shops—that's the equivalent of walking from London to Nottingham—averaging out at 2.77 miles per week, burning 193 calories and covering 4,059 steps in that time. Going shopping with a friend is even more beneficial, as two tend to cover greater distances than a lone shopper!

Which is something of a comfort...but not much once you take into account the biggest danger of all linked to compulsive shopping: debt.

Britain's debt time bomb

Britain is officially the most debt-ridden country in Europe, possibly the world. According to the latest studies, people in the UK are borrowing on average almost twice that of citizens in other Western European countries.

Much of this debt comes about due to the ease by which one can obtain and use credit cards. Something about those little pieces of plastic means that we are far happier to spend greater amounts with them than if we had to hand over hard cash. But, as everyone knows, there's a catch. Fail to pay off your credit card bill quickly enough and you can suddenly start to face extortionate amounts of interest, not to mention late payment fees, which all stack up. To compound matters, many people try to play the system by using yet more cards to pay off existing cards and increasing the overall debt. In some cases, debts have spiralled so far that those owing have been unable to cope and have committed suicide.

At the heart of this huge increase in debt is the ease with which we can now get credit. At one time, if you went and asked your bank manager for a £1000 loan (unless you were already wealthy) you'd be lucky to walk out with £300. These days, that apparent caution has been turned on its head and our letter boxes are full of mail shots assuring us that we've been pre-approved for a super new credit card or loan deal. In one embarrassing instance, the Royal Bank of Scotland even sent a pre-approved Gold credit card with a £10,000 limit to a dog!

And finally, it's perhaps worth bearing in mind the words of Barclay's CEO Matthew Barrett, who stated in October 2003 before a Select Treasury Committee investigating Barclaycard's extortionate interest rates that: "I do not borrow on credit cards. It is too expensive."

Good advice from one who knows?

Nick Hobbes
© John Good

The statistics on Britain's debt problems are truly frightening:

- Although there are only 59 million people in Britain, there are currently over 67 million credit cards in circulation.

- Unsecured lending on credit cards etc in 2005 totalled £216bn.

- The average Briton owes £3,175 excluding mortgages.

- Including mortgages, Britons have a combined debt of over £1.2 trillion.

- Outstanding balances on credit cards have gone up by 383% since 1994.

- The average debt of clients seen by the Consumer Credit Counselling Service has risen from £27,566 in 2003 to £33,000.

- Advice services such as Debt Free Direct say they received 275% more calls per day in December 2004 than they did a year earlier.

- Britain's bailiffs are enjoying 70% more work than they did two years ago.

- 15 million people struggle with repayments every year.

- 170,000 deceased people a year receive direct mail, much of it offering credit cards or loans.

- On average, people seeking help from Citizens' Advice were £13,153 in debt.

- According to the CAB, it could take 77 years on average for most people who come to them to get back into the black.

Our home cost just 50p, now it's going for £145,000

Owners reap a windfall as inner city is regenerated

Lucy McDonald

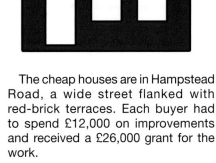

Houses that were sold seven years ago for 50 pence each in a desperate attempt to regenerate an area plagued by high unemployment, crime and antisocial behaviour are now being sold for up to £145,000 each.

The homes in North Benwell, a rundown area of Newcastle upon Tyne, have increased in value by about 29 million per cent compared with the national average of 162 per cent over the same time. When the houses were sold eight years ago by the city council there were more than 250 applicants for each one.

Mohammed Naeem, 41, was one of the lucky ones. The restaurant manager moved from a cramped flat to the spacious terraced home with his wife Yaqoob, 32, and their growing family.

He was initially warned off: 'My friends told me not to buy in Benwell – even for 50p. It had a terrible reputation, but we like it. Our neighbour's just sold his house for £145,000. But that doesn't shock me. I'm happy. I bought a house for 50p. Now look what it's worth.'

In 1999, while homeowners in most of the country revelled in record property prices, the market in Benwell had collapsed. Although it is just a mile from the affluence of Newcastle city centre, poverty and despair seeped out of every burnt-out car, broken window and boarded-up home.

Home ownership levels were low, unemployment high and most residents were living on benefits. Kerrie Clarke, a local estate agent, said: 'North Benwell used to be grim. It was all right by day, but by night it was a different story.

Good people used to shut their front doors and hope for the best.

'Investment buyers snapped properties up for next to nothing. I remember one auction where a man bought three flats on his gold card.'

Today it is still more Coronation Street than Acacia Avenue, but Benwell's fortunes have improved. Crime and the number of empty homes have dropped by a third. There are hanging baskets, recycling boxes and even a communal compost heap. Drivers used to park in their backyards to protect cars from vandalism, but now the streets are lined with vehicles.

But according to the 2001 census this still ranks among the country's most deprived areas. Four in 10 of its adults have no qualifications and its population has fallen by 33 per cent in 20 years. More tangibly, the barbed wire on back gates, bursts of graffiti and local troublemakers indicate that its insalubrious past has not entirely departed.

Salik Uddin's family is the first of the original 50p owners to move. They have sold up for £145,000 and are leaving later this month. They are grateful for the chance to make their start on the housing ladder but glad to go.

'I can't wait to get out,' said Salik, 22, a waiter. 'We're moving to Middlesbrough, to an area that's really posh. Our new home is lovely – four bedrooms, a garden and a shed the size of a house. The streets are safe. I've never lived anywhere like it. Our house here was worth 50p. I can't believe what it costs now.'

The cheap houses are in Hampstead Road, a wide street flanked with red-brick terraces. Each buyer had to spend £12,000 on improvements and received a £26,000 grant for the work.

All of the 50p houses were originally two flats, but a condition of purchase was that they be converted into family homes. From the outside the Naeems' three-storey home looks like a normal terrace house, but inside it is startlingly roomy. There are seven bedrooms and a huge bathroom. The walls are cream, the floors wooden and the sofas L-shaped, all a far cry from the boarded-up shell they bought eight years ago.

Next door lives charity worker Sahina Begum, 30, with her husband and their three sons. She said: 'The area's changed. There's less racial crime and vandalism. No one used to want to live here, but now we get offers for our house all the time.'

Sir Jeremy Beecham, a local councillor of 40 years, said: 'It was a device to encourage interest in Benwell which suffered from a preponderance of poorly managed, rented accommodation. It was a slightly two-edged approach. On one hand it drew attention to the collapse of the area, but it also began a renewal.'

The Observer 7 January 2007

How to live to be 150

Experts believe that the first person to live half way through their second century has already been born. Jeremy Laurance, health editor, reports on the stunning breakthroughs that science promises, while Sarah Harris outlines 10 ways to extend your life

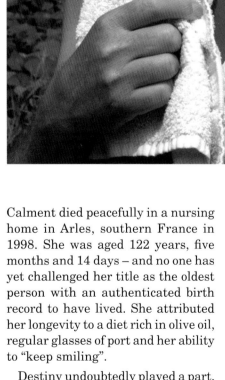

For today's centenarians, living to be 100 is an achievement marked by a message from the Queen. Within two generations it could be as routine as collecting a bus pass.

The first person to live to 150 may already have been born, according to some scientists. Worldwide, life expectancy has more than doubled over the past 200 years and recent research suggests it has yet to reach a peak.

What will the world be like when people live long enough to see their great-grandchildren and great-great-grandchildren? Extending life by adding extra years of sickness and growing frailty holds little appeal. Increased longevity is one of the modern world's great successes, but long life without health is an empty prize. The aim is for humans to die young – as late as possible.

It is eight years since Jeanne Calment died peacefully in a nursing home in Arles, southern France in 1998. She was aged 122 years, five months and 14 days – and no one has yet challenged her title as the oldest person with an authenticated birth record to have lived. She attributed her longevity to a diet rich in olive oil, regular glasses of port and her ability to "keep smiling".

Destiny undoubtedly played a part, too. If you want to grow old, choose your parents carefully. The genetic determinants of long life are gradually being unravelled, in recent years at least 10 gene mutations have been identified that extend the lifespan of mice by up to half. The good news is that these super-geriatric mice are no more frail or sickly than their younger brethren.

In humans, several genetic variants have been linked with longevity. They include a family of genes dubbed the Sirtuins, which one Italian study found occurred more commonly in centenarian men than in the general population. Researchers at Harvard Medical School in the US, convinced they have discovered a "longevity gene", are now studying whether adding an extra copy of the gene extends the lives of mice. The long term aim is to find a way of manipulating the genes to add an extra decade or two to the human lifespan.

Other gene variants affect the production of growth hormone and insulin-like growth factor (IGF), both of which increase metabolism – organisms with higher metabolism tend to die sooner. Blocking receptors for growth hormone and IGF, so slowing metabolism, provide possible targets for anti-ageing drugs.

Also promising, but still far from yielding concrete results, are telomeres, which are present in every cell. Telomeres shorten with every cell division, like a burning fuse; when they can shorten no more, the cell dies. Inhibiting the enzyme telomerase to prevent the shortening of the telomeres in effect extends the lifespan of the cell, and, as we are comprised of millions of cells, could extend life.

Ageing cannot be reversed but it may, perhaps, be delayed. The emergence of the extremely old population has only happened in the past 50 years and is chiefly due to improvements in the health, lifestyle and environment of the elderly that started in the 1950s – how we eat and drink, where we live, what we do.

Ageing is an irresistible target for snake oil salesmen and the pharmaceutical industry. Several hundred medical compounds that can boost memory and learning ability are being investigated. Research teams are examining genes for Alzheimer's disease, mechanisms that cause cells to age and die, and brain interfaces that promise to pump new life into aged or diseased limbs. The aim here is to add life to years, as well as years to life, but ageing itself is taking over as the new target for therapeutic innovation.

One promising avenue of research is to increase the resistance of cells to the stresses caused by free radicals, unstable molecules that disrupt cellular processes. There is no evidence that the sort of anti-ageing compounds sold over the internet containing anti-oxidants that promise to tackle free radicals actually slow ageing. However, delivering antioxidant enzymes direct to the cell has been shown in mice to extend lifespan by 20 per cent – pointing the way to future research.

> The aim for humans is to die young – as late a possible

> Adding life to years, as well as years to life, is the new target

But the optimism comes with a warning – that the consistent increase in life expectancy we have enjoyed for the past 200 years could be about to go into reverse. Some Jeremiahs in the scientific community claim ours could be the first generation in which parents outlive their children. The greatest enemy of extending life further is growing obesity, they say. Its effects could rapidly approach and exceed those of heart disease and cancer. Calculations by US scientists suggest that life expectancy would already be up to a year longer but for obesity. As Jeannne Calment indicated, wisely if unexcitingly, on her 122nd birthday, those who live moderately live long.

TEN THINGS YOU CAN DO TO HELP INCREASE YOUR LIFE EXPECTANCY

Exercise regularly

Keeping fit is the elixir of youth. Even 30 minutes of regular gentle exercise three times per week, such as walking or swimming, can add years to your life expectancy. Aerobic exercise preserves the heart, lungs and brain, elevates your mood, can help ward off breast and colon cancer and prevent atrophy of the muscles and bones. Gareth Jones of the Canadian Centre for Activity and Ageing in London, found that for an over-50 who has never taken part in physical activity a brisk 30-minute walk three times a week can "basically reverse your physiological age by about 10 years." Not exercising can knock off five years. A 1986 study at Stanford University found that death rates fell in direct proportion to the number of calories burned weekly.

Eat the right foods

Certain foods delay the ageing process and may increase life expectancy. Green leafy vegetables such as spinach and broccoli are rich in antioxidants and beta-carotene. Diets high in fruit, vegetables, fibre and omega-3 oils, and low in fat may prevent high blood pressure and heart disease. In their low-fat diet of fruit, vegetables and rice, the long-living people of Okinawa also consume more soy than anyone on earth, and soy is linked to low cancer rates. Eating cooked tomato daily can slash your risk of heart disease by 30 per cent, found research at Harvard.

Find God – or friends

It's official: having religion pays off – and not just in the after-life. Nearly 1,000 studies have indicated that those who go to a place of worship are healthier than their faithless counterparts – and live an average seven years longer. One in 10 of the nuns of the convent of the School Sisters of Notre Dame in Minnesota have managed to reach their 100th birthday. But atheists should not despair: experts believe that a sense of community, and of belief in something larger than yourself, are vital ingredients in a long and happy life. Jeff Levin, author of God, Faith, and Health: Exploring the Spirituality-Healing Connection, argues that a place of worship provides a social network and a source of comfort to the ageing, ill and needy.

Live dangerously

Mild sunburn, a glass of wine and some low-level radiation sounds like a recipe for disaster, but many researchers believe that small doses of "stressors" can reverse the ageing process. While this "hormeosis", is not a licence to lie on a hot beach all day swigging vodka, mild exposure to certain harmful agents can trigger the body's natural repair mechanisms. The body is tricked into producing particular DNA-repair enzymes and heat shock proteins to fix the damage that has been caused. Sometimes the body's repair mechanisms overcompensate, treating unrelated damage – "rejuvenating" as well as repairing it. Hormeosis could stretch the average healthy life span to 90.

Be very successful

The more rich, privileged, successful and educated you are, the longer you will live. The Whitehall Studies, 1967-77, examined the health of male civil servants between the ages of 20 and 64, and found that men in the lowest-paid positions had a mortality rate three times higher than those at the top level. The study proved that the more important a task a person is asked to perform, the longer they are likely to live; that the person at the top with the big office, shouting orders will have a more relaxed and pleasurable existence than his frustrated underlings. And it's not only civil servants: Canadian researchers found that Oscar-winners live longer than other actors because of am increased sense of self-worth and confidence. And if you can't manage an Oscar, then only one extra year in education could increase your life expectancy by a year and a half.

Reduce your calories

One hundred years of hunger is what you can look forward to if you follow the Calorie Restriction philosophy. Practitioners of CR believe that by reducing your calorie intake (by between 10 and 60 per cent) you can extend life expectancy by lowering your metabolism and the production of harmful free radicals. It sounds like torture, but there is research to suggest that it works. One study reported that participants who ate 25 per cent less for three months had lower levels of insulin in their blood, a reduced body temperature and less DNA damage. Brian Delaney, president of the California-based Calorie Restriction Society, is aiming to live to 122 with a diet of barely 1,800 calories per day (2,500 is the normal for men).

Challenge yourself

An active mind is as important as an active body. Studies show that you can boost your immune system and delay the onset of conditions from depression to dementia by keeping your brain engaged and stimulated. Leonard Poon, director of the University of Georgia Gerontology Center, found that people who reach three figures tend to have a high level of cognition, demonstrating skill in everyday problem-solving and learning. And Marian Diamond of the University of California, Berkley, found that rodents who were given problems to solve and toys to play with, lived 50 per cent longer.

Get your health checked

To last a century, stay ahead of life-threatening illnesses. It is possible with regular blood tests to detect the first signs of prostate cancer, one of the commonest causes of cancer deaths in men over 85. You can have free bowel cancer screening between 60 and 69, cervical screening for women aged 24 to 64, and mammograms for women aged 50 to 70 are also free. Figures show that 95 per cent of women who had invasive breast cancer detected by screening are alive five years later.

Live in a good area

It is not only how you live, but where you live that matters – and the residents of Okinawa in Japan seem to know the secret.

These Japanese islands are home to the world's largest population of centenarians. At 103, the daily routine of resident Seiryu Toguchi included stretching exercises, a diet of whole grain rice and vegetables, gardening and playing his three-stringed instrument, the sanshin. The clean-living Seventh Day Adventists of Utah also do pretty well, living on average eight years longer than their fellow Americans. Worst off are those living in poor, polluted urban areas such as Glasgow, where residents of the poorest suburbs have a life expectancy of only 54. Overcrowding, dirt and noise all contribute to high blood pressure, anxiety and depression, which reduce lifespan.

Enjoy your life

Good relationships are the key to longevity. Social contact staves off depression, stress and boosts the development of the brain and immune system. Most research shows that people with family, friends, partners or pets, live longer than those who don't.

Marriage is also a good idea if you want to meet the 100-mark, adding an average of seven years to the life of a man, and two to a woman. Indulgence, too, can be good for you. Chocolate can enhance endorphin levels and acts as a natural antidepressant, wine contains natural anti-oxidants, and laughing is good for your immunity.

The Independent on Sunday
7 January 2007

Senior citizens head for the sun!

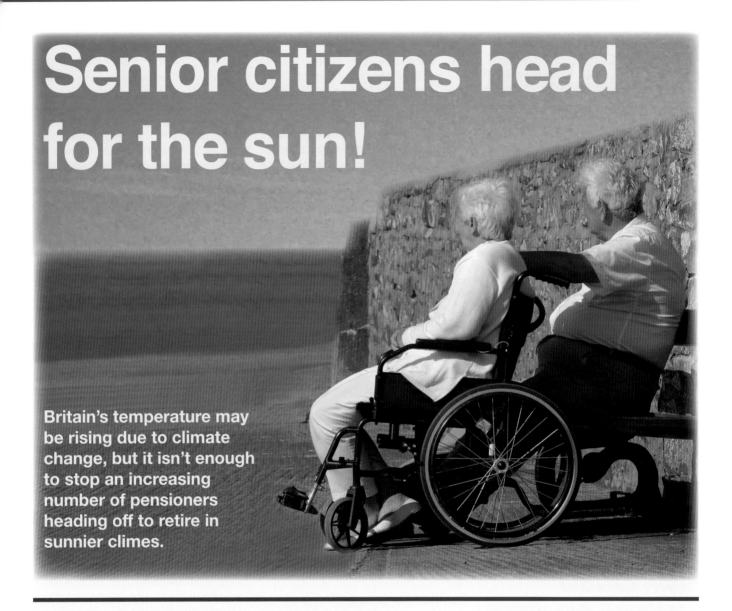

Britain's temperature may be rising due to climate change, but it isn't enough to stop an increasing number of pensioners heading off to retire in sunnier climes.

According to figures published in the recent report 'Brits Abroad', conducted by the Institute for Public Policy Research (IPPR), there are currently approximately 1 million British pensioners living abroad. IPPR researchers spent nine months collecting census information and other data from nearly 200 countries, in order to make a comprehensive assessment of the number and profile of Britons living abroad. They found that in 1981 there were just 252,000 British pensioners living overseas but by 1991 that number had more than doubled to 594,000. This figure had risen to 1 million by the start of 2006, which means that one in 12 British pensioners are now

"22% of Britons would retire overseas if money were no object"

living abroad. If this trend continues, then 19% of British pensioners, an estimated 3.3 million, will be based overseas by the year 2050.

Australia ranks as one of the most popular destinations with 1 in 5 of those retiring overseas heading there, while the US, Spain, Ireland, Canada and France make up the five other top retirement destinations. As well as those retiring abroad, an increasing number of Britons are

living abroad for part of the year, largely because of the increase in second home ownership. Due to properties abroad becoming more affordable, the number of British people buying second homes in the sun has soared. Danny Sriskandarajah, Associate Director at IPPR said, "Our report shows more people are moving from country to country: to study, to work and increasingly to enjoy their retirement. This 'silver flight' is the result of more Brits being increasingly willing and able to spend their retirement in Adelaide rather than Accrington."

According to a recent survey by Ipsos-Mori on behalf of estate agency King Sturge, 22% of Britons would retire overseas if money were no object with 21% agreeing that retiring abroad

"Often Britons come up against linguistic and cultural barriers that they haven't prepared for"

would be the best way to make the most of their retirement. While the majority of expatriates settle well into their new communities, evidence shows that a small but significant minority find the emigration experience much more challenging. Often Britons come up against linguistic and cultural barriers that they haven't prepared for and in response cluster together away from their host society.

"It's not fun in the sun for every British pensioner abroad. Our research shows that some find it difficult to adjust to life overseas and struggle to access healthcare or find themselves lonely without local language skills. Not every Brit enjoys their retirement in Benidorm more than they would have if they'd stayed in Bournemouth," explains Danny Sriskandarajah.

The charity Age Concern is aware of the many problems faced by elderly people living abroad and offers advice on its website to those who are considering it. They recommend that "If you have been to the country as a tourist you may need to see it out of season as well, and if the climate is a reason for moving, find out what to expect in all seasons." People's needs as residents are often very different to their needs as tourists and so Age

Concern recommend people live abroad on a trial basis first to fully understand the social and practical differences they will face. They also suggest, "If you know someone who has already moved there, get in touch with them and ask them about the things you're interested in."

The IPPR research sheds new light on to the implications of Britain's increasingly ageing population,

a topic of much government concern. Interestingly the findings also reveal that the dominant motivation for emigrating is the positive attributes to be found abroad as opposed to the negative attributes of the UK, with a small minority (12%) saying they would leave because they didn't like what Britain was becoming.

Source: various

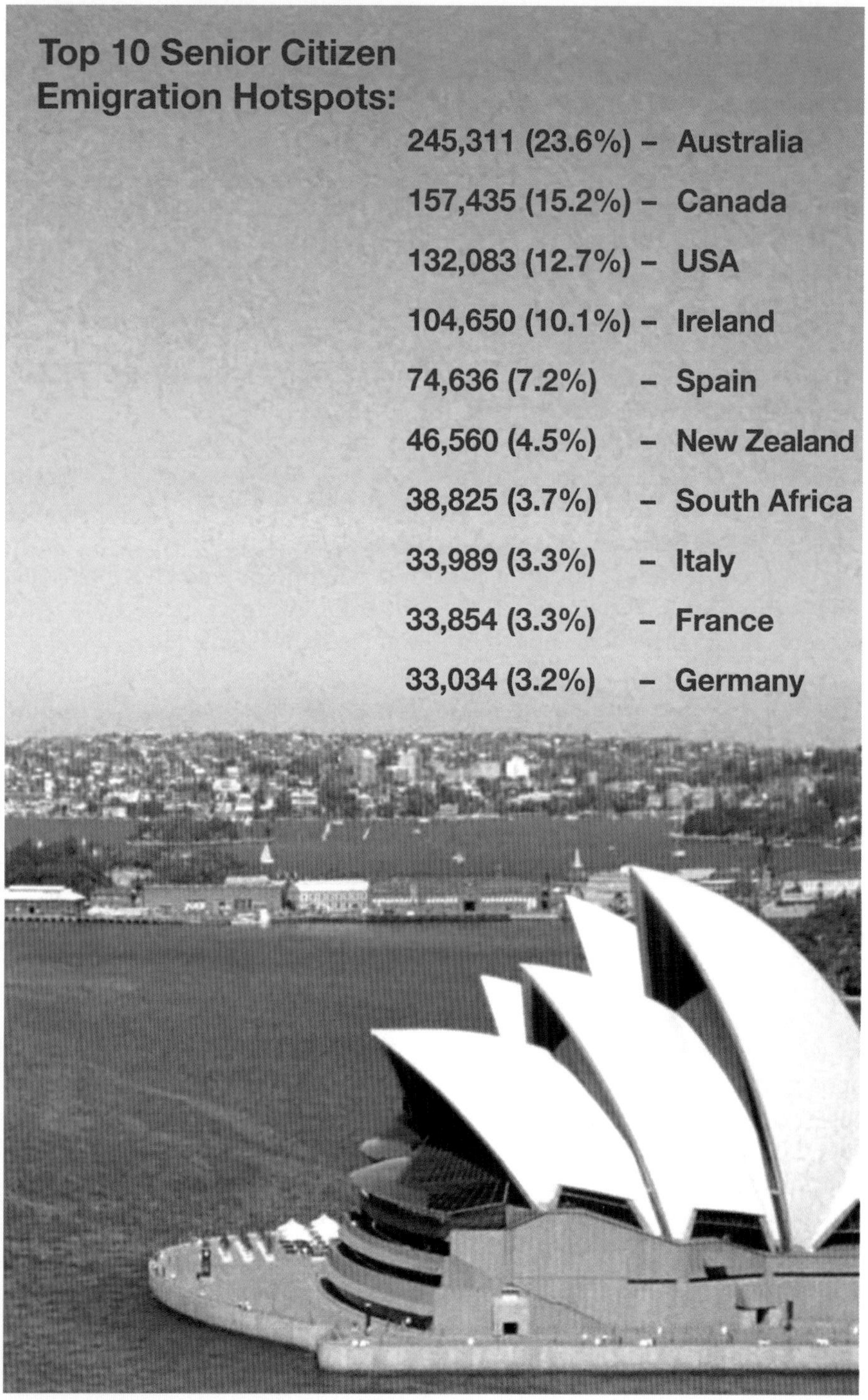

Top 10 Senior Citizen Emigration Hotspots:

245,311 (23.6%) – **Australia**

157,435 (15.2%) – **Canada**

132,083 (12.7%) – **USA**

104,650 (10.1%) – **Ireland**

74,636 (7.2%) – **Spain**

46,560 (4.5%) – **New Zealand**

38,825 (3.7%) – **South Africa**

33,989 (3.3%) – **Italy**

33,854 (3.3%) – **France**

33,034 (3.2%) – **Germany**

Marianne Talbot looks after her elderly mother. Her blog on the *Saga Magazine* website details the lows and not-infrequent highs of a carer's life

Helping hands

14 February 2007

In London for the day, with a carer booked until 6pm. By 5pm I had spent an hour and a half in the same traffic jam and saw no likelihood of early release.

I rang the carer (thank goodness for mobiles!). But she had to get home. One neighbour was out but the other – who has two children – plugged the gap (an hour and a half's worth). Came home to find mum in her element, in a tangle of arms and legs, tickling toddlers.

These relatively small crises are nothing compared to those I had before mother moved in. Compared to caring from a distance, having mum living with me is a doddle. I used to feel permanently guilty, not least because mum was lonely, but mostly because I worried about her so much. This worry was usually unfounded but occasionally it reached fever pitch.

Once, for example, I was away at a conference. Checking my answer-phone late in the evening I found an impassioned plea from my mother's vicar, telling me mum's alarm was ringing and she wasn't answering it, or the telephone. He had been to the house but all the curtains were closed. It was then midnight. I rang the vicar (poor man), but no answer.

Heart thumping I considered whether to ring the police, the social services and or her doctor. I went for the social services and was amazed that they answered the phone on the second ring, agreed to send someone out immediately, and said they'd phone me back as soon as they had news.

Heart fluttering, I settled down to wait.

Twenty minutes later (!) they rang back. When they had got to the house the police were there, with two neighbours and the vicar. This lot trooped upstairs together and went into my mum's room, the alarm still ringing. Waking up she turned on them a beatific smile and said how pleased she was to see them! She simply hadn't heard the alarm.

A happy ending. But it was incidents like that that made me realise that mother really couldn't go on living alone, 200 miles away from me (and neither of us with a car). Since she has lived with me the guilt and the worry have largely gone, to be replaced by organisational angst and occasional frustration.

But thank goodness for the social services. Both where mum lived before and here, they really are marvellous. They are usually efficient, always kind, sometimes saint-like and extremely knowledgeable. It is easy to carp – especially at the end of one's tether (and carers spend a lot of time there) – but without them the job would simply be undoable.

One of the joys of caring, actually, is meeting so many people who devote their lives to helping others, cheerfully and competently. Humbling really.

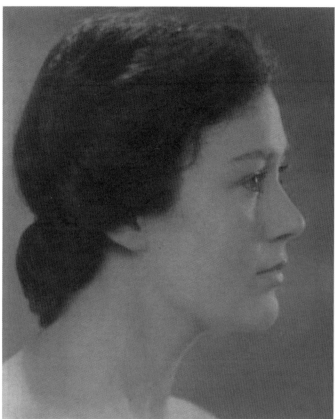

Lesley Talbot
All photographs courtesy of Marianne Talbot

Keeping Mum

23 April 2007
....

Mum used to be a great story-teller. She'd tell the same story over and over again, but everyone forgave her because they'd be newly embellished each time, and she'd tell them with such verve.

One of her favourites was about the birth of her twin brothers, Ian and Bryan. Mum was 14 at the time, and by all accounts (well, hers at least) an innocent of the first order. She hadn't been expecting anything out of the ordinary when, going into her mother's bedroom to say goodbye before school, she was told to look in the cot beside the bed.

She looked. There was a head the size of a coconut. 'Very nice.' she said dismissively, and started to leave. 'You could look at the other end,' said her mother. So she did. There was another one, exactly like the first. She had twin brothers!

Now that was interesting. Satisfying her curiosity, however, made her late for school. This was a serious offence, but mum thought that for once she had the perfect excuse.

'My mother had twin boys last night!' she told her forbidding headmistress. But twins in those days were unusual and her headmistress didn't believe her. The outrage in mum's voice at the injustice of being kept in after school was the climax of the story.

Mum's Alzheimer's was quite advanced before she lost her story-telling ability. At first the stories just got more outrageous. Then they started to blur into each other.

The story about the twins' birth, for example, would be merged with a story about being so late for school she forgot to put on her tunic and was made to wear a bright green science overall in which she stood out like a sore thumb.

Then it was as if the telling of a story would stand, for her, as a reminder of the story, so the minute she finished it she'd start it again.

I remember a particularly embarrassing lunchtime with friends at which she told the story of the twins' birth about four times, then started it another 20 times, before being cut off by me saying 'you've just told that one'.

Mum had – and still has – a good antennae for when she is behaving inappropriately. I fear I must have said 'you've just told that one' often enough for it to have inhibited her.

But it wasn't entirely me. She had started to lose the thread of the stories. She'd start one, then get lost in it, either tailing off into embarrassed silence, or making it up as she went along, so the whole was senseless. One day she just stopped.

The world is a sadder place.

Saga Magazine
www.saga.co.uk.magazine

Welcome to Eastbourne,

Sodom and Gomorrah by the sea

Jasper Gerard

Our youngsters are the worst-behaved in the world, but what of our oldsters? More than 55 per cent of Asbos in Eastbourne are reportedly slapped on the elderly. I'd assumed the nearest this arthritic town came to crime was seagulls dive-bombing pensioners' Eccles cake. Asbos? Surely less a problem than irritable bowel syndrome?

Now we learn the lives of Eastbourne's upstanding young are blighted by marauding gangs of Saga louts. Are pensioners foregoing meals on wheels for wheelies in nicked Cosworths? Or at least joyriding on other's stair-lifts, before legging it on their Zimmers? David Cameron will be visiting to launch his latest crime initiative: hug a granny. Hell, Eastbourne suddenly sounds so exciting, I might move there.

But bro', before you check out the 'hood, a warning: this is antisocial behaviour Eastbourne style. One Asbo was imposed for 'blasting out Des O'Connor at four in the morning', which should surely carry a custodial sentence. Another went to a grandad sunbathing in a 'seethrough, heart-shaped ladies thong', which sounds more Brighton but is a half-cogent argument for castration.

Typically, crime is not black on black but Black & Decker on patio extensions, which kills hope of hearing *The Archers*.

You can probably cop an Asbo in Eastbourne for not being a member of Ukip. The ambience is more Tring than bling, with fights not over mobile phones but the siting of mobile homes. And threats to slap a bitch? That will be because a labrador has been hangin' with a neighbour's shih-tzu.

Still, the Home Secretary should remind these feral grannies about the respect agenda. Where are their role-models? The elderly of today need a good clip round the ear. It's the only language they understand, squire.

The Observer 25 February 2007

Sadly, there is no human right to be happy

Photo: Lewis Whyld/PA Wire/PA Photos

Natallie Evans was refused permission by the European Court of Human Rights to use her frozen fertilised embryo without the consent of her ex-partner

The case of the British woman denied the right to use her frozen embryos is a cautionary tale of our times.

Mick Hume reports

It is coming to something when judges in Strasbourg have the power to rule on whether or not a woman from Wiltshire can have a baby.

Most commentators seem to agree that the European Court of Human Rights (ECHR) was correct to rule that the British woman, Natallie Evans, could not use her frozen fertilised embryos to get pregnant without the consent of her ex-partner. But there are bigger questions to be asked about the human rights culture that brought such a sad case to court in the first place, and put those judges in a position to make her pregnant or not.

Evans embarked on IVF treatment in 2001 after she was diagnosed with ovarian cancer. Embryos fertilised by her partner, Howard Johnston, were frozen to protect them during her cancer treatment. But after their relationship broke down, Johnston withdrew consent for her to use the embryos.

Evans has since pursued her legal battle to get pregnant, first through the UK legal system and then the European courts. Throughout, it appeared clear to many that she had little chance of winning. The law covering IVF in the UK is explicit on the principle of shared responsibility for the embryos and the need for both parties to consent to treatment. But the UK

It seems as if any notion can be legitimised by being cast in the magic language of human rights

Human Rights Act (HRA), and the European Convention on which it is based, allowed the lawyers to drag out what must have been a traumatic process for both Evans and Johnston for five years.

Evans claimed that the law's insistence on consent – of which she had been clear from the start – constituted an infringement of her human right to a family life, as established by the HRA. The ECHR's final judgement this week tried to put the case in the tortuous language of balancing human rights. 'We did not consider,' the judges wrote, 'that the applicant's right to respect for the decision to become a parent should be accorded greater weight than [Johnston's] right to respect for his decision not to have a genetically-related child with her.'

Evans' response was in a similar vein: 'Whilst a lot has been said about the rights of Mr Johnston, what I was fighting for was my right to be a mother and the rights of the embryos.'

The right to respect, the right to be a mother, the rights of embryos? This is where we have ended up today, when it seems as if any notion can be legitimised by being cast in the magic language of human rights.

It is worth recalling that, when the HRA 1998 was first introduced by New Labour with cross-party support, there was much high-minded talk about how the grand moral sweep of the new law would make Britain a better place. Ministers claimed that it would enshrine the general principles of equality by helping to create a 'universal human rights culture'. One of the authors of the legislation wrote a book describing the Act as nothing less than a code of 'Values for a Godless Age', a sort of ersatz set of moral commandments.

In practice, however, the HRA has turned into something very different – a kind of 'I'm Always Right Act' that has done much to cement the 'me, me, me' culture. It has often seemed that any personal complaint can assume the authority of universal values by being couched in the language of human rights law. By the same token, people can appeal to the courts to trample on laws, conventions or principles that have served society as a whole perfectly well by demanding their supposed human rights.

Thus one woman's claim that the break-up of her relationship effectively infringed her human right to get pregnant could call into question the principle of consent – a legal bedrock of the infertility treatment system in the UK and elsewhere. That the Euro-judges rejected her appeal should not distract from the potentially dangerous consequences of this state of affairs.

And nor has the impact of the human rights culture on infertility treatment always been so benevolent. The UK authorities' insistence on upholding the 'right' of children born by IVF to know the identity of their biological father, even if he was simply a sperm donor at a clinic, has led to a predictable collapse in the numbers of such volunteers.

The harsh fact is that nobody can be granted the human right to have a baby or a family life. Nobody can be guaranteed the human right not to be unhappy. Of course it is sad if women who want to have children cannot do so. But it is not the job of the courts to make their personal wishes come true or their private life more fulfilled.

The end result of this legal fetish, of course, is that it is not really the individual complainants who are empowered, but the judges. They are granted the authority to act as a cross between King Solomon and Jeremy Kyle, meddling in people's private affairs in the name of human rights. That is as inhuman as it is wrong.

Who really wins (apart from the lawyers) in a case like that of Natallie Evans? It is a stark warning of the destructive consequences of making society's laws on the basis of it's-all-about-me. And at a time when 'the politics of happiness' is becoming a big issue in the UK, it

The harsh fact is that nobody can be granted the human right to have a baby or a family life

should remind us all of what can happen when private lives and emotions are turned into the stuff of public debate and policy.

One 'universal value' that is worth fighting for is liberty – from the tyranny of the courts as much as any other. The American revolutionaries, founding fathers of the fight for individual freedom, promised their people only the right to life, liberty and the pursuit of happiness. The success or otherwise of that pursuit is a matter of common human endeavour. It cannot be assured to any aggrieved individual by calling on God, or His modern substitute, the Human Rights Act.

Mick Hume is editor-at-large of spiked.
13 April 2007
www.spiked-online.com

'What is done easily is done frequently'

Easy access to abortion was supposed to improve lives. It failed in that purpose and is now just another form of contraception, argues **Mary Kenny**

When 10th Baroness Howard de Walden – described as "a devout Roman Catholic", which is media-speak for "dotty extremist" – let it be known this week that clinics in Harley Street are no longer to be allowed to perform abortions, the abortion rights lobby denounced her as a sinister opponent of "choice".

But the lady is merely exercising her own choice – to do what she pleases with her own private property.

The event is not without irony. Harley Street, part of the large swathe of Marylebone run by the Howard de Walden Estate, which owns the freehold, has been the site for "society" terminations since the time of Lillie Langtry.

In the 1960s, when the Abortion Law Reform Association – the lobby that made David Steel's Abortion Act possible in 1967 – was at its most energetic, some of its adherents regarded Harley Street as a deplorable example of hypocrisy and class bias.

The rich went to Harley Street while the poor went to the back streets. I remember hearing the MP Lena Jeger make that point in an impassioned plea for abortion rights in 1966. Harley Street, she said, should be closed down because it provided abortions for the rich. Now it has been, thanks to Lady de Walden.

Abortion law and practice is full of such paradoxes. The original campaigners for abortion law reform emphasised the scandal of back-street abortions: they also claimed that legal abortion and better access to contraception would mean (a) no more unwanted children; (b) no more children in care; (c) no more cruelty to children; (d) a reduction in "teenage mothers" – the figures had reached a shocking 4,000 in 1966; (e) a reduction in all "illegitimacy"; (f) a reduction in "subnormal" – that is, low IQ, mothers – giving birth; (g) the disappearance of "subnormal" children; (h) a reduction in child murders and attacks on children.

In the mid-1960s there were some 5,000 children abandoned to local authority care. Access to abortion would solve all that, campaigners believed.

Forty years on, there are now some 50,000 children in care, and 40 years after the Abortion Act was supposed to decrease "illegitimacy", Britain has the highest rate of single teenage mothers in Europe, and a third of all births are now out of wedlock. As for improving conditions for children, a report from Unicef this week put the UK bottom of the developed nations' league for child wellbeing.

Meanwhile, Britain's official abortion figures increase by more than two per cent, year on year, with a special surge after Christmas, which this year even surprised one of the major providers, Marie Stopes. It carried out 5,992 terminations in January – a 13 per cent rise year on year and the highest figure in the organisation's 32-year history – and blamed the rise on an excess of binge drinking and partying.

In all social change, nothing ever turns out quite as predicted. Campaigners tend to believe, Pollyanna-like, that human nature is endlessly perfectable, and all will be solved when new laws are put in place. In truth, human nature is rather better described by Dr Johnson, who observed that: "Whatever is done easily will be done frequently."

And that, I suggest, is the short answer to those who wring their hands asking why Britain's abortion rate climbs annually, despite the wide menu of contraceptive choice. Abortion is relatively inexpensive today: it is easily accessed and the acceptable social attitude is that it is simply a personal choice, with no moral or ethical dimensions. This is not quite how it always works out, but that is broadly the way it is seen.

Easy, cheap and accessible – why wouldn't it increase each year? More than one in 10 women in their late twenties to early thirties has had an abortion, according to a survey earlier this week. Moreover, some women actually prefer abortion to contraception as a means of controlling their fertility. An experienced abortion practitioner once told me: "Some women do not know whether they want to be pregnant until they are. They want to exercise that choice after the pregnancy has occurred, not before.

'Abortion was expected to reduce the number of teenage mothers from 4,000 a year'

"They are then in a better position to judge their own mood, choice, circumstances, and to test the reactions of a boyfriend or partner. They are also satisfied that they are able to get pregnant. A lot of 'accidental' pregnancy is fertility-testing. Women who have been on the Pill for years want to find out if they can get pregnant. So a pregnancy, though unwanted, confirms their fertility."

This is not what some of the abortion reformers had in mind. Their purpose, they said, was to halt illegal abortion, help overburdened mothers of large families, and reduce teenage pregnancy. David Steel made it clear at the time that he did not favour "abortion on demand".

He believed in a strictly limited Act, which would rescue women in difficult situations, be it poverty, health problems or rape. The suggestion that party-loving hedonists might use abortion as a convenience was dismissed as "moral panic" by "Roman Catholic bigots and a few elderly Anglicans".

Neither did the birth control campaigners of the 1920s and 1930s – Marie Stopes and her American counterpart, Margaret Sanger – ever envisage that abortion would be a routine part of "family planning". Stopes was a eugenicist of almost Third Reich perspectives, desiring to

sterilise not only the inadequate, but anyone who wore glasses. However, she did believe in contraception – that is, fertility control in advance of sex. In her own lifetime she steered clear of abortion, preaching that "birth control" actually meant taking proper precautions.

Who would contest that Stopes won a battle for women (and men) in establishing entitlement to fertility control and rescuing it from the stigma of the squalid? Yet she, too, was a kind of Pollyanna in imagining that once contraception was widely available, abortion would fade away and all would practise responsible birth control.

Many do practise responsible birth control. Many women time their pregnancies and control their fertility with irreproachable integrity. Yet an increasing number, it seems, just regard abortion as part of the "contraceptive menu". Abortion providers will say that women choose abortion for a vast number of individual reasons: and if that also includes the post-Christmas party-binge, so be it. It's a personal choice.

And a cultural one: we have lived through a major cultural change, from "family planning" and "birth control" – words emphasising old bourgeois virtues of planning, deferred gratification, and self-control – to the era of fast data, instant feedback, and the "delete" button on the computer. The post-hoc decision of whether to continue the pregnancy, or press that "delete" button, reflects the spirit of our age.

So will the abortion figures – now standing at 186,000 a year – simply climb inexorably? Certainly, legal efforts to curtail abortion have repeatedly failed. In addition, the procedure is likely to get even cheaper and easier, and an abortion pill could soon be available over the internet, offered like Viagra.

The campaign for legal, safe abortion   *Photo: PA Archive/PA Photos*

Yet there remains a dislike of casual abortion among the general populace, and few really believe that abortion is a good way for a woman to control her fertility. Pro-choice campaigners and doctors who routinely carry out the procedures deplore the fact that in Russia, for example, 55 per cent of pregnancies are terminated. Social historians view a high rate of abortion in any society as a sign of social failure.

And on the other side of the coin is the frantic pursuit of fertility: it is anecdotally reported that perhaps a third of women seeking IVF have previously terminated pregnancies. This is not necessarily because abortion has made them infertile – more likely the passage of time. But for women entering repeated cycles of IVF, it can still be a rueful reflection that "the right to choose" is not always available.

An increasing number just regard abortion as part of the "contraceptive menu"

Sheer demographics may eventually bring about a sea change. The pro-natalistic societies are now in the majority Islamic, and the countries that are falling short of replacement level are mainly "post-Christian": even in France, where mighty efforts are made to maintain the birthrate, the popularity of Muhammed as a boy's name indicates that it is Muslim women who are providing the future generations. Eventually, this lack of young people will hit us where it really hurts – the economy.

In railing against Lady de Walden's personal decision about her private property, the abortion rights campaigners are displaying a wrong analysis of the situation – and not for the first time.

Daily Telegraph 16 February 2007
© Telegraph Group Limited 2007

I want a baby for my sister

Dear Miriam

Dr MIRIAM STOPPARD

FOR some time I have wanted to offer myself as a surrogate mum for my sister.

My sister has lost three babies and has always longed to be a mum.

My husband and I have talked it over and we both feel we should consider it as an option.

But before I talk to my sister, I want to gather as much information as possible so we're as well prepared as we can be.

I don't want to disappoint her in any way as she's had enough setbacks to cope with over the years.

Are there any surrogacy support organisations we can contact and what do you think of my being a surrogate mum for my sister?

Your Verdict:

You're too close to do this

❏ I'VE been a surrogate four times. I also have children of my own.

I find it very rewarding to have a baby for a couple who have waited so long for one but I don't think I could do it for a sibling.

I wouldn't be able to stop myself interfering with the child's upbringing which would lead to so many arguments.

If your sister does agree to surrogacy, use a stranger.

Mrs M Smith, Leeds

❏ DON'T you think you're being a bit hasty? I'm sorry your sister has lost three babies but there are other routes. Has she considered IVF, adoption or even fostering?

I'm only saying this because I think it would be difficult for all of you if you offered to be a surrogate mum for your sister.

Mr C Sands, Bridlington, E Yorks

❏ MY cousin, who can't have children, has asked me if I'd be willing to be a surrogate.

I've researched this thoroughly and I'm still in two minds whether to go through with it.

One part of me wants to help and the other thinks there will be huge problems with ours being such a close family.

Maxine, Dagenham, Essex

❏ I THINK there could be big problems having a child for your sister. Could you really watch it grow up having no say in its future?

It's a nice thing you want to do for your sister but I hope, for your sake, she refuses your offer.

Mrs G Roberts, Widnes, Cheshire

❏ SUPPOSE you do become a surrogate mum for your sister.

Have you considered the fact that any child you have will also be your niece or nephew?

Could you really cope with that?

Elizabeth, North London

❏ MY biggest sadness was that I couldn't have children. I'm a widow now and I wish there had been such opportunities around when my husband and I were trying for a baby.

It would have been wonderful to know that another woman would have been willing to have a baby for a childless couple.

I hope your sister agrees to your suggestion of help.

Mrs M Martin, Cambridge

Miriam's Verdict:

Go slow
– there are hard choices ahead

'When a family member offers to serve as surrogate, it may seem like a dream come true.

It's comforting to have personal knowledge of the surrogate's medical history and background. It's wonderful you're contemplating helping your sister to have what she wants.

However, the closeness of the family relationship can lead to difficulties so evaluate the situation carefully. Many authorities openly disapprove of family surrogates.

While the surrogate may view her participation as an act of love and adamantly refuse any financial compensation, the intended parents may feel uncomfortable with this imbalance.

Alternatives to a surrogate fee include a donation towards her children's education costs or paying for a holiday for their family after the birth.

Family members may prefer to keep their dealing on an informal level, but remember – surrogacy involves an important legal transaction. The surrogate is placing herself at risk physically and financially. How many cycles will be attempted? How will the obstetrician be selected?

Will the surrogate be expected to make lifestyle changes in areas such as diet, exercise and alcohol consumption?

Who will be present at the birth? You, your husband – your sister and her husband need to be together in this decision.

When we move into an area that involves another person making a commitment to us, you and your partner must share the same readiness and desire. Without this, an uncommitted spouse can undermine the effort. So go very slowly.

If you're are determined to pursue this option, find out more about it by calling the *COTS surrogacy information line on 01549 402401*.

Alternatively, talk to *Infertility Network UK*, an organisation giving general advice to people with infertility problems, on *08701 188088.*

You might want to contact the *Human Fertilisation and Embryology Authority on 020 7291 8200* too.'

The Daily Mirror 20 January 2007

Listen to the mother who wishes that her son had died at birth

An informed decision to let life go may be more humane than saving a severely ill baby without considering its future

Polly Toynbee

'Baby Butchers Launch Attack!" That was how pro-life campaigners reacted to the Nuffield Council on Bioethics' well-reasoned new guidelines on withholding treatment from premature babies. Their objections were echoed more politely by other religious groups: the Society for the Protection of Unborn Children called it "nothing short of eugenics". The BMA opposed any "blanket rules": it wants decisions left to the widely divergent practices (and beliefs) of individual doctors.

The Daily Mail's front-page photo of a five-year-old – "Now doctors say babies like her should be left to die" – found one of the infinitesimally few healthy children born at 22 weeks' gestation who survived against all odds. Her mother says: "Medical staff are not God and they should never be allowed to decide if a baby lives or dies."

But others will remember the baby Charlotte Wyatt. Her case was much championed by the Daily Mail, which no doubt encouraged her parents' fateful decision to demand every medical intervention to keep her alive. The Mail was unabashed by this story's less than happy ending. Charlotte was born three months premature with severe brain and organ damage, and her case became a right-to-life legal battle between her parents and doctors. Now aged three, she is still in hospital with oxygen and other tubes. Social services are searching for a foster home: her parents have separated and her mother visits infrequently as she has three other children. But with a shortage of 10,000 foster parents, the child may stay for ever in hospital. Few would think this a life well saved.

The Nuffield's eminent group of professors of law, medicine and ethics drew up the guidelines in response to the rising number of premature babies and the wide variation in their treatment. They recommend that babies born before 23 weeks should not be resuscitated, as only 1% of these survive and a high proportion of those will suffer severe disabilities. Between 23 and 24 weeks the prognosis is poor – most die and two-thirds of the survivors end up disabled – but they say parents should make the final decision. Once a baby reaches 25 weeks, intensive care should normally be given, and half will live. (An unintended consequence of this report will be an end to the anti-abortion lobby's claim that the abortion laws need tightening to lower the current 24-week cut-off: this report does not suggest a 24-week foetus is viable.)

Parents may be deceived by care in a baby unit. If they imagine the same kindness awaits outside, they are in for a shock

At the report's official launch Dr Jane Campbell, the distinguished campaigner and convener of the anti-euthanasia group Not Dead Yet, complained that no disabled person was on the committee. Why didn't they consult those who wouldn't be there now if they had been allowed to die at birth? How does anyone else know what is or isn't a tolerable life? She is one of those campaigners who regards letting any life go on the grounds of extreme disability as akin to genocide of the less than perfect. They see abortion and non-resuscitation on the grounds of disability as an assault on the validity of their own lives. But that leaves out the wishes and the lives of parents. When it comes to foetuses and newborns, their fate depends on their parents' willingness or ability to sacrifice themselves to bring up a child whose own quality of life may be very poor.

At the heart of this report is the message that parents must be given written information explaining the risk of severe disability. Doctors have trouble describing probability; parents have trouble estimating it, often investing too much hope in slender odds. As in baby Charlotte's case, parents often can't predict their own ability to cope. Worse still, they may be deceived by the round-the-clock, one-to-one care in an intensive-care baby unit. If they imagine that anything resembling that kindness awaits them outside the hospital doors, they are in for a shock. Hospitals spend a fortune on each day in intensive care, but social services have no such funds. Only in an ideal world would money never be a consideration in life-and-death decision-making, whether in providing drugs or care; the report is graphic about the costs involved.

All these new parents should be given copies of Henrietta's Dream by Henrietta Spink, a warning of the battle ahead to get the necessary care. Thinking about the Nuffield report, here is what Henrietta wrote to me yesterday about the birth of her second severely disabled son, who was saved by massive medical interventions: "Had I known what we would be put through over the next 15 years of his life – even though he is my passion, my life and my joy – I would have wished he had died at birth. With a first profoundly disabled child who, aged nearly 19,

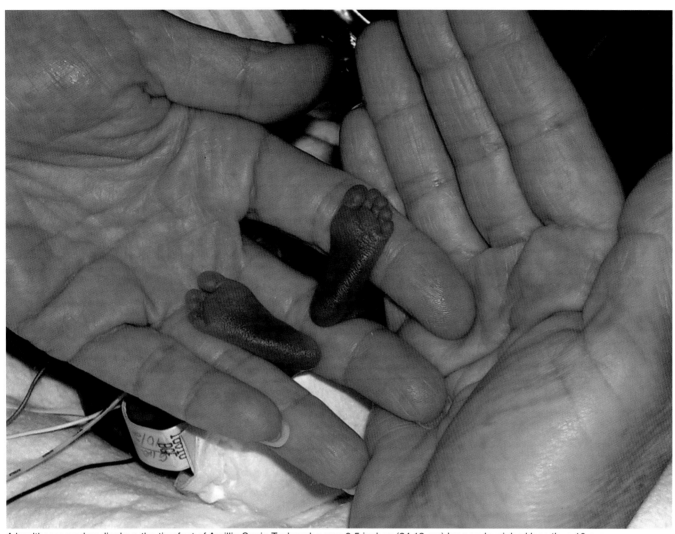

Photo: AP/PA Photos

A healthcare worker displays the tiny feet of Amillia Sonja Taylor who was 9.5 inches (24.13 cm) long and weighed less than 10 ounces (284 grams) when she was born at 22 weeks of pregnancy. The Nuffield Council on Bioethics has recommended that babies born before 22 weeks should not be resuscitated. (Amillia remained in hospital from her birth in October 2006 until February 2007.)

has not developed further than 3-6 months, I would know we could not survive without support with a second profoundly disabled child. We have lost our house, our jobs and any form of stimulating lives for ourselves. We don't get holidays and we hardly socialise. For 19 years we have put our children first and I have no regrets – my love for them will never die – but oh I so wish for just a little life for myself. To give us all quality of life by providing a proper care package would only cost half the amount of abandoning the boys into full-time care.

"If the government intends leaving people like us in a downward spiral of no existence then the very least they could do is legislate that euthanasia becomes legal. There is no point in spending hundreds of thousands of pounds to save a life and then sending the individual home with no support. It's inhuman, degrading and soul-destroying, and I would rather not exist if the next 19 years are going to be the same."

She has taken her local authority to court, only to discover that the law leaves it to councils to decide what level of help to offer, with the money not ringfenced. But local directors of children's services face an ever-increasing number of severely damaged children in need of help, and it's breaking their budgets. David Hawker, Brighton's children's director, now has one child costing £9,500 a week and another costing £4,500, with more in his care every year: it is not just premature babies but many more disabled full-term babies who used not to survive. So he is now cutting his youth services, the ones that will protect other troubled children from care or jail before long. He and the other children's

directors now want a ringfenced fund to pick up the bill for each severely disabled child, to protect the rest of the children's budget. Meanwhile, the government's strategy-unit survey showed that 77% of families could not get basic equipment such as wheelchairs and hoists: they soon become the very poorest families.

Shellshocked new parents are unlikely to have thought about any of this at the sudden arrival of a very sick baby. They probably never met a family falling apart under the strain of a severely disabled child: even the best help of the state would never take that away. Suddenly confronted with a tiny baby fighting for breath, they need all the information these guidelines can give before making decisions. Sentimentality or right-to-life rhetoric is no guide.

© The Guardian 17 November 2007

Too Much Choice Can Be A Dangerous Thing
Says Robert Matthews

We all love choice, don't we? It is surely everyone's basic right to be given the widest possible choice of everything, from consumer products to political parties. Well, at least politicians think so. For them, the right to choose is up there with motherhood and apple pie as an Inherently Good Thing.

It's time they were put straight. Sometimes choice isn't a good thing at all. Sometimes it is just a pain in the neck. Or, in my case, heart. After a bit of trouble with my ticker, I was contacted recently by someone saying she was from the NHS 'Choose and Book' scheme. Apparently, this is part of the multi-billion-pound programme to computerise the health service, and is designed to give us all more choice over when and where we see an NHS consultant.

Within about 20 seconds of getting the phone call, I was more in need of a defibrillator than an NHS consultant. I was told that I had a choice of cardiology departments, consisting of four hospitals: my local one, plus three others, all more than 20 miles away. This seemed like a no-brainer. Why should I want to travel miles to see just another cardiologist in a white coat when I could simply stroll down the road instead? Then I had a brainwave – maybe one of the other hospitals had a brilliant cardiology department and had come out top in some or other league table. So which of the four hospitals had the best team? "Oh, I can't tell you that," the Choose and Book

 Psychologists are concerned about the way that people respond when presented with choices

person replied. "But I can tell you about the restaurants and car-parking."

Oddly, the availability of tuna sandwiches and parking spaces had not struck me as key criteria in chooing a cardiologist, so I tried something else. "What about waiting times?" I was told they were all much the same – 40-odd days. So I ended up doing what I would have done anyway, and chose my local hospital. Apparently most people end up doing precisely that – which does seem to back the view of many doctors, which is that the whole Choose and Book scheme is some politically driven gimmick that will do little apart from make some IT companies rich at the taxpayers' expense.

Walking away

Actually, it may be worse than that. Psychologists have become increasingly concerned about the way that people respond when presented with choices. They are finding that people often deal with lots of options by making no choice at all. A few years ago, a pair of American psychologists set up an experiment in a California supermarket centred on an in-store jam stall. When a modest selection of six varieties of jam were on offer, around 40 per cent of customers stopped to take a look. When the range was increased to an eye-popping 24 varieties, the proportion of customers visiting the stall soared to 60 per cent. So far, so obvious – anyone who has been to a supermarket in the last 20 years knows more is better.

But here's the twist: only three per cent of visitors to the 24-variety stall actually bought some jam, compared with a whopping 30 per cent of those visiting the more modest display. The reason? Confronted with so much choice, customers at the stall simply felt overwhelmed, and their fear of making the wrong decision led them to make no decision at all. Meanwhile, those at the smaller display felt confident about being able to make a sensible comparison.

It's a finding that ought to give supermarket managers pause for thought, and politicians as well, as the same phenomenon can have a dire effect on weightier issues than jam-buying. One of the researchers behind the original study, Professor Sheena Iyengar of Columbia University, has been looking into the looming problem of millions of workers in the US who are failing to take out retirement plans. According to Prof Iyengar, one of the key reasons is the sheer range of plans available, with companies falling over themselves to offer a host of options, thinking this makes their plans more attractive. In fact, many employees just feel overwhelmed by it all, and walk away from any decision. The result is a financial time bomb set ticking by a misguided belief in the benefits of choice. The consequences of offering people too much choice in healthcare hardly bear thinking about. But I hope someone is.

BBC Focus Autumn 2006

Robert Matthews is Visiting Reader in Science as Aston University, Birmingham

"Thank you for choosing Greenfields Hospital. Today your peritoneal dialysis comes with salmon en croute, new potatoes, and a cheeky Chardonnay"

Telling porkies to the brain

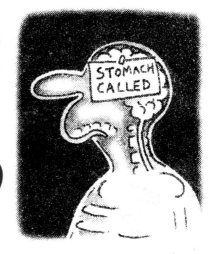

Oliver Pritchett

Let me, explain, as simply as I can, how this new chewing gum would cure obesity. Scientists believe that the hormone pancreatic polypeptide, placed in the gum, would send a signal to the brain saying that the stomach was full. So the person chewing would eat less and lose weight.

That's it, in a nutshell. The stomach sends a message saying, "Hi there, this is the stomach. That was absolutely delicious, but I really couldn't manage another single mouthful." And the brain probably replies: "Are you sure? Just try one more roast potato – they're cooked in goose fat, just as Nigella recommends."

"No, I couldn't possibly," the stomach insists. "It was lovely."

"Right, let's move into the other room and catch up with the gossip."

"I mustn't stay long," the stomach says. "I've got an early start tomorrow for a working breakfast."

The risk is that there will be physiological readjustments in the brain. To put it in layman's terms, it becomes suspicious. Next time the stomach gets in touch to cancel its order for chips, it says: "Not so fast, sunshine! You're up to something. I've just had the lower left molar on the line telling me it's not aching any more, but there's something fishy. I bet it was actually a couple of Nurofen impersonating the molar."

"Would I deceive you?" the stomach protests. "I'm just a simple stomach. You're the clever one. I've just had enough chips and that's the honest truth. It's a gut feeling. May I never rumble again if I tell a lie."

The brain is not convinced. It has a nasty feeling that various parts of the body are ganging up on it, trying to deceive it. Come to that, the twisted knee has suddenly gone very quiet. And what has happened to that reassuring dull throb in the right shoulder? Something is definitely up, the brain decides.

An impairment of receptors may then occur. A simpler way of expressing this is to say that the brain folds its arms, turns away and says: "La, la, la, la, I'm not listening to you. La, la, la." Or to put it another way, the stomach sends messages to the brain, via the pancreatic polypeptide, but the brain never returns its calls. The stomach complains: "There's been a total breakdown in communication in this body. And, in the meantime, what am I supposed to do about this slice of Genoa cake?"

Scientists now believe they may have the answer to this problem. It is a drug (in the form of a large, oblong yellow pill) which makes the stomach's messages appear more convincing to the brain. I suppose you could say it makes pancreatic polypeptide appear "sincere". Obviously, in order to deceive the brain, it has to be administered surreptitiously. Inside a doughnut, for example.

Meanwhile, I expect you are wondering about that twisted knee. Feeling its signals to the brain are being ignored, it starts clamouring for attention, sending out all sorts of contradictory signals, It's hot, it's cold, it's itchy, and so on. Finally, in desperation, it brazenly informs the brain that it is hungry. Obviously, it's a little more complicated than that, but essentially it means we are going to get millions of slim people suffering from the affliction known as "hungry knee".

Fortunately, we have a solution. We can implant a small device in the brain which has a similar effect to a spam filter on a computer. So, when contacted by the hungry knee, it sends back a message saying, "I am not in my skull at the present time, so I am unable to deal with your message. Please make other arrangements."

You can also have a daily injection of a drug that causes signals from your molar, your shoulder and the rest of the body to be diverted to the stomach, which evaluates them before forwarding them to the brain, accompanied by what you might call a neurological Post-it note saying: "These are genuine messages for your urgent attention."

I hope this has made things clearer.

The Daily Telegraph 17 January 2007
© Telegraph Group Ltd

'There are strong indications of intelligent design'

Stuart Burgess is Professor of design and nature in the department of mechanical engineering at Bristol University. He argues that intelligent design is as valid a scientific concept as evolution.

Nick Jackson

Current scientific philosophy is to rule out completely the possibility that a creator was involved. But there is no scientific justification for making such a sweeping assumption. Science should always be open-minded.

Newton, Kelvin, Faraday and Pascal had no problem with a creator and with design. There is no reason why a modern scientist cannot take the same position as these eminent scientists. Three hundred years ago, there was so much support for intelligent design that life could be difficult if you were an atheist. Now the opposite is true; life can be difficult if you show the slightest sympathy for intelligent design.

Evolution cannot be taken as a fact of science because of the ambiguities in the evidence. The fossil record can be evidence for and against evolution because of the gaps. Similarities in DNA code can be just as much evidence for a common designer as for evolution. Most significantly, scientists have failed to reproduce the spontaneous generation of life for 60 years.

I've been designing systems like spacecraft for more than 20 years. One of the lessons I've learnt is that complex systems require an immense amount of intelligence to design. I've seen a lot of irreducible complexity in engineering. I have also seen organs in nature that are apparently irreducible. An irreducibly complex organ is one where several parts are required simultaneously for the system to function usefully, so it cannot have evolved, bit by bit, over time.

The mammalian knee-joint is an organ that appears irreducible. Everyone has a four-bar linkage in their knee. Engineers know that for this to work, you need all four bars to be present. Every time we walk, we're using irreducible mechanisms. Evolutionists have not been able to explain how the knee joint evolved step by step. We cannot prove that an intelligent being designed these, but at present no one can prove that they evolved, either.

There is a real difference between

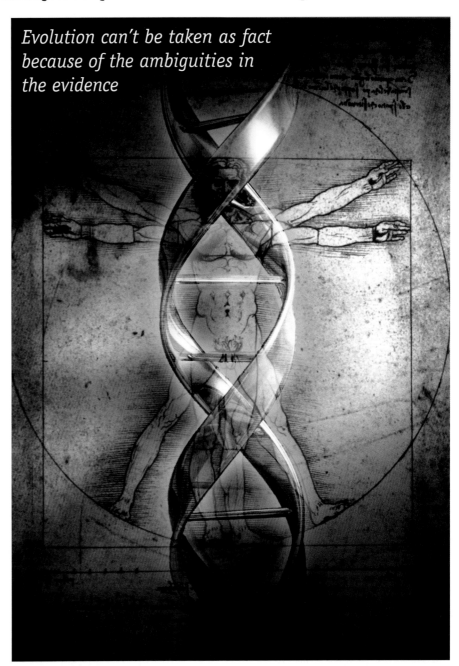

Evolution can't be taken as fact because of the ambiguities in the evidence

intelligent design and creationism. Creationism is about who the designer is and why he created the world. For this reason, I don't think creationism should be taught in a science lesson. But the question of intelligent design is completely different. It only addresses the question of whether an intelligent designer is needed for life to have been possible. The possibility of a designer should be mentioned, however briefly.

I can understand that some people are worried about the implications of the existence of a creator, but it's not science to rule something out because you don't like the implications.

The Independent 8 February 2007

Why I hate Intelligent Design.
It's simply IDiotic

"It's so we can get some peace up here"

Richard Fortey

A snare has been cleverly set by the proponents of Intelligent Design in their quest to prove that Charles Darwin got it wrong.

The vast majority of scientists feel nothing but distress that the teaching of Intelligent Design (ID) has been promoted in a number of our schools, particularly the faith schools beloved by Tony Blair.

Fundamentalists of both Islamic and Christian persuasion meet on this rather implausible common ground. Both these groups of religious hard liners deplore Darwin and all his works.

Scientists tend to get angry when confronted by what they see as the gross distortion of truth promulgated by Intelligent Designers. This has come across badly in "balanced" debates in the media. As was the case with arguments over the

MMR vaccine, the scientist when provoked can unwittingly appear to be a fulminating zealot. By contrast, many of the proponents of Intelligent Design have contrived to appear to be in favour of free speech. Aren't those scientists spluttering with rage and crying "nonsense" the very picture of a threatened Establishment? On this platform the evolutionary scientist rather than the ID enthusiast can seem to be the less reasonable of the two.

The trouble stems from the use of the weasel word "theory".

Successive Presidents of the United States have got themselves off the hook with the Christian fundamentalist lobby by the deployment of this useful but traitorous word. Ronald Reagan would flash his aw-shucks smile and amiably reiterate: "I guess Evolution is just a theory." This has become a mantra among ID proponents. If evolution is one theory – then ID is another, or so the argument goes.

The crux of ID is that evolution is purposeful, and that an "invisible hand" has operated at crucial stages to direct the course of life onwards and upwards.

The Intelligence of the Designer is manifest at certain critical points – such as the creation of life itself. On the other hand, the scientific "theory" of evolution actually breaks into two components. The first part is to assert that descent of all organisms from a common ancestor has, indeed, happened. To deny this is the equivalent of believing that the earth is flat, or that the sun goes round it. Both could be described as theories, though nobody has taken them seriously for hundreds of years.

Some fundamentalists still believe that creation happened a few thousand years ago. No respectable scientist believes this. Since the unscrambling of the genome has recently been added to evidence from the fossil record, it might be said that descent is simply a fact. We share genes with bananas and bacteria. At this deep level, DNA proves that humans are joined to all other life.

This ought to awake nothing but wonder in all of us, but some find the thought of such a brotherhood of life scary. The other part of Darwinism says that natural selection is the driving force behind evolution. This is where the ID protagonists come in. They accept the long timescale required from what we know of the age of the earth, but substitute supernaturally directed selection at critical points in life's long history. They might say that proteins are too darn complicated to have arisen by natural selection alone. This kind of assertion drives rationalists crazy, because it is impossible to refute by a critical experiment.

There will always be another protein, another example of that supposed extra, guiding ingredient. The problem for scientists is that when this additional design factor is added it serves only to suppress questions – and science is all about tackling questions head-on. Why should we spend money on setting up experiments to simulate the creation of the first living cell if the motive force was a "designer"? No experiment can detect such metaphysical seasoning in the primeval soup.

Science has always been about tackling new areas of knowledge, with theory and experiment interacting creatively. If God's influence is invoked for any breakthrough in life's story, research is simply stopped dead in its tracks: no point in investigating further. ID therefore becomes a brake on discovery, not a way of enriching it.

In my view, God has overly got mixed into the argument. Scientists are often presented as the champions of atheism. This is typified by Richard Dawkins's views of theistic "delusion". Although I might agree with much of what Dawkins has to say, it might be that his almost theological espousal of atheism has served to up the stakes in the ID debate. In fact, there are many world-class scientists who are also believers. But they also believe that God should not be introduced into the explanation of nature.

A worthwhile theory always suggests new lines of investigation, and on this criterion Darwinism has passed with flying colours. Field and laboratory studies helping us to understand how evolution works are beyond counting. The behaviour of Darwin's finches on the Galapagos Islands has been studied for decades.

A million generations of fruit flies have given up their lives to unravel the mysteries of the expression of genes. In the process many debates have opened up – like the relative importance of sex or geography in generating new species.

This does not mean that Darwin is in trouble. It just means that the science is still vigorous, that understanding is honed progressively. So that is why biologists get so mad at the propagation of ID.

It wastes time. It suppresses research rather than encouraging it. It's not really a theory, it's a story. It serves to kill curiosity rather than encourage it. Sometimes it is right to get angry in the face of unreason. Darwinists are readily labelled. There should be an equivalent term for the proponents of Intelligent Design.

May I suggest IDiots?

Richard Fortey is a senior paleontologist at the Natural History Museum in London and a Fellow of the Royal Society. He won the Royal Society's Michael Faraday Prize for the public communication of science in 2006.

The Daily Telegraph 30 January 2007
© Telegraph Group Limited 2007

Where Dolly went astray

Ten years ago the first mammal cloning seemed to herald a new era of medicine – then nothing happened. **Robin McKie**, who broke the story, meets the pioneer who says Britain let another breakthrough slip away

It was a breakthrough decades ahead of its time. On 23 February, 1997, the world learnt that British scientists Ian Wilmut and Keith Campbell had created the first clone of an adult mammal. 'They have taken a cell from a sheep's udder and turned it into a lamb,' ran The Observer's front-page story. Dolly the Sheep had arrived.

The creation of Dolly – at the Roslin Institute, the agricultural research centre near Edinburgh – opened up the prospect of an era of new medicines and treatments for conditions such as Alzheimer's and Parkinson's. It also triggered a fierce debate about the prospects of cloning humans and creating armies of Saddam Hussein doppelgangers.

Yet, despite the fuss, neither medicines nor cloned dictators have materialised. For a technology that promised to transform the world, this absence is startling. Indeed, most recent headlines have focused on South Korean scientist Hwang Woo-suk. He once claimed to have cloned human embryos and extracted stem cells, which have the potential to be used as life-saving medicines. However, Hwang has since been revealed to be a fraud.

Controversy, but not results: not much of an epitaph for Dolly. She died in 2003 and her stuffed remains are now displayed in Edinburgh's National Museum of Scotland. Will we soon wonder what was so special about her? Why have we not seen more scientific breakthroughs emerging – particularly in Britain?

It is an issue that vexes Wilmut. At present the best use of cloning has been the creation of a herd of cows that can make human antibodies, he believes. 'This has really important implications,' he said in an interview with The Observer last week. 'If a virus or a cancer gets past a person's immune system, he or she is in trouble. Soon we may be able to use cattle to provide antibodies that would pick up such a tumour or microbe. It has great potential.' The trouble is that the herd is the creation of Jim Robl of Hematech, a company based in the United States.

In fact, Wilmut has moved on from the Roslin Institute, where he did his pioneering work, to become director of Edinburgh University's centre for regenerative medicine. In effect he has turned his back on agricultural research and moved into medical science. A major motivation seems to have been the failure of Roslin to take advantage of his cloning work for use in agriculture, though Wilmut is reticent on this issue.

A few years ago the companies set up by the institute to exploit his cloning techniques were sold to the US biotechnology giant, the Geron Corporation. With those companies went the rights for Wilmut and Campbell's cloning technology. As a result, if a scientist or company wants to make a cloned animal as a part of a commercial enterprise today they have to pay Geron for the privilege. Even Wilmut would have to stump up – though only if he wanted to use it for commercial purposes. Scientists doing basic research do not have to pay.

'We are not entrepreneurial in this country,' Wilmut said. 'This is another technology that has walked, which means we miss out from the point of view of return on investment, on employment and in getting good access to profits.'

Thus the rights to use cloning techniques, and the best example of its exploitation, reside on the other side of the Atlantic. It is not a healthy position.

On the other hand, Britain retains the whip hand when it comes to the use of cloning in medicine for humans. Human embryos can be made by cloning and then be used as sources of stem cells, which have great promise as treatment for diseases such as Parkinson's and Alzheimer's. However, work like this is banned in federal laboratories in the US, giving Britain a clear advantage in ground-breaking research in this field.

A classic example of the potential cloning holds for humanity is provided by one of the crippling – ultimately fatal – illnesses, motor neurone disease. Wilmut was recently given permission to create human embryos from the DNA of victims of the disease, which strikes people at an average age of 56 and affects about 1,200 people in Britain every year. The aim of his research was simple. He intended to grow embryos taken from motor neurone patients, then remove the stem cells – the cells that eventually grow into the bodies' different tissues. In this way, key insights into the development of the disease would be gained, raising hopes of developing new drugs.

However, the gods of cloning again conspired against Wilmut. He was persuaded by Hwang Woo-suk – then hailed as the world's greatest cloner

'This is another technology that has walked and we all miss out'

– that this approach was wrong and doomed to failure. So Wilmut gave up the programme and let his licence lapse. 'I should have known better,' he said. 'We'd visited Hwang in Korea on a couple of occasions and he had all these invalids in wheelchairs lined up in the audience in front of the platform that he was speaking from. He would tell them he would have them walking in no time. It really wasn't on.'

Now Hwang has been disgraced and Wilmut's approach vindicated. However, the licence has expired, which means his research plans into motor neurone disease have been set back by about five years. However, he remains determined. Indeed, his commitment is touching. In America, he pointed out, motor neurone disease is known as Lou Gehrig's disease, after the baseball star who died of it in 1941. In this country the disease should, by the same logic, be known as Jimmy Johnstone's disease. Johnstone was the Celtic winger who helped his team win the European Cup in 1967 and whose dazzling bursts on the right earned him the Glaswegian accolade of 'Wee Jinky'. Last year Johnstone died of motor neurone disease.

'I had the privilege of meeting him and his wife a few months before he died. He and I were roughly the same age, but he was completely paralysed from the neck down.' The recollection stopped Wilmut in his tracks, and for a couple of minutes he seemed on the cusp of tears. 'I am not normally lost for words. It was extremely moving meeting someone like that. Why are we not doing what we can for them?'

As head of his university's new regenerative medicine centre, Wilmut intends to do just that and aims to regalvanise his efforts in seeking breakthroughs in the treatment of motor neurone disease: 'That would be the best possible way to celebrate Dolly's life.'

Cloning will ultimately be extremely valuable to medicine, Wilmut added. It is just proving hard to exploit. It took 270 attempts to create the embryo that resulted in Dolly. 'That represents an efficiency of 0.3 per cent. Today we have got that up to about 3 per cent. But it is still very low.'

There are other reasons for our failure to follow on swiftly from Dolly's creation, however, as Simon Best of the UK Bioindustry Association pointed out: 'Dolly's creation was simply so far ahead of its time it caught scientists out. If you had taken a poll of scientists in 1997, the vast majority would have said there was no prospect of cloning a mammal for another 15 to 20 years.

'Wilmut and Campbell caught everyone by surprise. This field was considered so unpromising only a handful of scientists were working in it. There were therefore no promising young scientists, expert in the field, to take up this work and follow through with new breakthroughs. That is why we are still having to wait.'

Look at other great scientific discoveries and you see a similar picture, added Best. When Crick and Watson discovered the structure of DNA, it took more than 20 years for their work to be translated into biotechnology products including human growth hormone, blood clotting treatments and other drugs.

And the science behind DNA's structure was much less revolutionary than that involved in Dolly's creation. Crick and Watson indulged in a great deal of scientific detective work to make their discovery, of course. But Wilmut and Campbell carried out hundreds of highly complex biological experiments before they succeeded. To create Dolly they removed a cell from an adult sheep. Then they took an egg from another sheep, scooped out its DNA and inserted the first sheep's nucleus. After a series of chemical treatments, they then placed this artificial embryo into a third sheep and coaxed it to grow into Dolly. This is cloning or nuclear transfer technology.

'Until then, we all thought it was impossible to reprogramme an adult cell and persuade it to act like an embryo,' said Cambridge cloning expert Roger Pedersen. 'Wilmut and Campbell showed that was wrong. They turned back the arrow of time. And we are still trying to come to grips with the implications.'

Wilmut looks an unlikely scientific revolutionary. He has an amiable, avuncular demeanour and describes himself as 'a rather shy, reserved middle-aged Englishman'. It is a fair description. His casual, bearded appearance makes him look more like a Yorkshire farmer than a researcher whose work frightened the living daylights out of politicians round the world.

'I hadn't expected all that fuss,' he admitted. 'Even in the middle of it, I thought it would all die down. I remember being on holiday, walking along a beach in Scotland, six months after the story broke, thinking: "Oh, well, at least it is now all over and I can got on with my work." But of course, it wasn't all over. It has never gone away. It just shows what I knew about my work's implications.'

The Observer 18 February 2007

Ian Wilmut and Dolly

Photo: Maurice McDonald

Stem cell timeline

1981
Gail Martin at the University of California, San Francisco, and Martin Evans, University of Cambridge, isolate embryonic stem cells in mice for the first time.

23 Feb, 1997
Dolly the Sheep (born at the Roslin Institute) is revealed to the world. It is the first clone of an adult mammal.

July 1998
Noto and Kaga, the first cloned cows, are produced by the Ishikawa Prefectural Livestock Research Centre, Japan.

2001
The UK becomes the first country to legalise therapeutic human cloning for research.

Feb 2003
Dolly the Sheep dies.

April 2003
The sequencing of the human genome is completed.

Feb 2004
South Korean scientist Hwang Woo-suk and his team claim to have created 30 cloned human embryos and extracted stem cells.

August 2005
The first dog clone, an Afghan hound called Snuppy, is born in South Korea, also created by Dr Hwang.

Jan 2006
Dr Hwang's work exposed as fake.

July 2006
President Bush uses his veto in order to kill a bill to increase federal funding of stem cell research.

Luc Torres

WORLD'S WORST INVENTIONS

⑩ Religion

Many blame religion for starting or fuelling wars. It has often had a difficult relationship with science. Many early scientists believed in a deity – Sir Isaac Newton recognised that the Sun's gravity caused the orbits of the planets, but believed God created the Solar System. Science and religion sit uncomfortably together today, with the theories of intelligent design and natural selection battling it out.

⑦ Television

The square-eyed among us are doubtless surprised by this one. But it's actually reality TV that's the main offender with three per cent of the total vote. Making its debut in 1948 with Candid Camera in America, reality TV's popularity has soared in the 21st century – in the US there are two television channels devoted to it. Why it's so unpopular is anyone's guess, but then Z-list celebrities are so last year, darling.

⑨ Speed Cameras

Ironically, the speed camera prototype was invented in the 1950s by rally driver Maurice Gatsonides, who wanted to monitor his speed. The first film-based cameras hit the roads in the 1960s, with digital units introduced in the late 1990s. Department for Transport research claims up to 42 per cent fewer people are killed or seriously injured at sites with cameras – although these figures have been disputed.

⑥ Cigarettes

Potent carcinogens in cigarettes mean that men who smoke are 22 times – and women 12 times – more likely to develop lung cancer than those who don't. Smoking is also linked to other cancers and heart attacks. Pregnant smokers are at greater risk of miscarrying or giving birth to underweight babies. The World Health Organisation says up to 29 per cent of British men and 19 per cent of women smoke.

⑧ Fast Food

Americans are the ultimate fast food junkies, spending an estimated $142 billion (£73 billion) on it in 2006. But it seems our days of blithe over-indulgence in fatty, cholesterol-rich grub may be numbered, as we gradually wake up to the health risks. In 2002 some obese US teenagers filed a lawsuit against McDonald's accusing the fast food chain of fattening them up. A judge later threw out the claim.

⑤ The Car

The car haters out-voted the petrol heads. Developed in the late 1880s, the modern automobile was initially the toy of the wealthy, but falling prices have made it a key part of family life. The motor industry is now booming – 63 million cars and light trucks were produced globally in 2005. But a green fuel is unlikely to take over from petrol soon, so the car continues to add to our burgeoning carbon footprint.

The Focus top 10… Fast food, Sinclair C5s and speed cameras all rank in the top 10 most loathed inventions of all time. But what really gets you riled? Thousands of votes were cast on the Radio Times website and the results make for a surprising read…

(4) Sinclair C5

Is it a buggy? Is it a go-cart. No, it's the Sinclair C5. This three-wheeled-battery-powered-commercial-disaster of a vehicle was invented by Sir Clive Sinclair and launched in Britain in 1985. Even at just £399, only around 17,000 were sold. The original C5 topped out at 24km/h (15mph) – and was even slower uphill. This speed was intentionally chosen so a driver's licence was not needed.

(2) Mobile Phones

A surprising silver medal for the gadget that's revolutionised communication. Mobiles have been available in the UK since 1985, and have been widely used since the late 1990s. Almost three quarters of Britons now own one. Despite health scares linking mobile phone usage to brain tumours, most studies have found there is no increased risk. Maybe it's those annoying ring tones that have put mobile phones here.

(3) Nuclear Power

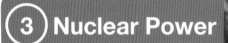

Accidents like the Chernobyl disaster blight nuclear power's CV. Reactor meltdowns are rare, but have devastating effects. Nuclear plants have higher construction and operating costs than their fossil fuel contemporaries, and are supported by large subsidies courtesy of the taxpayer. Waste storage is also a concern. But advocates promote nuclear power's green status as it produces no carbon dioxide directly.

(1) Weapons

Bombs, bayonets, biological weapons, you name it – innovations that go bang or cause bodily harm were the most widely frowned upon in our survey. Nuclear weapons were the worst offender, getting 11 per cent of the total vote. They've only been used twice in wartime – in 1945 the US dropped 'Little Boy' on the Japanese city of Hiroshima, followed three days late by 'Fat Man' which fell on Nagasaki.

Focus March 2007

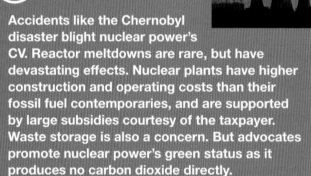

"I can think of a worse invention than the car... the car alarm!"

WEEOO WEEOO WEEOO!

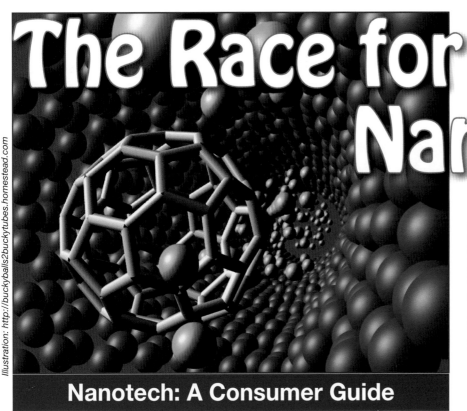

Illustration: http://buckyballs2buckytubes.homestead.com

The Race for Nanoland

Nanotech: A Consumer Guide

Is 'grey goo' about to eat the planet? Probably not, but there are real dangers with the development of nanotechnology that are not being addressed

Toby Shelley

A $1 trillion market lies just over the horizon. Not a previously undiscovered continent whose resources can be pillaged and inhabitants trained to labour and consume, nor a nearby planet where the little green men will trade in platinum for bottle tops – here we are talking about nanotechnology.

The claims and projections for this emerging basket of processes and products suggest its impact could be as major as finding a new land mass or trading with planetary neighbours. And nanotechnology is going to affect our lives, bringing benefits but also broken promises and serious dangers.

Nanotechnology is the systematic exploitation of the properties materials display at the scarcely conceivable scale of billionths of a metre, far smaller than most contemporary commercial chemical processes operate. At this scale many materials act very differently from how they behave at a larger scale. Basic science teaches us that diamonds and charcoal have different qualities but are both made of carbon. Similar disparities are exploited by nanotechnology. For example, materials that may not conduct electricity at a larger scale may

be highly efficient at the nanoscale, or the colour or transparency they display may be different, or they may be massively stronger. They may gain or lose toxicity.

The manipulation of these properties has applications in just about every area of life – from the very mundane (and already commercially available), such as translucent sun lotion and self-cleaning windows, to the highly targeted delivery of drugs specifically to infected cells, massive increases in the efficiency of solar power and fuel cells, and advances in computing that could both extend the limited lifetime of the current chip-based paradigm and take us way beyond it into the realms of DNA and quantum switch computing.

The spin is that nanotechnology will feed the hungry, power the energy-poor, and conquer disease. Its applications do indeed have the potential to bring great benefits. Tiny and highly efficient diagnostic kits capable of instantaneous scanning for hundreds of conditions and illnesses could be made from nanoscale components called quantum dots, housed in a latex bead and exposed to a light source. Solar panelling that can be rolled out like roofing felt could

power the most remote communities while water is efficiently filtered to eradicate a range of diseases. The most appalling pollution of land and water might be reversed using nanoparticles of iron.

We have been here before. Biotechnology was going to feed the world but what it has done is to tie millions of farmers to the products supplied by a handful of powerful corporations, speeded up the plunder of seed varieties from the developing world, and raised health and environmental concerns that have seen Europe refuse US foodstuff that Washington has then attempted to dump on African countries.

While some developing countries do have niche nanotechnology research programmes of their own, the spend on R&D is inevitably concentrated in the institutions and corporations of the rich world. Indeed, there is fierce competition between corporations and states to dominate nanotechnology. In 2000-2003, worldwide government spending on nanotechnology research was some $3 billion, more than three times that of the previous three years. The US federal spend for last year was estimated at nearly $890 million, and that excludes direct military spend and state level expenditure. Committees and hearings regularly assess the dangers of being outpaced by others.

At the same time, there is scarcely a major manufacturer in the world that does not have a nanotechnology strategy. For some it is a matter of wanting to exploit new materials and processes ahead of competitors. For others it is a matter of understanding emerging technology that might render their current processes and products obsolete. Some invest in in-house research, others farm it out to universities, or buy in to small specialist companies, or purchase patents or licences from players too small to exploit their discoveries.

With US government agencies touting a market value for nanotechnology of $1 trillion by 2015 (a more cautious $220 billion by 2010 is used by one German bank), there is little wonder at the excitement among corporate strategists. For the car industry, just the probable savings on rare metals used for catalytic converters is forecast to bring early savings of $1 billion a year and more accurate engineering another $2.5 billion. High-tech sensors at the nanoscale will have applications for medicine, transport ergonomics and security with a potential 2012 value of $17 billion, according to some estimates. And so it goes on for industry after industry, perhaps the most impressive being the semiconductor industry, where the value of nanotechnology could be $300 billion before 2020.

And what of curing malaria or lighting and heating fuel-poor communities? If there have been any studies of the market potential, we can be sure they are considerably less attractive than putting investment into treatment for obesity in American teenagers or supplying light-sensitive, power generating glazing for European office blocks.

Inevitably the military is deeply implicated in nanotechnology, particularly the US military. The quadrennial defence reviews that are the road maps of US strategy highlighted the importance of nanotechnology in 2001. Ambitions include the development of 'smart

dust', minute sensors deployed by the billion to monitor battlefields or entire regions. Missouri University has an army contract to marry nanoparticles and microchip technology into miniaturised warheads.

Meanwhile, the flip side of the promises held out for medical treatment using nanoparticles and understanding and manipulation of their properties is the threat of hitherto unimagined varieties of chemical and biological warfare, a concern already identified by the British MoD. The US military talks of 'bionanobots' that might identify enemy combatants by DNA analysis and then self-destruct in the brain, and of nanobots that could destroy hardware by eroding metals or rubber.

> **The spin is that nanotechnology will feed the hungry, power the energy-poor, and conquer disease**

We have become accustomed to the disparity in armour and firepower between the Palestinian stone thrower and the Israeli soldier, between 'Rolling Thunder' and the culvert bomb in Falluja. At MIT, the Institute for Soldier Technologies, partnered by Raytheon and DuPont amongst others, is using nanotechnology as part of the Future Force Warrior project 'to create a lightweight, overwhelmingly lethal, full-integrated individual combat system, including weapon, head-to-toe individual protection, netted communications, soldier-worn power sources, and enhanced human performance'.

One of the reasons that biotech food reached the shelves before environmental and health questions had been addressed was because regulatory agencies were not up to the task of assessing new products. The expertise was concentrated in the higher-paying corporate sector. Additionally, where a new technology

brings a paradigm shift, regulation is not geared up to ask the right questions.

This is the case with nanotechnology, and it means that we, as workers and consumers and inhabitants of our environment, are unshielded from the potential dangers of nanoproducts and processes. Materials manipulated at the nanoscale may well be familiar to regulatory authorities and have been passed as safe without those authorities having any proper understanding of the different properties – and potential hazards – of these materials at the nanoscale.

As late as 2005, there was no coordinated surveillance of new products anywhere because of their use of nanoparticles. Staggeringly, the US Food and Drugs Administration declared, 'Particle size is not the issue.' Even after the scandals and rows over GM foods, campaigners at the Canadian-based ETC Group found no regulation anywhere in the world governing the entry of nanoscale particles into food products. Treatments so small they can pass through the blood-brain barrier are a Holy Grail for researchers into Alzheimers, but what are the dangers of particles so small they can worm into every cell in our bodies? For a century communities have fought the blight of asbestosis. We do not know whether the rush to profit will unleash a hazard far more pervasive.

I have not touched on some of the more distant ambitions for and fears arising from nanotechnology – self-replicating products, factories in a shoe box, grey-goo consuming the planet. But if nanotechnology is to be anything like as transformative as governments and business believe, there are compelling reasons for civil society rapidly to involve itself. We need to be sure that profits are not put ahead of potentially catastrophic environmental and health risks, and that we are not at the starting line of a new arms race. More positively, we must demand that the benefits of an exciting new dimension in scientific research accrue not to those who need them least but to those who need them most.

Red Pepper September 2006

Our sexual obsession damages boys as well as girls

Rachel Bell

It's official: sexualisation harms girls. Of course it does. It harms all of us. It doesn't just make girls ill, it harms boys too, teaching them to be sexually violent.

The American Psychological Association's findings – that the portrayal of girls and young women as sex objects harms girls' mental and physical health – should be addressed at the root cause: the media. Powerful and profit driven, they are left to self-regulate with their own voluntary codes. Not only is this not working, it's harming society. The Government needs to introduce responsible media regulation, in which social responsibility and harm are not compromised for free speech. Only then will we see diverse representations of females in positive roles.

As a society, we should be extremely worried. The saturation of sexualised images of females is leading to body hatred, eating disorders, low self-esteem, depression, high rates of teen pregnancy and unhealthy sexual development in our girl children. It also leads to impaired cognitive performance. In short, if we tell girls that looking "hot" is the only way to be validated, rather than encouraging them to be active players in the world, they underperform at everything else.

But the consequences of sexualising girls are far more devastating than this. Rape is at crisis levels, and one in three women will be a victim of stalking, sexual harassment or sexual violence in their lifetime.

But who are the mysterious perpetrators of these crimes? Much of the media, the justice system and one-third of the public seem to think

> The number of young men using prostitutes has doubled in a decade to one in 10

alcohol is raping girls. That by getting drunk, dressing sexy and flirting, girls and women are responsible for the horrific violence committed against them.

Only 8% of rapes are stranger rapes. It is ordinary boys and men who are committing these sexually violent crimes against girls and women. It is appalling that when another rape or sexually violent crime is reported on the news – so ubiquitous it is unremarkable – it is never followed by a report asking: "Why are boys and men sexually abusing and raping girls and women? Where do they learn to film this abuse on their mobiles? Where do boys and men learn that having power over women and being violent is an acceptable way to be a man?" Instead, the onus is on girls and women to curb their behaviour and lives.

The sexualisation of girls and the normalisation of the sex and porn industries have made it increasingly acceptable and "fun" for women to be viewed as sex objects, and for men to view women as sexual commodities. To speak out against this trend is framed as "anti-fun" and "anti-sex". The pressure group Object has documented how men's "lifestyle" magazines and lad mags do not merely objectify women, they trivialise trafficking, sex tourism and prostitution. The number of young British men using prostitutes has doubled in a decade to one in 10 in 2000.

The charity the Lilith project has found that the increasingly mainstream pole and lapdancing and porn industries are careful to hide their links with prostitution, trafficking and sexual violence. A five-year-old boy can buy a lad mag and learn that women are only sex objects and he has entitlements to their bodies. If he logs on to Zoo magazine's website, he can watch videos of girls stripping and lap-dancing, one set up as if the woman is being stalked and secretly filmed in her bedroom while she strips, another of a "ridiculously hot" girl being so frightened, she is screaming and crying uncontrollably in a ball. This is not just about sexualisation. Sexual harassment is being eroticised.

The sexualisation of girls exploits girls and boys. All children and young people are under immense pressure to accept it. Boys who are not enthusiastic about it, or speak out against it, run the risk of being ignored or ridiculed, of being labelled "gay", "unmanly", or not liking sex. Boys and young men are under pressure to act out masculinity in which power and control over women, and men, is normal. In which violence is normal.

The absence of positive role models in boys' immediate lives is showing. If the adult men around them do not challenge sexism and traditional masculine behaviours, boys won't either. And with absent fathers, boys are

A five-year-old boy can buy a lad mag and learn that women are only sex objects...

left with celebrities and sports heroes to look up to. Music videos largely follow a template of an individual man possessing a group of sexualised women, gangsta rappers promote sexist and violent notions of masculinity, many young footballers and other sportsmen behave like playboys, enjoy group sex, get away with rape and keep their "hero" status.

Damian Carnell who works to prevent anti-gender violence, says: "From boyhood, men read into the messages that we see around us, from men's institutionalised superiority over women, and privileges of being male, to negative stereotypes of girls and women. It's no wonder that 35% of boys aged 11-16 believe it is justified to abuse women."

The sexualisation of girls is not just shattering the lives of girls and women, it is preventing boys and young men from relating to girls and women as complex human beings with so much to offer them. It is preventing boys from forming healthy friendships and working relationships with girls and women. Instead, it is nurturing potentially violent abusers, rapists and johns. Ultimately, it means boys are not free to be themselves, to know their own humanity.

The Independent 22 February 2007

It could have been me

By Elton John

It's been 40 years since homosexuality was decriminalised in Britain, yet around the world gay people still suffer abuse and discrimination because of their sexuality

In association with Amnesty International

On 21 December 2005 I was legally bound to the man I love, on the first day that civil partnerships were possible. It's my legal right and my human right and I wanted everyone to know – I wanted to shout about it but I still felt nervous about the public's reaction. I was, therefore, delighted and relieved on leaving the register office in Windsor to find the crowd outside cheering and supporting our union as I had feared that abusive, banner-waving bigots would try to spoil the occasion. I felt so proud that day to be British.

There has been substantial progress on gay rights in Britain, but we can't be complacent, not when homophobia still exists here and not when people around the world live in fear solely because of their sexuality. In some countries, my voice would have been drowned out – maybe even stamped out. For many, basic rights are still a matter of life and death.

There are individuals suffering because of their sexuality every day. Last year, William Hernández

had a gun pressed against his neck outside the San Salvador offices of his gay rights organisation, the Asociación Entre Amigos. William and his colleagues who speak out for gay rights in El Salvador had been protesting against moves to amend the constitution formally to prevent gay marriage.

"We will kill you before you can get married," said his attacker.

The offices of Entre Amigos had been broken into and ransacked two nights before. Nothing of value had been stolen, but details of planned events were taken and written homophobic threats were left in the offices. It was the seventh such break-in in five years. These are not isolated incidents in El Salvador – attacks on gay, lesbian, bisexual and transgender people are commonplace. And those responsible are seldom brought to justice.

Men and women are persecuted and attacked every day all over the world, just because of whom they love and whom they make love to. Gay sex is criminalised in more than 80 countries.

Homophobia impacts on health education. Information that could help prevent the spread of HIV and Aids (a subject close to my heart as founder of the Elton John Aids Foundation) is suppressed, or those providing it or seeking it out are persecuted. Indeed, William and his colleagues are targeted partly because they provide sex education for gay people in El Salvador. In Uganda, a radio station was fined when one of its programmes discussed the need for HIV/Aids services for gay men. In India, people have been arrested, beaten and charged under anti-sodomy laws for giving out information on safe sex. Gay people in many African countries are at greater risk of HIV/Aids because they are less likely to receive information and treatment.

In some European countries, the bigots have a loud voice and they're not being shouted down. Pride marches are still banned in some cities in eastern Europe (including Moscow, whose mayor recently described gay parades as "satanic"); gay people in Latvia were attacked

Photo: Ian West PA Archive/PA Photos

Elton John and David Furnish arrive for the annual Elton John Party at the Pacific Design Centre in Los Angeles.

and spat at when they tried to march last year.

In September 2006, on stage in Warsaw, I decided to use a concert to make a statement about homophobia in Poland: "Twenty-two years ago I came to Gdansk and went to the home of Lech Walesa who ... fought for freedom and his own human rights ... and I will never ever forget that moment and to see him again tonight makes my heart full of warmth and love.

"I am just a musician. I come and I play and I hopefully make everyone's troubles disappear for a couple of hours ... and I am also a gay man ... and I know that in Poland recently there has been a lot of violence towards gay people ... and I urge you ... this is a time for compassion.

"There is enough hatred in the world. Leave gay people alone. We are just trying to be ourselves. We do not mean any harm.

"Love is what it's all about ... and the Polish people have always been full of love."

This month I celebrate my 60th birthday. It is 40 years since the decriminalisation of homosexuality in the UK, and yet it is still sadly outlawed in many parts of the world. I want to shine a spotlight on William Hernández, his colleagues and the many, many individuals who stand up for human rights around the world, at great risk to their personal safety. People like William are a lot braver than me, because when the bigots shout abuse, he shouts back at them. And the more visible he and others

are, the louder their voices become. Eventually, with support, they'll shout the bigots down.

So, today, I shout out to William, a brave guy doing a dangerous and vital job. My voice has served me pretty well over the years; I hope maybe it can do him some good, too. But we need more voices. Whether the bigot is in our local pub or a thousand miles away, we should all stand up and speak out for basic human rights. I want to ask you, today, to add your voice.

Sign up to Amnesty's campaign:
www.amnesty.org.uk

New Statesman 26 March 2007

WHAT IS SLAVERY?

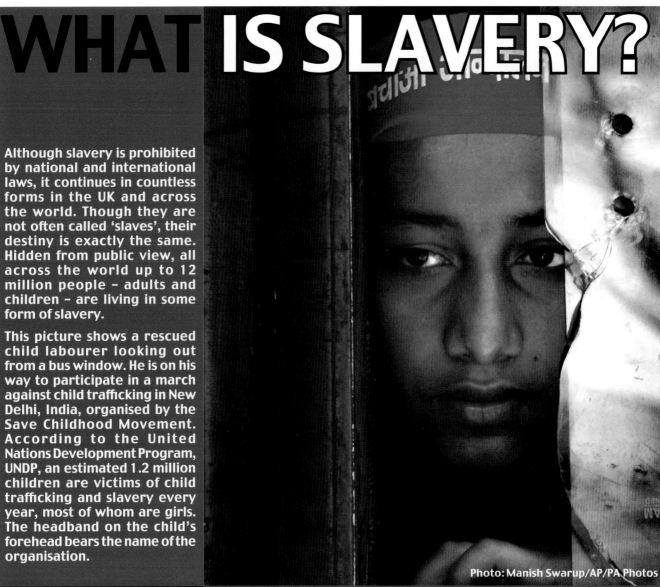

Although slavery is prohibited by national and international laws, it continues in countless forms in the UK and across the world. Though they are not often called 'slaves', their destiny is exactly the same. Hidden from public view, all across the world up to 12 million people – adults and children – are living in some form of slavery.

This picture shows a rescued child labourer looking out from a bus window. He is on his way to participate in a march against child trafficking in New Delhi, India, organised by the Save Childhood Movement. According to the United Nations Development Program, UNDP, an estimated 1.2 million children are victims of child trafficking and slavery every year, most of whom are girls. The headband on the child's forehead bears the name of the organisation.

Photo: Manish Swarup/AP/PA Photos

Common characteristics of slavery

There are things that distinguish slavery from other human rights violations. A slave is:

Forced to work through mental or physical threat;

Owned or controlled by an 'employer', usually through mental or physical abuse or threatened abuse;

Dehumanised, treated as a commodity or bought and sold as 'property';

Constrained, either physically or has restrictions placed on his/her freedom of movement.

What types of slavery exist today?

Bonded labour affects millions of people around the world. People become bonded labourers by taking or being tricked into taking a loan for as little as the cost of medicine for a sick child. To repay the debt, many are forced to work long hours, seven days a week, up to 365 days a year. They receive basic food and shelter as 'payment' for their work, but may never pay off the loan, which can be passed down for generations.

Early and forced marriage affects women and girls who are married without choice and are forced into lives of servitude often accompanied by physical violence.

Forced labour affects people who are illegally recruited by individuals, governments or political parties and forced to work, usually under threat of violence or other penalties.

Slavery by descent is where people are either born into a slave class or are from a 'group' that society views as suited to being used as slave labour.

Trafficking involves the transport and/or trade of people, women, children and men, from one area to another for the purpose of forcing them into slavery conditions.

Child labour, worst forms of which affect an estimated 126 million children around the world in work that is harmful to their health and welfare.

Source: Anti-Slavery International, ILO

THE FOUL STENCH OF FIRESTONE

SLAVERY ISN'T DEAD, WRITES ROBTEL NEAJAI PAILEY. ITS MODERN-DAY VARIANT IS JUST FOUND ON A DIFFERENT KIND OF PLANTATION

Emmanuel B is 30, a slender five foot three, and a labourer whose piercing brown eyes tell unspeakable truths. He's not the kind of slave-labourer we're familiar with from 19th-century plantations in the Deep South of the United States. Instead, Emmanuel is a modern-day plantation labourer in 21st-century, post-conflict Liberia, and the Firestone Tire and Rubber Company is his unyielding master. Like many workers on Firestone's largest rubber plantation, Emmanuel was born in Harbel, has lived in Harbel all his life, and will most likely waste away in Harbel.

As westerners drive around in their heavy-duty SUVs, propelled along on the black gold of Firestone tires, Emmanuel wakes up at the crack of dawn to tap raw latex from 800 rubber trees daily. His clothes are tattered and his shoulders covered in red puss-infected blisters from carrying buckets full of raw latex suspended from an iron pole to the Firestone processing plant two miles from his tapping site.

Emmanuel was gracious enough to demonstrate what a tapper does from sun-up to midmorning. With a pitchfork suspended in the air, he extended his long wiry arms to ease the raw latex out of the trees and into the small red cups that catch it. The drip-drip-drip of the whitecoated liquid was almost as laborious to witness as Emmanuel's daily task – another 799 trees still to go after this one. For Emmanuel and his fellow tappers, a 5am start is the only means of meeting their daily quotas; their wages are reduced by half if they fail to do so. Some have begun to use their children to complete the Herculean task.

I visited the Firestone rubber plantation for the first time in December 2006 while on a research fact-finding mission. I decided to take a break from high browed academic work, and visit the sprawling modern day encampment I had heard so many horror stories about. It's what I imagined the South to look like during the century or so of chattel slavery in the United States, with the hustle bustle activity of plantation life and the accompanying strokes of exploitation.

As my brother-in-law, Christopher Pabai, and I pulled into the one million acre – and constantly expanding – plantation, we were welcomed by an ungodly stench, a stench I can only compare to the smell of rotten cheese. Not just ordinary rotten cheese, but the kind that has been drenched in burning oil, steamrolled on a conveyor belt, and neatly packaged for nonhuman consumption. That's what raw latex smells like when it's being processed.

Rather than wearing masks to protect their noses from the assault, the plantation workers ingest the foul stench day in and day out. It took all my willpower not to retch all over Firestone's perfectly manicured lawn or lush green golf

SOME HAVE BEGUN TO USE THEIR CHILDREN TO COMPLETE THE HERCULEAN TASK

course that senior management frequents while on hiatus from their back-breaking overseeing.

But the foul stench is the least of the workers' worries.

While England celebrates its 200th anniversary of the abolition of the slave trade, plantation workers in Liberia are trapped in a time warp of monumental proportions. They exist in the parallel universe of multinational corporate checkmate, where the prize goes to the highest exploiter. Firestone has been playing the chess pieces of Liberia's rubber pawns since the company signed a concession agreement with the Liberian government in 1926 to lease one million acres of land for six cents per acre – an abominable exchange given the astronomical dividends garnered from rubber sales then and now.

In 2005, Liberia's transitional government signed another concession agreement for an extra 37 years of rubber slavery. Rubber is Liberia's largest export, and Firestone its largest international corporate exploiter, I mean employer, to date. The country and its people have paid a high price for the asymmetrical relationship.

History challenges us to stay on a forward moving dialectic of change. The Firestone example shows us that an ironic distortion of that dialectic is taking place right under our noses. Slavery isn't dead, it's manufactured in the rubber we use daily. We owe it to Emmanuel and his comrades on the Firestone Rubber Plantation to change the course of history, to make a clean break from modern-day slavery and its peculiar 21st century manifestations. We owe it to ourselves.

For more information on the struggle against Firestone the Stop Firestone Campaign website at:
www.stopfirestone.org
Liberian native Robtel Neajai Pailey is a ... at the University of Oxford and a multi-... Fahamu/Pambazuka News (www.pamb... published a longer version of this a...

After 200 years, fight to end slavery in the world goes on

Mike Pflanz reports

UNDER the battlements ringing Cape Coast Castle, Britain's former colonial seat in Ghana, a guide showed two dozen schoolgirls the underground passage linking the slave dungeons to the Door of No Return.

Until Britain led the world in outlawing the transatlantic slave trade 200 years ago, countless Africans shuffled through here to cramped ships waiting beyond the pounding surf.

But hundreds of Ghanaian girls, the same age as those on their school trip to Cape Coast, still live in conditions echoing the 18th century plantations in the Americas.

An ancient practice still strong in the country's north and east allows mystic priests to demand virgin brides as servants as atonement from families deemed to have offended ancestral gods.

Wrenched from their parents, the girls are kept captive in the priest's shrine and, even as children, are forced to work in his fields and clean his compound. When they reach puberty, they become his trokosi, or wife. Most are raped or sexually abused, many are beaten, campaigners have discovered.

for no reason. If I ran away, I feared more people would die."

A campaign by local human rights organisations forced a change in Ghanaian law in 1998, prompting the liberation of 3,500 women and girls from the trokosi system, including Mrs Tordzro.

She now runs a village hairdressing business. "Now people respect me, that is the freedom I feel," she said. But 1,000 more trokosi are still enslaved and fear among lawyers and the police means that the law is rarely enforced. To date no one has been prosecuted.

"People might not be in chains but there's a very close semblance with the old style of slavery," said Rev Walter Pimpong, the director of International Needs Ghana, which led efforts to outlaw trokosi.

"Before, you had men with guns rounding up people who couldn't defend themselves. Now it's the priests who use their spiritual authority and power."

Close to Mrs Tordzro's village, 80 miles east of the capital Accra, her former master, Torgbi Mama Venanua, sat under a neem tree spilling schnapps on the ground as an offering to the gods. Mr Venanua, a smiling man in a white cotton robe and a woven reed mitre, was among the first trokosi priests to agree to give up his wives. "At first we didn't understand why we should change our traditions," he said, surrounded by village elders.

"But we consulted the deities and it became clear we could find other ways to compensate

How one man stirred the nation's conscience

MORE THAN two centuries ago, Thomas Clarkson spent seven years riding 35,000 miles on horseback across Britain, whipping up the campaign against the slave trade. He collected stories from sailors and drew posters detailing the horrors aboard the slave ships which shocked the public.

In 1787 he persuaded the MP William Wilberforce to take the fight into Parliament and helped form the [...]y for Effecting the Abolition of the Slave Trade. [...]n, some 24 million Africans had been sold to [...]traders. They were collected at oceanfront [...]ike Cape Coast Castle then loaded on to [...] Only 10 million are thought to have survived [...]ree-month Atlantic voyage and one in three [...]eached the Caribbean plantations died within [...]ears. Parliament passed The Abolition of the [...]Trade Act in 1807. The Slavery Abolition Act [...]assed in 1833, giving all slaves in the British [...]e their freedom.

graduate student
edia producer for
azuka.org), which has
ticle

Red Pepper June 2007

185

ne, visit

st

for the crimes. People can give us money or cows, we do not need wives any more."

Those who have yet to be set free are among the 12 million people who Anti-Slavery International estimate still suffer forms of enslavement.

These include boys forced to be camel jockeys in Gulf states; West African girls used as domestics; men forced to clear Amazon rainforest; and women trafficked to Western Europe.

"Slavery is found in every region of the world, including Britain, even though it is illegal," said Beth Herzfeld, a spokesman for Anti-Slavery International.

"The bicentenary is of course an important milestone to commemorate on the path towards the total abolition of slavery worldwide, but the fight goes on."

The Daily Telegraph 1 February 2007
© Telegraph Group Ltd

Enyonam Tordzro, who was a trokosi from 1983 to 1998 in payment for the crimes of her grandfather

Slavery: the hard numbers

Asia Pacific	9,490,000
Latin America & Caribbean	1,320,000
Sub-Saharan Africa	660,000
Industrial countries	360,000
Middle East & North Africa	260,000
Transition countries (Baltic States, Central & Eastern Europe & the Commonwealth of Independent States)	210,000

Source: ILO Special Action Programme to Combat Forced Labour (SAP-FL).

Short tragic life of an Iraqi baby

Asma Ibrahim tells Hala Jaber of her tormented experience giving birth amid Baghdad's anarchy

Photo posed by model

WHEN I realised I was pregnant within a month of being married last June, I could barely contain my joy. I'm an ordinary young Iraqi woman, aged 26, with commonplace dreams of building a home and family. It seemed last summer that even in Baghdad, such dreams could come true.

My wedding had been different to most in the world. I wore a simple white dress and the closest members of my family came, but no friends. Strangest of all, my husband-to-be Samouel al-Rawi could not be there.

Samouel, who's 30, was in hiding after receiving a death threat a few days earlier. He worked for a Canadian cargo company transporting goods for the US military, and some Sunni extremists told him that unless he supplied the names of employees and dates of cargoes being moved out of the airport he'd be killed. So he just stayed in the airport, day and night, for safety.

Luckily the groom doesn't have to be present at a Muslim wedding so we went ahead without him. But we didn't feel like celebrating. It's hard to celebrate in a city where people are afraid of showing happiness for fear of hurting the feelings of others or arousing the suspicions of those who want Iraqis to live in sorrow and darkness.

Finding out that I was pregnant made me forget the lonely weekday nights of waiting to see Samouel at weekends. Suddenly we were making plans and counting the days until our baby was born, determined to give him the most stable life a family can provide in a time of war.

Even so, mundane details that would be taken for granted elsewhere became big issues for us. How would I find a good doctor when most have fled or been driven out? Which hospital would I go to when most have become hunting grounds for militias? How would I cope with the birth without my baby's father at my side?

I tried to concentrate on the happiness each month's appointment with the doctor would bring. Hearing the baby's heartbeat transported me away from the daily bombings to a seemingly brighter future.

Given the relentless pressures, it is perhaps not surprising that I started having small contractions in my seventh month of pregnancy. But I never imagined I would have to give birth like an animal in the forest.

It was eight weeks ago, the night of December 12, and I was alone in my bed when the serious contractions started. I rang my mother and my parents-in-law, who lived nearby, but although they were there in five minutes flat there wasn't much they could do.

There was a curfew so they couldn't take me to hospital. They called for an ambulance but were told it wasn't safe to come to our district, Amiriya. The police response was the same: "Sorry, we cannot come to your area."

My brother walked to an Iraqi military checkpoint 10 minutes away, but the soldiers fired warning shots at him.

"They called for an ambulance but were told it wasn't safe to come to our district"

For two hours I screamed with the pain as my family sobbed with me. I was bleeding heavily by the time I felt my tiny baby slipping out of me. Suddenly there he was, lying on the sitting room floor at the end of the umbilical cord. He was blue and still.

"Please do something, please, help him," I cried. "I want him to grow up with me."

My mother and mother-in-law didn't even go to him. He looked stillborn to them so they concentrated on trying to stop me bleeding to death.

It was only now that someone remembered a surgeon who lived one block away. When he arrived at 4am to

shrieks of Allahu Akbar (God is greatest) the couch and carpets were drenched in blood and my son was still on the floor. The surgeon, who'd brought some basic instruments, immediately set about trying to staunch the flow of my blood.

But while everyone else's attention was focused on me, I kept staring at my son, willing him to live. And then a miracle happened. He seemed to choke for a moment and started crying out loud.

"Oh God, he's still alive," I shouted as all eyes turned to the child. "Please save him."

Still attached to me, he was wrapped in a blanket and at 5am the surgeon decided to drive us through the checkpoints to the hospital in Yarmouk, a Sunni district 20 minutes up the road.

I thought the hospital would be a safe haven for Sunnis like us. Imagine my horror when we were greeted at the entrance by Shi'ite gunmen.

They waved us through but I knew we wouldn't be able to stay for long.

The umbilical cord was severed at last and my son was placed in an incubator. I looked at him and in my exhaustion I believed for a moment

that he was smiling at me and all my anguish faded away.

I had to leave him there. They said it wasn't a safe place for Sunnis. The nurse gave me a mobile number to call so that I could check my boy was all right. But when I rang the following night he was suffering from jaundice.

"His blanket, nappy and a bag of clothes we'd brought were missing"

I had to see him, however briefly. I went in the morning and found him in a terrible state, struggling to breathe and with little blue bruises all over his body. His blanket, nappy and a bag of clothes we'd brought were missing.

Later, when I rang the nurse to complain, she slammed the phone down on me. But there was another call that evening — the call to tell me my son, Ahmed, had died.

The pain that gripped my heart that night may never go away. I had to phone my husband and he was practical, though I know he must have

felt the same. He arranged for a good Shi'ite friend of his to collect our son's body for us.

The friend found him in the hospital morgue. Our boy was wrapped in a thin white sheet and placed in a small box for his homecoming.

Even then, there was no end to our ordeal. When the time came to bury him, the road to the cemetery was too dangerous. We went to the mosque in Amiriya but the people there wouldn't take Ahmed. My husband and I thought we'd better put him in our garden, but our families said that wouldn't be right.

In the end we had no alternative but to bury our little one in a patch of wasteland. We've cried about this every day since, thinking that it was perhaps a sin to leave him in such a place.

Last week we abandoned him altogether when we left our country for the safety of Jordan. I've had an operation and now I'm left with just my thoughts.

My suffering is multiplied countless times across Iraq every day. The Americans said they came to liberate us. Is this the freedom they promised?

The Sunday Times 11 February 2007

Judicial killing demeans all

T he strongest argument for the death penalty was the simple invocation of the name of Hitler – or in more recent days, Saddam Hussein. What fate but death could possibly be appropriate for the world's most wicked men? But the appalling images and stories from Saddam Hussein's actual execution chamber in Baghdad have dramatically reversed the argument. Here was irrefutable proof that execution dehumanises not just its victims but its perpetrators. It was a disgrace not just to the present Government in Iraq but also to those who put it in power, which has to include the British. If the ex-dictator of Iraq will be remembered for anything, it is the personal dignity he preserved in the face of taunts and insults even as the trap door opened beneath his feet, his prayers strangled in his throat.

Everything was wrong about the way Saddam was dealt with. The execution for the mass murder of 148 Shias in Dujail in 1982 was allowed to take precedence over the continuing trial of those, including Saddam, accused of responsibility for the deaths of thousands of Kurds later in the same decade. The Dujail trial itself was little more than a parody, though the evidence indicating Saddam's guilt was never really challenged. It was manifestly "victor's justice", a show trial, an opportunity for the Americans to gloat at the discomfiture of their old enemy. Certainly no alternative verdict could have been countenanced in Washington, whose own reputation for fair and just dealing in Iraq has been damaged yet again.

The idea that his execution was the judicial act of a sovereign government that had to be respected even if one disagreed with it – the British Government's line – was undermined by the way it was carried out as an act of sectarian vengeance, almost a public lynching, with several of those watching shouting out the name of the Shia leader Moqtada al-Sadr, and jeers in Arabic of "go to hell". The impious and disrespectful shambles was officially videoed, silently, for state television; and on mobile phone cameras, with sound-track. They were on the internet within hours.

The Catholic Church opposed the execution of Saddam Hussein on principle, as did the European Union and the British Government. In the latter cases, politicians admit that moral sensitivities have changed since the Second World War, not least as public opinion has come to see judicial execution as degrading both to those who carry it out and to those on whose behalf they act. The Catholic Church says that while capital punishment was once justified to preserve the common good, that is no longer true. This is not yet a powerful enough argument to swing opinion in the United States, even among Catholics, whose pro-life inclinations are somewhat selectively applied.

The fact that opinion in America was genuinely shocked by what it saw in Baghdad suggests that consciences may be awakening at last. The degrading scenes from Saddam's death chamber came just days after Catholic convert Jeb Bush, the Governor of Florida and the brother of the US President, halted all executions in his state after a prisoner took 34 minutes to die. What happens in the places of execution in Florida, or in Texas or Oklahoma, or indeed any of the 37 American states where judicial execution is permitted, is in principle neither less cruel nor demeaning to the executioners and those they purport to act for than what happened in Baghdad. At least Saddam Hussein did not have to endure the inhumanity of 20 years on death row, as some of those executed in America have done.

The Tablet 6 January 2007

WOMEN AT WAR

THE DEBATE CONTINUES

Joanna Dyer was killed while serving in Basra

Photo: Crown Copyright/MoD 2007/PA Wire/PA Photos

For over a century women have played a vital part in the armed forces. Manpower shortages in both World Wars made it necessary to allow women into the military and gave women the opportunity to prove that they could successfully perform work previously only done by men, although there were still many areas that were inaccessible to them.

Since the 1990s, when the separate Women's Services were abolished, women have been fully integrated into almost all aspects of military life. They now serve alongside their male counterparts in nearly all specialities but are excluded from units whose

> **Since they now deploy alongside their male colleagues, they are being killed, captured and wounded alongside them too**

primary duty is "to close with and kill the enemy" as well as from service on submarines or as mine clearance divers (for health reasons). This means that more than 70% of jobs in the Army and Navy, and more than 96% of jobs in the RAF, are open to females.

Women have not been slow to take up their opportunities. There were 17,900 females in the armed forces in 2006, making up 9.1% of the total number of personnel. The number of women officers has increased impressively to 3,670, 11.3% as compared to 6.5% in 1990. Being able to serve in a wide range of positions has inevitably taken many women to the front line. Since they now deploy alongside their male colleagues, they are being killed, captured and wounded alongside them too, sparking ongoing media debate over the role of women in the forces.

The first female casualties in Afghanistan and Iraq further fuelled this controversy. On 5 April 2007, a Warrior armoured vehicle on patrol in Basra was destroyed by a huge explosion. Four soldiers were killed: Corporal Kris O'Neil (aged 27), Kingsman Adam Smith (19), Private Eleanor Duglosz (19) and Second Lieutenant Joanna Dyer (24).

Amidst the tragedy, press attention focused mainly on the young women killed, particularly on Joanna Dyer. It was Eleanor Duglosz' job to provide patrols with immediate medical support. Joanna Dyer however held a less traditional role. Involved in the gathering and coordinating of intelligence that informed the planning and conduct of ground operations, Joanna had carved out a role in the army that put her close to the heart of combat. Coming from a military family, Joanna served at Sandhurst alongside Prince William, a factor which heightened media interest.

The deaths – effectively deaths in combat - of the two female soldiers intensified the debate on the role of women in the modern armed forces. This discussion was already being extensively conducted about Faye Turney, one of the naval personnel captured and held by the Iranians for an alleged trespass into their territorial waters, The presence of a woman and her role as a mother were both exploited as propaganda.

In most cases, the particular attraction of the armed services for women seems to be the opportunity to have a career that involves action. Faye Turney is quoted as saying, "I'm too up-and-about to sit behind a desk." Colleagues paid tribute to Joanna Dyer as someone who "seized every chance to get involved" and was "determined to make the most of her deployment" while Eleanor Duglosz is said to have "enjoyed the challenge of being a military medic".

There is no societal pressure on young women to serve in the armed forces. Those who do so make a positive choice in full knowledge of the risks which may await them. For the general public, however, each death raises the question of whether this is a choice they should be allowed to make.

Sources: Various

FOR

WOMEN AT WAR

Bill Duff

IN 30 YEARS of service in the Parachute Regiment and the Royal Ulster Constabulary I have observed women's roles and contribution expand considerably and attitudes revolutionised. The issue of "the front line" is increasingly difficult to define. It is not and never will be again as simple as the trenches in the Great War.

I believe that women do have the right to contribute to the maximum of their ability and if necessary to accept the risk of making the ultimate sacrifice for their country and their comrades.

If they are pregnant or have young children perhaps their responsibilities, for a time at least, should lie elsewhere.

Modern war demands an ever-increasing range of skills and for many of these women are well suited. Electronics, computers and communication spring to mind but no longer are these technologies confined mainly to base stations. They are to be found well up into the front line.

I have also observed women bring a different perspective to addressing issues. Women do address issues from a different angle and are less likely to have tunnel vision. They can exert a calming effect on male colleagues. Some women are excellent problem solvers and good at prioritising.

It is a fact that women are not as physical as men and I would never advocate their employment in the infantry. But I have observed women police and soldiers working against ruthless terrorists as surveillance operators and agent handlers. I only wish we had more.

If a woman has the ability and the inclination to sign up and endure the training and disciplines of service then they should, within common sense boundaries, be permitted to serve in the front line. There are many able-bodied young men who don't have the gumption to do so.

Bill Duff is a former detective superintendent in the RUC. He is a Fellow of the Royal United Services Institute.

Kate Adie

I HAVE only occasionally encountered a front line - trenches, enemy lined up opposite, fighting for territory. Today's front lines are in the market place, the back street and the lonely countryside road - and they can be as deadly as any traditional battlefield.

Nor are these modern front lines the product only of war. Peacekeeping, insurgency, UN deployments and terrorism all have the potential to deliver mayhem and harm.

Women who sign up to serve these days know this. They don't expect to be like their mothers and grandmothers, "doing their bit" in the two world wars, in uniform but confined mainly to cookhouse and admin. They accept what might happen on operations and anyway, they live in a world where equal pay, employment opportunities and financial independence are a right and backed by the law. With rights come responsibilities - and that this should include serving your country, and if necessary, defending it, is the logical conclusion.

Against this, you can hear the voice of Winston Churchill and his Cabinet, utterly opposed to women bearing arms and being anywhere near combat: "It would demean men." This emotion is both romantic and conventional - but women's status has changed and the Armed Services have adjusted rather more swiftly than perhaps some of the media.

Today's headlines are identical to those which greeted the first nine members of the WAAC returned in coffins from France in 1918, after a German air raid. I suspect the public is more accepting, knowing that recruitment depends on women signing up in significant numbers and that there is still a barrier to their joining units which may involve high-intensity close combat. Besides, rape, kidnap and death are not unknown in peaceful civilian society. So when risk and danger do arise just listen to servicewomen's families saying: "She loves the job, and she's good at it." Let's give her our support.

AGAINST

WOMEN AT WAR

Col Bob Stewart

NO MATTER how the so-called politically correct brigade spins it, most people are disquieted by the thought of women serving in the disgusting business of front-line fighting.

Of course I know that women cannot officially serve in an infantry platoon but does this prohibition matter a damn if they are allowed to work alongside front-line soldiers on operations?

The two servicewomen would not normally be expected to be so far forward. But they were and now they are dead – along with two male companions and an Iraqi interpreter whose deaths are an equal tragedy.

In the chaos of fighting in Iraq, it is hardly surprising that brave and professional women soldiers just do anything they can to help their male compatriots.

As well as being present when several male soldiers have died I have also witnessed the deaths of two women.

I can just manage when men are killed but the deaths of the women, particularly one of 18 with no legs and only one arm, haunts me to this day.

At the time I remember I blubbed and was incapable of command for several minutes. I was not alone; my soldiers wept too.

Yet we were surrounded by dead and dying men.

Most men think of women as being not only equal but also very special too. The last words once whispered to me by a soldier dying of his injuries were: "Tell my Mum I am all right and I love her." His words show exactly how the majority of men view women when the ultimate chips are down.

For me it will be a very sad day when we live in a society where men and women are so equal that the death of a serviceman or servicewoman is not a tragedy and the death of a servicewoman an especial additional hurt.

Col Stewart is former commander of UN troops in Bosnia and the Cheshire Regiment.

Mary Kenny

EQUALITY dictates that women may be recruited just as men are to the Armed Forces. And women have often proved to be brave in wartime – playing a heroic role in such services as SOE during the Second World War. Yet, there is something in us which does not want women to be exposed to the fiercer aspects of soldiering, and when there is an engagement in which personnel are killed, news reports automatically regard it as a more distressing fact when those slain include women.

Feminists might call it "conditioning", but others might claim, with reason, that it is less in woman's biological wiring to go to war, and to be exposed to the horrors of combat.

Experience, too, has not favoured the equality argument. The Israelis have put women in the front line of battle, but have now withdrawn from that position. The Soviets found that women were not equal, physically, to the heavy tasks expected of men. Male soldiers have also testified that if a female squaddie is wounded next to them, their instinct is to stop and assist, rather than to move on and let her die, if need be.

And then there is motherhood. If men as fathers are permitted to serve, then women as mothers do so too. The image of Faye Turney, mother and Marine held in captivity by the Iranians, amplified the anxiety that we feel about a mother in these circumstances.

It is not anti-woman to say that it is worse to lose a mother than a father at a very young age.

Free societies accord free choices, so you cannot disbar any female whose passionate desire is to serve in the Forces. But it remains a self-evident truth that women are more vulnerable in combat, that their presence can disturb male discipline, and that we find it more distressing when women are killed. There may sometimes be grounds for exceptions, but it should not be the norm to appoint women to the front line in defence duties.

The Daily Telegraph 7 April 2007
© Telegraph Group Limited 2007

Sane, ordinary Muslims must stand up and be counted

Yasmin Alibhai-Brown:

These nihilists undermine our fundamental right to belong in this country

As they wake up to news of the foiled car-bomb attack on Glasgow Airport, I know what millions of my compatriots - atheists, Hindus, Sikhs, Jews and Christians - will be saying, their easy Sunday ruined by yet another alleged Islamicist plot: "What's wrong with these crazed Muslims?" "Why the hell are they here if they hate it so much?" "When will we be rid of the lot of them?" "What do they want?" "Other minorities also have a hard time, they don't blow up nightclubs and airports".

What these aggrieved Britons don't realise is that exactly the same conversations are taking place in most Muslim households too, with many more expletives flying. Sane, ordinary British Muslims are even less forgiving of such nihilists, whose barbarism undermines our fundamental right to belong to this country as absolute equals. These are hobby terrorists with screwdrivers and screwed heads; they appropriate legitimate concerns, turn them into excuses on their own violent reality shows, sure to be broadcast again and again on screens around the world.

With no politics, no aim, no dreams, no noble imperative, for these Islamicists and their ideological masters, the means is the end. They are at once satanic abusers of our faith and social misfits unloved by all except their own reject band of brothers. Scorned by those they claim to defend, the dreaded sociopaths now seem determined to wound fatally the social contract made between this country and Muslim citizens. Only each assault deepens our sense of nationhood. We still rail against racism and unethical government policies - and I do so incessantly, as you know. Unlike self-righteous neocon liberals, we see how our young are profoundly affected by Iraq and Palestine. However, when bloodthirsty Islamicists strike, we experience a collective intensification of our attachment to Britain. There is no place like this home for us, the only place we want to live and die in.

> **What these aggrieved Britons don't realise is that exactly the same conversations are taking place in most Muslim households too, with many more expletives flying**

On Saturday night, at a lavish Shia wedding in Hertfordshire, Muslim guests were livid about "these bastards giving us a bad name". "Send them packing to the Middle East or Pakistan," said a solicitor to much cheering at one table. "Time to say we love this country. For Muslims, no better country - that's why so many want to come over," added a businessman, who had come here penniless and turned his fortunes around within 10 years.

The father of the bride, too, arrived in Britain with little and joined a small English family firm. He brought entrepreneurial energy; they gave him encouragement and support. This ultra-loyal immigrant for many years led the pre-dawn prayers at our main mosque in Kensington.

As we enter another hyper-crisis period, the danger is we will again succumb to the dystopian nightmare of irreconcilable clashes and culture wars. Calls for draconian laws are sure to ring through the nervous land, although thus far the new government sounds more temperate.

The measured response is an acknowledgement that few Muslims now excuse the killing brigades. The apologist Muslim Council of Britain, whose leader was knighted by Mr Blair, is a spent force. It tried to incite rage and riot over Salman Rushdie's knighthood and failed. Muslims realise what a disaster that confrontation was for both sides. Now,

There is no place like this home for us, the only place we want to live and die in.

the MCB grovels and seeks rehabilitation. Ex-militant Ed Hussain and Hassan Butt have written denunciations of fellow jihadis. The hardline Hizb-ut Tahrir asks Muslims not to "fuel dangerous political agendas". These organisations have been humbled and discredited.

One Independent reader, a graduate, described how Islamicists operated on campus. An idealistic young woman, she fell for the leader, a charismatic man who all too soon did her head in and wrapped it up in a cloak of his choosing: "He commanded me to declare I hate this country and got me into a niqab. Then one day I heard him chatting up this new student and he was saying exactly the same things to her as he said to me when we met, about beautiful eyes, and how he loved women with spirit. I told him to bugger off." Her hair is lovely in the photo she sent me, free now as she is.

I am not naive. Islamicists are cunning and well-connected. Their backers pretend to believe in liberal democracy while plotting its demise. But there are now passionate Muslim democrats standing up to be counted.

Imran Ahmad, young trustee of British Muslims for Secular Democracy, writes in Unimagined, his evocative memoir: "I have had great opportunities and choices. There still is racism in the indigenous society, it's undeniable ... but [compare] Britain to all those so-called Islamic countries, where tribalism is endemic and anything is used as an excuse for discrimination, hatred and mistreatment: village, clan, family, sect, province, class, money, gender, occupation, even shade of skin. At least Britain is committed to implement the highest ideals - personal freedom, social equality, human rights and justice."

With friends like these, Britain can beat its enemies within. Have faith; a time will come when jihadis will terrorise our lives no more.

The Independent 2 July 2007

Should soldiers be able to opt out of wars?

Today is the start of the court martial of a US officer who has refused to serve in Iraq, offering instead to be posted to Afghanistan. Last June, army lieutenant Ehren Watada became the first commissioned officer to publicly refuse deployment to Iraq on the grounds that he found the war illegal and immoral. In the UK, we have already jailed an RAF officer for the same thing.

In the free world, the best armies are volunteer professional organisations. You join as a free person but submit to military law. When the commanding officer of a British unit calls the soldiers together to tell them where they are deploying, he does not expect any discussion. It is not a holiday: you don't get a choice of where to go. On rare occasions some have tried to avoid active service, but this tends to be one way of ensuring you are sent to the thick of it.

Watada can take no comfort from his objection on legal grounds. The legal case against the war is unproven conjecture and, in any case, by submitting to military law, you surrender your citizen rights for the order and discipline of the military. If you have a problem of conscience, you resign your commission. I was careful not to criticise the war – about which I have severe reservations – until after I left the colours in 2004. The odd prima donna believes that what they think matters more than duty. In service life, it does not. There is a clear option to resign.

Watada's mitigation that he would serve in Afghanistan instead holds no water. If only we could all pick and choose our battles. Were it so, such a military would be as much an army as a pile of building materials is a house. It is not about blind obedience; it is about duty and sacrifice and a cause greater than oneself.

Tim Collins

Colonel Collins was commander of the Royal Irish Regiment in Iraq.

*© The Guardian G2
5 February 2007*

"The war's been stopped for health and safety reasons"

CATHY REAY – The new columnist for Disability Now who will be writing every issue about disability and the media, says it's music journalism or bust, and probably both...

Introducing myself on this dauntingly blank sheet of cyber-paper is proving quite the thorny task. Whenever and however I attempt to weave my vital statistics into one sentence, it reads more like a personal ad than a column. Perhaps I am selling myself short (warning: that was the first of what will hopefully be few very poor puns).

So without further ado: I am Cathy, I have achondroplasia, a form of restricted growth, and I'm one of those tax-thieving, living-off-rice student types. I'm in my third year studying journalism at London Metropolitan University, and, with this part of my life speedily and frighteningly drawing to a close, I'm supposedly just about ready to enter the real world and find a job.

Or not. You see, whilst my peers simply delight in filling me in on their long ago concreted career plans, I have absolutely no clue as to what direction I should take. I had this same feeling about a year ago, and, in my panic, booked half a

"My main interest is music; ok, I lie, my only interest is music"

dozen internships with various magazines in the capital. My main interest is music; ok, I lie, my only interest is music, so naturally most of my work experience was completed in the relevant specialist magazine offices. This was all fine and dandy, until it dawned on me that every British music magazine has a ratio of 1:100 in terms of full-time writers vs freelancers. In order to earn enough money to be able to stay comfortably in London, I would have to have ten years more experience that I do now: experience that I could only gain by firstly becoming a freelancer at these magazines and then slowly working my way up.

"It's a vicious cycle," the one and only Kerrang! in-house writer helpfully told me when I picked his brain. Alternative suggestions have included a change of career (also useless, as, as previously mentioned, I only have one interest) and moving back home. Back home being the barren retirement county of Norfolk (I think not).

A journalist friend of mine mentioned local papers. Having spent considerable time interning at a Norfolk paper last Christmas, my general impression was that I'd have more fun weighing dog droppings for a living.

So, with four months of studenthood left, I feel just as unprepared as every other time I've had to make a big decision. I'm thinking that this time, the blindfolded random elimination technique might not work so well...

Source: Disability Now
www.disabilitynow.org.uk
February 2007

A day in the life of a doctor

The team building day

"The main purpose of a team building day is to build a team", the Facilitator begins smugly. A team building day is a cliché building day. The Facilitator can cram more clichés per square sentence and mix more metaphors than George W Bush. The Facilitator has a capital F, and the self satisfaction of believing that the profundity of his or her insight knows no depths. The word Facilitator has the same derivation as the word facile.

"A problem shared is a problem solved." Another purpose of a team building day is embarrassment. "Let's all begin by telling our names, two things about us that no one else knows, and, if you were a dog, what breed you would be." A Rottweiler, you think, longingly.

"There is no 'I' in team." Unless you are dyslexic. You resist the temptation to point out that there is a "me" in team. You also resist the even bigger temptation to point out that we would all be better off it there was no F in Facilitator.

"Mates is an anagram of teams. By the end of today, we will all be mates." Or meats. Or steam will be issuing from our ears.

"You use more muscles to frown than you do to smile." You wonder how many muscles you would have to use to wipe that supercilious smile off the Facilitator's face.

"A happy team makes for a happy client." The Facilitator is referring to what we used to call patients because they needed plenty of patience. A client is a patient with attitude. A customer is a patient with health insurance.

"The team is bigger than the sum of its parts." Except the England World Cup football team, which was less than the sum of its parts. Other examples are possible.

"There is a resolution to every conflict." The team building day teaches you how to Deal with Conflict in the Workplace. Not, you regret, by improving your martial arts training. You are taught to deal with conflict by Mediation and Negotiation and Understanding and Mutual Goodwill. Sticking pins in wax images of the patronizing little toe-rag in Human Relations is not Dealing with Conflict.

There are upmarket team building days and downmarket ones. An upmarket team building day involves paintball fights and smoked salmon and avocado foccacio. A downmarket team building day involves pinball machines and salmonella.

Source: British Medical Journal
23-30 December 2006

David Isaacs *senior staff specialist, Department of Immunology and Infectious Diseases, Children's Hospital at Westmead, Sydney, Australia ,* Stephen Isaacs *consultant, Waltham Forest Child and Family Consultation Service, London,* Dominic Fitzgerald, *senior staff specialist, Department of Respiratory Medicine, Children's Hospital at Westmead*

Just listen to that…"Go, Doctor Farley, go!"…Now that's what I call team spirit.

One in ten employees injured at work

New research from AXA Insurance has revealed that as many as one in ten people have sustained an injury in the workplace in the past five years. AXA's study revealed that whilst employee injuries are most likely to be caused by work-related accidents (81%), for example, using machinery and tripping over, a shocking 8% of work-related injuries sustained by employees resulted from a physical assault by either a customer or colleague.

The study also revealed that employees who work for large companies (250 employees or more) are almost twice as likely to suffer an injury whilst working compared to those employed by small and medium-sized companies (10 to 250 employees). Like small to medium-sized enterprises, smaller businesses (one to nine employees) also had a better record for workplace accidents and injuries when compared with large companies – 17% of small business employees have suffered injuries at work compared with 47% in large companies.

Workplace accidents account for the most injuries at work and one third of all injuries are the result of falls and trips. Strains and sprains are the most common result of an accident – 34% of workplace accidents resulted in these types of injuries. The AXA study also found that employees aged over 50 are most likely to have a fall whilst doing their job (47%) compared with 28% of 18-29 year olds and nearly one in ten of those injured UK employees (9%) complain of repetitive strain injury (RSI) or other injuries by the working environment.

Most common accidents in the workplace	% who have suffered in past 5 years
Fall, slip or trip	33%
Kitchen accident	19%
Lifting	11%
Inappropriate working environment	9%
Industrial machinery accident	6%
Vehicle/road accident	4%
Contact with dangerous substances	3%

Most common injuries sustained	% who have suffered in past 5 years
Musculoskeletal disorder (back pain, strains and sprains)	34%
Cut(s)	28%
Burns(s)	21%
Broken bone(s)	11%
Loss of mobility	6%
Headaches	4%
Knocked unconscious	3%

Chilling statistics

In 2006, 220 workers were killed and 361 members of the public were fatally injured following a workplace incident. During this period 150,559 major and 3-day plus injuries were reported. Last year also saw 35 million working days lost overall (1.5 days per worker), 28 million due to work-related ill health and 7 million due to workplace injury.

Further information on HSE statistics can be found at: **http://www.hse.gov.uk/statistics/index.htm**

Sources: various

WHAT'S YOUR PROBLEM?

Jeremy Bullmore

Q: I run my own business, own a big house and car. I'm a successful businessman but I'm close to illiterate. This was fine when I was starting up the company, travelling around and selling, but now I'm deskbound it's getting difficult. My PA, who has been with me from the start, knows my problem, but no-one else at work. My wife wrote this for me. For the first time, this is becoming a real problem for me. How can I fix it?

A: Your achievement to date is remarkable. I hope you're proud of it; you certainly should be. But as you must already know, you now face a stark and simple choice. You carry on, with increasing difficulty and embarrassment, living a life in part based on pretence. Or you learn to read and write with fluency and confidence.

That last thought may fill you with fear; it would be odd if it didn't. But you're clearly a man of high intelligence and strong will. I believe you would surprise and delight yourself with the speed with which you progress. I have no idea how long this will take, but a year from now this problem could be behind you forever. Your sense of achievement (and relief) will be quite overwhelming.

Tell your wife and your PA of your resolve – and ask them to do some thorough research on your behalf. I'm no expert in this field but they might like to start with the National Literacy Trust – www.literacytrust.org.uk – and see where that takes them. Explore all possibilities before plumping for one: you're bound to feel deeply uncomfortable at first, so it's essential you put yourself in hands that you trust. I do hope you'll let me know how you get on.

Q: I run a medium-sized business close to an open prison. I was recently approached by a charity that helps place offenders into local businesses and I'm considering taking some on. I'm feeling a bit wary about doing this but it's time I put something back into society. My colleagues are not happy about my suggestion. How far should I champion this, especially as I run the risk of it backfiring?

A: If I were one of your colleagues, I think it would be your use of the word 'some' that alarmed me. How easy for the imagination to race ahead and envisage this relatively small business suddenly being overwhelmed by dozens of unqualified people, and all of them with criminal records.

Equally, I don't believe you should be deterred by their initial hostility. I think you should go back to the charity and say you'd be very happy to give work experience to just one of these offenders, subject to a preliminary meeting. Take one of your colleagues with you – and if the candidate seems to you both to be a reasonable bet, take him or her on.

Resist the temptation to be the offender's personal godparent yourself: much fairer and more effective to invite one of your colleagues to do so. Keep it all fairly low-key and most of that early suspicion will soon be forgotten.

Management Today January 2007

Stop moaning
and take action to save our youth

Yvonne Bailey

I'm sick and tired of reading and hearing about people tearing us apart. We're already falling apart and don't need this constant negative barrage especially from other black people. These people are forever harping on about what we don't do to pull ourselves up. But what are they doing to improve the situation? They expect to get something out of nothing.

Bill Hendon (The Voice, November 27 – December 3, 2006) for instance mentioned that he felt uncomfortable when he saw a young boy displaying anti-social behaviour on the train. So why didn't he as a grown man, do something about it? This is one area where we have gone wrong. Incidents like this wouldn't have happened years ago as our cultural upbringing wouldn't have allowed it.

Unfortunately, children today are far removed from their culture and as a result, they have lost all the manners and respect that we once prided ourselves upon. All the things that many of these gripers admire in other cultures were qualities that were admired in us not so long ago.

Why did the British government invite black people here to build up Britain after WWII? Was it because we were lazy, no-good, low-life criminals who wanted an easy life by thieving and mugging their little old ladies? Or was it because we were seen as cheap labour willing to do dirty, manual, low-paid work just like the Eastern Europeans that Mr. Hendon and the whole British government are now praising to high heaven? And despite the fact that we were not all from the same background, a number being 'small island' people, wasn't there a camaraderie, a sense of togetherness, that enabled people to share cramped, over-crowded dwellings as seen in the Asian community who are now held up as our role models.

Weren't we the trend setters in elegance despite our meagre wages, head held high with our respectable families? All the people in my family, bar one, who came in the 1950s later bought their own homes and owned cars, and many of my friends families were in the same position. All this, while sending money back home

"These children were not aggressive, but in fact opened up to me"

for their extended families. However, just like the British before us, as we got more affluent we began to move away from our families, our neighbourhoods and our culture. We became individuals – every man for himself.

The trouble is 'no man is an island' and with other factors working against us, that individuality began a trend of us working against ourselves, which we are still doing to this day and as a result we have no community. Nevertheless, it doesn't stop me from interacting with 'my people' young and old alike. In fact I started Kreative Culture Klub for young people eight years ago and try to motivate them to achieve academic success with the Young Gifted and Black award ceremony, the fifth being held on January 26, 2007 at Walthamstow Assembly Hall.

While out with some members this past summer, I approached a group of young people sitting at the back of a bus, who were not only loud but extremely coarse in their language. How shocked I was to discover they were only 13-years old? When I finished speaking to them they became very quiet and spoke in same tone among themselves for the rest of the journey and kept this up when leaving the bus and while walking on the pavement. These children were not aggressive but in fact opened up to me admitting they could not behave like that at home as they'd get 'some good licks' but did so because they were in a group.

I have also spoken to older youths engaged in 'territorial wars' a few mentioning they want to get out of that lifestyle knowing they'd die young, but need more people like me to assist. Who will assist? Not people who just moan and do nothing, so nothing will be achieved.

The Voice 4 December 2006

Photo: Neil O'Shea

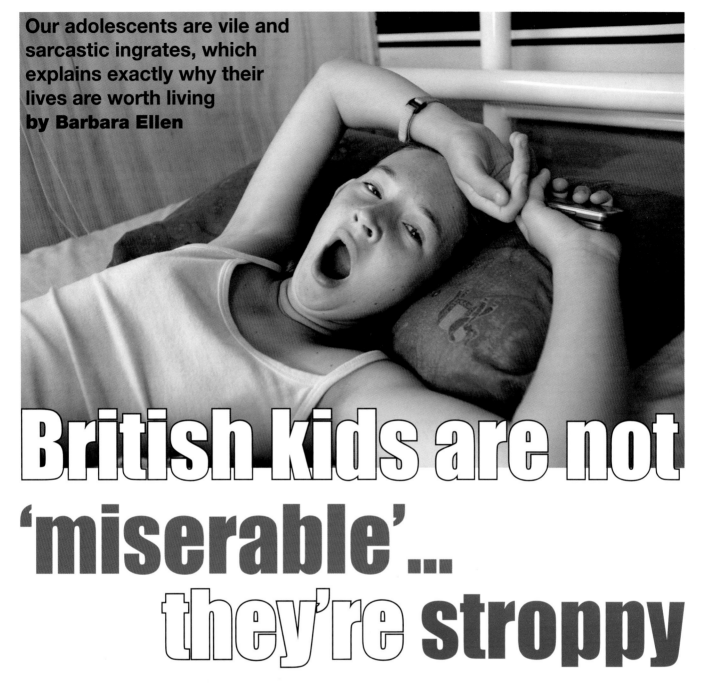

Our adolescents are vile and sarcastic ingrates, which explains exactly why their lives are worth living
by Barbara Ellen

British kids are not 'miserable'... they're stroppy

And so, in the only parents' race that really matters, we limp in last, egg fallen from the spoon, potato sack tangled around the ankles. Last week, the Unicef report (An Overview of Child Wellbeing in Rich Countries) placed our children overall bottom of the world's 21 most developed territories, behind the top-ranking Netherlands and Scandinavia, and countries such as Poland and the Czech Republic.

Not only were British children ranked 'worst off' in the developed world – with the highest rates of drunkenness, obesity, bullying, early sexual intercourse, cannabis-taking,

and teenage pregnancy – they made it clear that they felt worst off: unhealthy, unhappy with family relationships and friendships, more likely to feel left out, disenfranchised. Ultimately, the picture painted by the Unicef report was of British childhood as the 'toxic' equivalent of a nuclear-waste dump, oozing through the soil of this green and pleasant land – the makings of a true asbo nation. It was time for British parents to feel ashamed and responsible, and of course we did. At first, anyway.

Hand-wringing aside, are British children really the most deprived in the developed world? The last time

you looked in a school playground was it bursting at the seams with drunk, stoned, pregnant, friendless manic depressives? Would our adolescents really be better off cultivating acne in Holland or Sweden, or queuing for Clearasil in Poland? While no one would deny our tragic levels of child poverty, the devastating teenage pregnancy rate, and not least the recent child-shootings in south London, common sense dictates that this cannot be the whole story.

The Unicef report has already come in for criticism for ignoring younger children, and using out-of-date data, as well as (shame on them) seizing upon lone parenthood as a surefire barometer of social degeneracy (thereby branding huge numbers of children as 'failures' before they even begin). Unicef also chose to employ a bizarre 'relative poverty' grading system that conveniently ignored the fact that most of our children live the life of Master Brooklyn Beckham compared with children in less economically stable nations.

Neglected? Deprived? Those living below the poverty line are one thing, but the majority of UK adolescents are, if anything, spoiled brats. I would challenge anyone to fill a small car park with British 15-year-olds (from any social class) who don't own a mobile phone. It is also debatable whether our children are as 'disenfranchised' as depicted in the report. At one point, we're breathlessly informed that 'only 81 per cent of them really like school' (only?). But never mind that. When listening to British children talking about the spiritual wasteland that is their existence, those nice Unicef people with their clipboards failed to include the most crucial factor of all – the contrary bolshie nature of the people they were talking to; the fact that British teenagers have always loved nothing more than to pose, bitch, rebel, slag everything and everyone off, and blow endless anti-establishment raspberries.

Indeed, British teenagers are, have always been, by nature, rebellious, stroppy, and a lot less interested in being fair than they are in being interesting. Which to my mind is much less creepy and disturbing than the thought of all those sucky-up kids from Holland and Sweden (henceforth known as the apple-polishing nations) chirruping away about how much they respect their elders. Bearing this in mind, this was the only possible result for this study.

Unlike their Dutch or Swedish counterparts, British children were never going to answer such questions as 'Are your contemporaries kind and helpful?' with po-faced sincerity; to piously and publicly abhor the idea of sex, drugs, and other 'bad behaviour'; and pour anything other

than molten scorn upon the status quo. Indeed, the vast majority of British adolescents are as they always were, as most of us were – vile, stroppy, preternaturally sarcastic ingrates, who would doubtless be labelled dangerous, disaffected sociopaths in any other European country. And this is supposed to be a bad thing?

Some of us would say (cautiously) that it isn't. While no one could seriously argue that youth in Britain have it better than everyone else (not after a week when children have been found gunned down in their bedrooms), there is evidence to suggest that things are not as bad as they seem in Britain, or quite as wonderful everywhere else. For one thing, if the true litmus test of a successful childhood is a happy adulthood then it seems strange that no one has factored in that Scandinavian adult suicide rates are double ours. (What happens to all those happy children who end up killing themselves?)

For another, it may be that it's the very restlessness of British youth, its inbuilt disaffection (or, to call it by its technical term, 'arsiness') that keeps our cultural heartbeat healthy and racing, as it continues to be, in terms of everything from pop to comedy, from art to fashion.

While no one is claiming that it is easy to be young in Britain, neither are our young easy. As any parent of a teenager could tell you, one is all too frequently torn between calling for a psychiatrist and screaming for an exorcist. Moreover, Oliver James's theories on 'affluenza' certainly ring true with what often comes across as an unattractively needy/greedy bunch. However, frightening as it sometimes gets, and Unicef reports aside, maybe we should accept British adolescence for what it is, has always been – a whirling out-of-control carousel. You can only watch and hope that your particular (stroppy, nihilistic, establishment hating, maddening, indispensable) Brit teenager manages to cling on for the ride.

The Observer 18 February 2007

'We all want to be cool – bitching is the way it works'

Photo posed my models

Eliza Chubb, 15

I come from a comfortable, two-parent home in south London and go to a good school so I can't complain about having a deprived childhood. I've no idea what it is like to be a teenager in the Netherlands or Sweden, which come top of the list in Unicef's "report card", but I do have some idea why even fortunate children show signs of the unhappiness that puts the UK at the bottom of the table.

There must be something wrong with our society that particularly affects teenage girls, because many of my friends, who appear to have it all, act as if something is wrong with their lives. Everyone is obsessed by their weight: some try not to eat at all, others stuff themselves and then make themselves sick. Once we had to put up new wallpaper in the bathroom because one of my friends threw up on it. If they are not being sick because they want to be thin, it's because they are trying to be sophisticated by drinking, smoking or doing drugs. The peer pressure is enormous. Some get laughed at because they don't want to do those things so I'm not surprised that less than half the children surveyed say their peers are "kind and helpful" to them – compared with 80 per cent in Portugal. We have a culture of bitching. Whenever people are being discussed, the first thing mentioned is always the way they look. We all want to be considered "cool" so rather than say nice things we call each other "fat" or "ugly" or "stupid".

We move around in packs and cliques and there is always one on the outside who is ignored and made to feel an outcast. Humour is sarcastic and the endless private jokes are very isolating. My friends say that bitching is the way it works, that it's the norm.

Why do we behave like we do? It is partly, I believe, because we are so influenced by America – it is also bottom of the UN list and that doesn't seem a coincidence. British children and teenagers want to be like Americans. We speak the same language, read about American stars, listen to American music, wear American clothes and watch American TV shows.

Most children, including my 11-year-old sister, don't want to be at home with their families. They would rather be lounging by a swimming pool like the teenagers in *The OC*, or sitting around in coffee shops – like they do in *Friends* – acting as if they are 20. Among my friends, I constantly hear: "I wish I was older." We all want to grow up fast: we want to be 18 and go out partying, or go to bars and get drunk.

Also, so many children seem to want attention. British parents work some of the longest hours in the world, and that makes for loneliness. My friends are mostly lucky and have two parents – if you didn't see one of your parents it would make you very lonely – but even in two-parent families some friends never see their parents because they leave early for work and get back after the children are in bed.

In many cases, lack of love is replaced by an excess of material possessions. In language classes at school, when we are asked what we did at the weekend, there is rarely a pupil who does not say "shopping".

But although life in Britain isn't perfect, we are all entitled to a free education, a National Health Service, clean water, and freedom. Many children in places such as Africa do not have these things and we shouldn't forget that.

The Daily Telegraph 15 February 2007
© Telegraph Group Limited 2007

Teenagers leaving care are neither children nor yet able to find their bearings in the adult world. The season of goodwill can hit them hard, however brave a face they try to put on things.
By Alice O'Keeffe

Christmas in care

"For Christmas, I'll be going to stay with my mum for three or four weeks. I'll be leaving here around 16 or 17 December, and I won't come back until we've taken the decorations down. My dad will be there, too. He's a DJ so he travels a lot. He doesn't live with my mum all the time, but he's coming back for Christmas. We'll just watch telly and eat and all that; I'll get my presents. I want a surprise."

The family Christmas described to me by Karen, 17, seems normal enough. It is only later, when I speak to one of the carers in the children's home where she lives, that I find out it is largely a product of her imagination. She probably won't spend more than a day with her mother, if they see each other at all, as their relationship all but disintegrated two years ago. Presents and decorations do not seem likely, and neither does a family meal. Perhaps she gave what she thought was the "right" answer to a prying journalist – or perhaps she has convinced herself it is true. After all, constructing a fantasy must be easier than facing the reality of a Christmas without anyone who loves you.

"Christmas here can be very difficult. Sometimes they think their parents are going to turn up, and then they don't. Even if they do, they might get home and find that Christmas dinner is, you know, a tin of beans," says Jane Raby, a senior worker at a residential home run by NCH, the children's charity, for six 15- to 17-year-olds in the north west. "We have to try to manage their expectations, and give them as good a time as we can here. But it is hard." Clearly she is deeply committed to her work, as are the other members of staff I meet, and deals with Karen's outbursts firmly but with patience and warmth. But she won't be around on Christmas Day this year – she has children of her own and will be spending it with them. "You hear so many sad stories, but you have to be professional," she says. "You can't take everyone under your wing."

Even the best-adjusted person would find it difficult to get through this time of year without family, but those children and young people who actually have to do so are those who are least emotionally equipped to cope. Karen, who has learning difficulties, was fostered two years ago, when her adoptive parents split up and her mother couldn't manage her. The placement soon broke down and she became homeless, sleeping in hostels and on friends' sofas. By the time she was taken into care she had been involved with serious drugs offences and was being targeted by a paedophile ring. She looks too tough for her years, with her face set in an aggressive glare and her blonde hair scraped back into braids, yet her psychological vulnerability is only too obvious. "Don't even ask me about being adopted, because talking about it makes me want to slit my wrists and kill myself," she says at one point, in an almost matter-of-fact tone.

In the absence of any stable, constant adult presence in her life, Karen is surrounded by a continually shifting array of people who are employed to support her: she has her carers at the project, a social worker, an employment adviser, a "pathway planning" adviser, a doctor – and the list goes on. She spends much of her time playing them off against each other. "My social worker is much better than you lot," she tells Raby spitefully. Raby tells me later: "She makes an appointment with the doctor about once a week, and everyone knows her in the jobcentre. She was forever telling us that her social worker had given her permission to do something, and then we'd find out she knew nothing about it. I think she feels so out of control about her own life, that she puts a lot of energy into manipulating and controlling all of the people around her."

Lack of options

Although things are difficult, Karen is doing relatively well at the moment. The three months she has spent at the project is the longest time she has stayed in one place since she left her family home. She says bitterly that she hates it and would "rather be back at my friends' – at least there I could do what I want". However, here she has her own room, meals provided by staff, and access to leisure activities such as bowling and eating out, as well as services for helping her get back into education and plan her future.

"If she really hated it so much she would have voted with her feet," says Raby. "It's very difficult to know where she'll be in a year's time – she has the capability to live an independent life, but the emotional side of her will make things very difficult. But you do get surprises all the time; some people make huge progress. All you can hope is that at some point she'll want to get motivated and get her life together."

That is the hope – but the statistics for those leaving care are far from reassuring, and put Karen's prospects in doubt. Of the 6,000 children who leave each year, a quarter of the girls are pregnant before they go, and half become single mothers within two years; Karen is already obsessed with getting pregnant. Those who have been in care make up half of all prisoners under 25, and one-third of the homeless. Next year, when she turns 18, Karen will no longer technically qualify for "children's services", and may have to leave the project whether she likes it or not. She has self-destructive tendencies, no family support network, and only a

fragile grip on reality; she may nevertheless have to fend for herself in the adult world. Her new year, in other words, does not look promising.

The dearth of suitable options for those leaving care is the biggest frustration of the job for Jeff Moody, manager of the project. "We are lucky, because we have negotiated with the Leeds authorities that if there is no suitable provision in place for housing, young people can often stay until they are 19," he says. "But far too often children in care are pushed out too soon, and to somewhere inappropriate for their needs."

Often those expected to cope alone are the children who are least emotionally equipped

Our failure

Of those who have recently left the project, Moody says, the project managed to find suitable housing for only one young man. Another returned to his family, where the relationship broke down again, and he ended up in a hostel. A third was given hostel accommodation, and has now disappeared completely. "It's a big frustration because the work is validated by people coming back and saying, I'm doing OK." Moody says that the ideal transition for most young people would be into supported accommodation – independent flats with staff on hand to help and advise. "Setting them up with practical skills is the easy one," he says. "The more difficult thing is the level of emotional vulnerability. We need to address the care and support they still need, while accepting that they aspire to be adults and take their place in society as well."

Britain's failure to provide ongoing support for young people who have been in care was a key area examined in the Care Matters green paper, which was published in October. It stated: "It is time to move away from the unhelpful idea of 'leaving care' and recognise that every young person needs continuing help to make a smooth transition to adulthood." The paper proposed a raft of measures, including allowing young people to stay with foster carers until the age of 21 or beyond, and creating bursaries for those in care who want to go on to higher education. It referred to the "shocking" statistics on the education of children in care and the widening gap in "outcomes" between those in care and other young people, arguing that care should be "a bridge to a better childhood and a better future".

Consultation on the paper is still under way, after which some recommendations may be put into practice – if money is made available. "It is not impossible for looked-after children to go on to have successful lives," says Clare Tickell, chief executive of NCH. "We're delighted that the government is taking these issues seriously. But now we just have to make sure that these proposals are backed up with proper funding and that all the good intentions are translated into action."

How long will that take? Too long for Karen who, as the green paper clunks its way through the Westminster system, will turn 18 and will be making decisions that will affect the rest of her life. The government, however, now has a chance to ensure that by next Christmas, young people in care could be looking forward to a brighter new year.

The ideal transition for most young people would be into flats supported by staff

Some names have been changed

CARE BY NUMBERS
(all statistics relate to the UK)

60,000
children are in care at any one time

85,000
each year will spend some time in care

50%
of girls leaving care are single mothers within two years

25%
of girls in care become pregnant before they leave

⅓
of the homeless have been in care

50%
of prisoners under the age of 25 have spent time in care

63%
of children in care are there as a result of abuse

77%
of residential care staff are not qualified to government standard

Research by Preeti Jha

New Statesman 18 December 2006